For a
mother-in-law to
be thankful for.

Donald W Rowe
(i.e.) Don)

O Love
O Charite!
Contraries
Harmonized
in Chaucer's
Troilus

DONALD W. ROWE

*Southern Illinois
University Press*

Carbondale and Edwardsville

Feffer & Simons, Inc.

London and Amsterdam

Library of Congress Cataloging in Publication Data

Rowe, Donald W.
  O love, O charite!

  Includes bibliographical references and index.
    1.   Chaucer, Geoffrey, d. 1400.   Troilus and
Criseyde.   I.   Title.
PR1896.R65   821'.1   76–4816
ISBN 0–8093–0697–2

For my parents

Contents

Acknowledgments

Though I acknowledged all the specific scholarly debts of which I am aware in the notes, they are in many respects an inadequate expression of my obligations and gratitude. First of all I should like to mention the late Dale S. Underwood, under whom I first studied Chaucer and from whom I first heard many of the questions this study attempts to answer. His inspiration was perhaps the first sine qua non of this book. The second was no doubt the scholarship of D. W. Robertson. I should not like the differences of opinion which may seem to dominate in the text to obscure my very great debt to his work. A third was Donald R. Howard's judicious and perspicacious criticism of an earlier draft of the present book. The reader may particularly wish to thank him for helping to make many a rough place smooth. I should also like to thank a number of my friends and colleagues at the University of Wisconsin who at one time or another offered varying degrees of much-needed encouragement, criticism, and expertise, particularly Stuart Curran, A. N. Doane, Richard Ringler, Eric Rothstein, Jerome Taylor, Andrew Weiner, and Joseph Wittreich. For errors of fact, infelicities of style, or absurdities of fancy I alone am responsible.

Grateful acknowledgement is made to the Bodleian Library for permission to reproduce MS. Auct. F. 3 14 fol.7^v a graph illustrating the order common to *mundus, annus,* and *homo* in Isidore of Seville's *De natura rerum.*

Donald W. Rowe

Madison, Wisconsin
September 1975

Contraries Harmonized

1

The Dynamic Principle
of the *Troilus*

After falling in love with Criseyde but before committing himself totally to love, Troilus sings a song about love's mystery.

If no love is, O God, what fele I so?
And if love is, what thing and which is he?
If love be good, from whennes cometh my woo?
If it be wikke, a wonder thynketh me,
When every torment and adversite
That cometh of hym, may to me savory thinke,
For ay thurst I, the more that ich it drynke.

And if that at myn owen lust I brenne,
From whennes cometh my waillynge and my pleynte?
If harm agree me, wherto pleyne I thenne?
I noot, ne whi unwery that I feynte.
O quike deth, O swete harm so queynte,
How may of the in me swich quantite,
But if that I consente that it be?

And if that I consente, I wrongfully
Compleyne, iwis. Thus possed to and fro,
Al stereless withinne a boot am I
Amydde the see, bitwixen wyndes two,
That in contrarie stonden evere mo.
Allas! what is this wondre maladie?
For hete of cold, for cold of hete, I dye.[1]

This song, based on a sonnet by Petrarch, can be too easily dismissed as a conventional playing with paradoxes, an exercise in poetical oxymoron later so dear to Renaissance sonneteers. Confronted with love, Troilus finds it not only irresistibly powerful but intellectually incomprehensible as well. Much like the Christian God whom the mystics loved to contemplate and to whom the end of the poem directs us, love is

3

seen as a mystery which cannot be contained within the neat compartments of rational thought, where hot is one thing and cold is its contrary. To Troilus, at least, love seems to transcend such rational categories and to deny man's normal perception and experience of things, bringing opposites into a union which both he and we can only intuitively and darkly understand. Nonetheless, he decides to commit himself unequivocally to this equivocal mystery, in language echoing Christ on the cross: "O Lord, now youres is/ My spirit, which that oughte youres be" (I.422–23). At this point one is ready to confirm Troilus's opinion prior to loving that all lovers are fools, for who but a fool would commit himself to such apparent nonsense? A critic of *Troilus and Criseyde* cannot thus abruptly dismiss love, however, for though Chaucer's narrator does not dare to love, Chaucer committed the poem to an exploration of love's mystery. Since here, as in the *Canterbury Tales,* Chaucer's words are "cosyn to the dede," the poem is as much a mystery as the love it explores.

The poem's ironies and ambiguities have increasingly tantalized its critics. D. W. Robertson, perhaps the poem's most learned and controversial critic, considers it (until the epilogue) consistently and pervasively ironic, arguing that its apparent approbation of romantic love is in fact a moralistic denunciation of *cupiditas,* an exposé of the very irrationality of such love.[2] Indeed, for Robertson there is no ambiguity in the poem since neither the nature of the love it dramatizes nor Chaucer's intention is ever in doubt. In a recent, admirably close reading of the poem, *The Double Sorrow of Troilus,* Ida Gordon argues the presence of ambiguity at nearly every significant point in the *Troilus.*[3] She repeatedly demonstrates the simultaneous coexistence of conflicting and often contrary meanings in the language and action of the poem, and argues that Chaucer deliberately employs a somewhat simplistic narrator who unwittingly speaks in "amphibologies" in order to force the reader to make his own intellectual and moral choice as to what is true and right.[4] Though the experience of reading the poem as Gordon reads it is markedly different from that of reading it as Robertson does, they come to much the same final conclusion about Chaucer's ultimate intention. For Robertson, Chaucer's irony is a club which beats the unwanted truth into us; for Gordon, Chaucer's ambiguity is a trap which forces the reader to discover for himself the same unwanted but irresistible truth. For both, what Chaucer means is largely the negation of what he says prior to the epilogue. While I agree that much of *Troilus and Criseyde* is ironic and that Chaucer frequently employed ambiguity to force the reader to discover the truth for himself, such a general approach to the *Troilus* seems to me inadequate, for it ignores the poem's most basic characteristic, its union of contraries.[5] Both the world the poem describes and the poem itself are constructed of contraries, of opposites united. Thus, both the poem and its world are not so much ironic and ambiguous as paradoxical.

That Chaucer was consciously dealing in contraries in the *Troilus* seems evident simply from those contradictions in the poem which have so bemused its critics. In terms of character, action, and style, at times the poem seems to belong to the world of romance; at times, to border on the world of fabliau. Its hero is a fatalist; its heroine repeatedly asserts her freedom. Its third major character seems both pander and priest. Its narrator constantly expresses conflicting attitudes and takes contradictory stances toward his matter, as he is now sympathetically involved in the past, now detached in the present; now declaring that his subject is the double sorrow of Troilus, now exulting in Troilus's joy; now loving Criseyde, now rejecting her. Though the poem explicitly affirms sexual love as a good, it ends by denouncing it as a vanity. Though we are told that the poem is a tragedy, we last see the hero looking down from the eighth sphere of the heavens laughing. Anyone familiar with the poem can add to this partial list of its apparent contradictions. Before we can believe that such contradictions are central to the poem's art, however, we must answer Robertson's objection that our tendency to view the medieval world in terms of fundamental oppositions is a mistake, the result of an imposition of a post-Hegelian pattern of thought on medieval man.[6]

Robertson argues that many of the things that we persist in thinking the Middle Ages viewed as warring opposites, such as body and soul, were actually considered to be elements in a hierarchy, their relationship being not one of opposition but of superior and subordinate. Other apparent oppositions are merely illusions. For instance, he argues that to the medieval mind good and evil are not contraries, for all is ultimately good; evil is only a privation of good. One might respond with common sense: Though what Robertson says may be theoretically true, medieval man persisted in talking of good and evil as opposites, just as we persist in considering hot and cold opposites, though we all know that cold is only the absence of heat. The whole effect of Troilus's song on love's mystery depends upon our acceptance that such pairs as "quike" and "deth," hot and cold "in contrarie stonden evere mo." Though medieval man knew that the Fall was fortunate, he also knew it was a fall. One must not take the paradox out of the paradox that all is for the best.

Robertson does allow that *cupiditas* might appear to be the opposite of *caritas* since it creates disorder, the opposite of order. He judges this a mistaken impression, however, for "the disorder resulting from cupidity is a disorder only with reference to nature as it was created; with reference to God, it is a part of the Divine Order and is essentially harmonious with it."[7] It is true that medieval man considered good and evil parts of a harmonious whole; it is also true, however, that he considered them contraries. Indeed, it is a commonplace of medieval thought that the universe is a harmonious union of contraries, a *concordia discors*. Everywhere medieval man looked he managed to find order and harmony, but it was a concord that contained the discordant, the diverse, and the contrary. That was the wonder of it all. Arnold, Abbot of Bonneval and friend of St. Bernard, provides in his discussion of the first chapter of Genesis a typical statement of the basic idea of *concordia discors:* "He encloses all things, strengthening them from within, protecting them from without, nurturing them from above, supporting them from below, binding contraries [*diversa*] with perceptible art, joining opposites [*contraria*] into one and with marvelous moderating power enjoining peace upon them, holding down lightweight things lest they fly off, holding up ponderous things lest they crash downward. . . . By God's moderating rule diverse and contrary things meet in a unity of peace, and static and erratic things are brought into orderly line; huge things do not swell larger, and the smallest things do not disappear. The entire fabric of the world—consistent though made of such dissimilar parts, one though composed of such diverse things, tranquil though containing such opposed elements—continues in its lawful and ordered way, solid, harmonious, and with no dread prospect of ruin."[8]

Indeed, one finds the fact that the universe is composed of contraries used to demonstrate the existence of God, for, as Boethius phrases it, "This world . . . of so manye and diverse and contraryous parties, ne myghte nevere han ben assembled in o forme, but yif ther ne were oon that conjoyned so manye diverse thinges; and the same diversite of here natures, that so discorden the ton fro that other, most departen and unjoynen the thinges that been conjoynid, yif ther ne were oon that contenyde that he hath conjoynid and ybounden."[9] Neither Arnold nor Boethius intends any denial that the universe is hierarchically ordered; they are merely characterizing another aspect of the order of the cosmos. Medieval man saw his world in terms of both organizing principles. Ultimately, the idea of a universe full of warring contraries is implicit in the hierarchical concept of the great chain of being, for, as Lovejoy argues, the chain can never be full of all possible beings until the ultimate in diversity—opposition—has been generated.[10]

The Middle Ages gradually developed a systematic analysis of the contraries harmonized in God's creation and a number of literary conventions for representing this vision of universal order. Though the objectives of this study do not require an historical survey of the origin and development of the *concordia discors* tradition, they do necessitate an examination of this concept, especially as it was represented in medieval literature. By a happy coincidence, that literature which most insistently presents the *concordia discors* conception is by and large literature which it is generally agreed Chaucer knew. While I have not limited my investigation to this group of interrelated works nor completely ignored questions of origin, such a focus seems the most valid and proves, I believe, the most illuminating.

Although the *concordia discors* tradition has received considerable examination by contemporary critics of Renaissance and eighteenth-century literature, critics who sporadically

glance back to the medieval world to document a commonplace, it has been insufficiently appreciated by students of
medieval culture and literature.[11] The most important study of
the subject, Leo Spitzer's pioneering *Classical and Christian
Concepts of World Harmony*, is limited, as Brendan O'Hehir
observes, "by its failure to recognize the basically dyadic nature of the classical idea of harmony, and the continuance of a
dyadic sense into Christian thought on the subject,"[12] and, for
our purposes, by the generality of its treatment of harmony.
Though many of the tradition's elements are classical in origin,
it received its fullest elaboration in the Middle Ages. An order
formerly seen here and there was now seen everywhere, in
virtually all areas and on nearly all levels of the created, uniting
them by analogy. The idea of opposites united became a model
in terms of which all things were perceived and understood.

The *concordia discors* conception is especially important in
the thought and literature traditionally, but too narrowly, associated with the school of Chartres.[13] Consequently, this
examination of the subject concentrates primarily upon works
which either had a substantial influence on the Platonic rationalism of the first half of the twelfth century or were themselves significantly influenced by it. Especially important for
our purposes are Boethius's *Consolation*, Macrobius's *Commentary on the Dream of Scipio*, Bernardus Silvestris's *Cosmographia* (*De mundi universitate*), Alain de Lille's *Complaint
of Nature* and his *Anticlaudian* and Jean de Meun's portion of
the *Roman de la rose*. Though none of these works was actually
produced at Chartres, the *Consolation* and the *Commentary*
were important sources of that flowering of Platonic philosophy in the first half of the twelfth century which found its
principal literary expression in the *Cosmographia* and the
works of Alain in the twelfth century, in Jean's portion of the
Roman in the thirteenth. They are all important works in the
central literary tradition of the Middle Ages; they are also all
works Chaucer probably knew.[14]

Though the medieval world was heir to a rich and varied
Platonic tradition, the only dialogue of Plato's actually known
to the Latin Middle Ages was the *Timaeus*, and that only in a
partial translation with commentary by Calcidius.[15] Backed by
the immense authority of Plato's name and and supported by

such supposed compendia of Plato's thought as Boethius's
Consolation and Macrobius's *Commentary*, it had a profound
influence upon the philosophical speculation of the first half of
the twelfth century, when it was studied as a philosopher's
equivalent of the theologian's Genesis, with the two being accommodated in what we might call a less than perfectly successful harmony of contraries. It is, as Wetherbee asserts, "impossible to exaggerate the importance of the Timaean cosmos
as a model for Chartrian thought."[16] The *Timaeus* itself is radically dualistic; its cosmic model, a harmony of contraries. Its
myth of creation posits two independent and prior principles,
ideas and matter, from which the demiurge created the cosmos.
The created universe is similarly dualistic, having a body and
a soul. Both the world's body and its soul are constructed of
contraries, the body of the elements, the soul of the circles
of the Same and the Different. The harmony of the physical
universe reflects the harmony of the World-Soul, since it is the
visible and tangible copy of this invisible and intangible model.
Man himself is a microcosm and is thus comprised of the same
contraries similarly ordered as the macrocosm.

Though there is much in Plato's myth of the creation and
constitution of the cosmos which medieval orthodoxy could
not literally subscribe to, medieval Christianity never doubted
that the world's harmony reflected the archetypal exemplars
in the divine mind, whatever its precise relation to that mind,
nor that this harmony was a product of the union of the diverse
and the contrary. To call the order of the universe a harmony
was to be precise, not vaguely metaphorical. The following, for
instance, is Boethius's definition of the word "harmony" in *De
arithmetica:* "Not without cause is it said that all things, which
consist of contraries, are conjoined and composed by a certain
harmony. For harmony is the joining of several things and the
consent of contraries."[17] Though Genesis insured that the medieval world understood creation as occurring *ex nihilo* and
though other theories of how the universe was created, for
instance, Neoplatonic emanation theory, had considerable influence on the range of medieval thought on the subject, the
Timaeus insured that the *concordia discors* tradition pictured
creation as a union of contraries having prior existence. In this
tradition as it flowered in the twelfth century, creation was

understood as a binding and yoking together of opposites. The harmony of both the macrocosm and man, since he is a microcosm, was understood as the consequence of a cosmic marriage of the sacred and the mundane.[18]

An even more important legacy of the *Timaeus* is the simple fact that man was considered a microcosm. The medieval interest in the natural world and the laws that govern it, natural justice, is in part a consequence of the microcosmic conception of man.[19] Since macrocosm and microcosm are the same, to study one is to study the other. Natural justice, the subject of the *Timaeus*, was seen as a possible model for social and moral law, for positive justice.[20] Thus, Boethius could conclude his famous celebration of the love which binds together the contraries of the universe and insures its stability by asserting that the same love binds together society and ought, at least, to order man: "And yif this love slakede the bridelis, alle thynges that now loven hem togidres wolden make batayle contynuely, and stryven to fordo the fassoun of this world, the which they now leden in accordable feith by fayre moevynges. This love halt togidres peples joyned with an holy boond, and knytteth sacrement of mariages of chaste loves; and love enditeth lawes to trewe felawes. O weleful were mankynde, yif thilke love that governeth hevene governede yowr corages" (II.*m*.viii.16–26). Thus, it became possible to hope that man could order himself and his social world by following nature.

The basic concept of *concordia discors* is seen most clearly in, and no doubt derives in part from, the classical analysis of the physical universe as comprised of the contrary elements, earth, air, fire, and water, these elements being themselves united pairs of the contrary qualities, hot, cold, moist, and dry.[21] The idea that the material universe was composed of contrary elements made from the union of contrary qualities is everywhere evident in the Middle Ages. St. Ambrose, for instance, incorporates a traditional description of the elements and their bond in his *Hexameron*, his explanation of God's creation of the universe in six days.

We discover earth to be dry and cold; water, cold and humid; air, warm and humid; fire, warm and dry. Thus each and every one of the elements is bound together by qualities shared in common with some other element.

Since earth has a quality dry and cold, it is connected with water by association of its cold quality, and through water it is related to air because the air is humid. Hence, water seems to embrace with its two arms, as it were, cold and humidity, on the one side, the earth, on the other, air—the earth with its quality of coldness, the air with its quality of humidity. Air, by its nature, also forms an intermediary between two opposing elements, that is between water and fire, for it binds both elements together. It shares with water the quality of humidity and with fire the quality of warmth. Fire, too, since it is by nature warm and dry, is bound to air by its quality of warmth and, because of its dry quality, is turned back to form an association and a union with earth. In this manner these elements, by a circuitous process, meet together in a dance measure of concord and association. Hence the Latin *elementa* is found in Greek as στοιχεῖα, denoting agreement and harmony.[22]

Here we find, as is traditional, both contraries and hierarchy, for the contrary elements are linked in a continuous chain by their shared qualities in a hierarchy extending from the lowest and heaviest, earth, to the highest and lightest, fire. Nonetheless, they form a circle.

Given the medieval rage for order and man's habit of analogy, it should not surprise us to find similar concepts of order explaining other facets of life's diversity. The impulse to divide other aspects of the physical universe into four categories, paralleling the elements and sharing with them the same paired qualities, is everywhere apparent. For instance, we find a similar harmony of the seasons similarly linked: Spring is damp and hot; summer, hot and dry; autumn, dry and cold; winter, cold and damp.[23] Macrobius associates each of the seasons with a single quality (the first of the pairs listed above) and even manages, in an unempirical moment, to divide each month and each day into four such contrary parts.[24] To medieval man these parallel orders were united by more than analogy, for they were tied together through the virtue of the planets. Each planet was associated with one of the pairs of qualities, as was each sign of the zodiac.[25] The influence of like upon like bound all together. Virtually everything that could be was divided into four categories and assigned a pair of qualities that all might correspond.

The most important such analogous order is found in man
the microcosm. Though man was first and foremost a microcosm because he shared being with inanimate things, life with
plants, feeling with animals and reason with the angels, he
was also a microcosm in that he was made of the four elements.
Some thought various parts of the body formed from the different elements—the feet and the part whereon one sits, for
instance, were made of earth;[26] others employ a scheme like
that of Honorius of Autun: "Whence came the corporeal substance used in man's creation? From the four elements, and
for this reason man is called a microcosm, that is a lesser world,
for from earth he has his flesh, from water his blood, from air
his breath, from fire his warmth."[27]

The most common conception of man's microcosmic identity
with the four elements is found in the physiological psychology
of the humors.[28] Just as there are four elements comprised of
pairs of contrary qualities, so in man there are four humors
dependent upon the four bodily fluids, which were made of the
same pairs of qualities, with each humor producing a disposi-
tion at least poetically like its corresponding element. The harmony of the harmony of the elements, of the seasons, and of
the humors was simply represented by graphs such as those
used in medieval manuscripts of Isidore of Seville's *De natura
rerum* to illustrate his explanation, largely quoted from St.
Ambrose, of the union of the qualities to form the elements.
The included representation of the order common to *mundus,
annus,* and *homo* is typical.[29]

The essential similarity of macrocosm and microcosm is nowhere more elaborately presented than in the *Cosmographia,*
a difficult but historically important work in the *prosimetrum*
form of the *Consolation.*[30] However Bernardus intended it to
be understood, whether literally or allegorically, its literal content is radically Platonic. The first part, *Megacosmos,* describes
the creation of the universe by Noys, who identifies herself
as "the consummate and profound reason of God" (I.ii.69), in
response to Nature's request that she order and render more
beautiful discordant chaos, which exists prior to the poem's
account of creation.[31] First she must subdue chaos (Silva) by
"the bonds of a reconciling concord," recognizing that "the
only principles of arrangement" possible are "the reconciliation

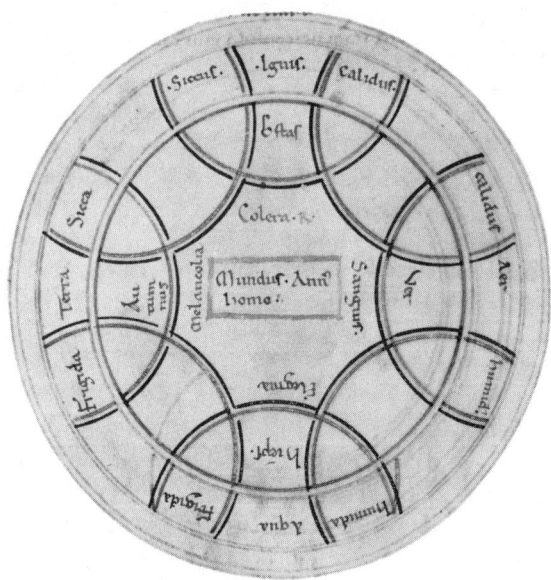

of discords, the aggregation of incongruities, and the yoking of mutually repellant forces" (I.ii.71). Then "reflecting inwardly upon eternal ideas," she proceeds to create "in close and intimate resemblance to these" (I.ii.72), by separating out the elements and assigning each its proper place, so that "warring factions" enter "into a condition of peaceful unity" (I.ii. 73). Then she vivifies the whole by joining it to Endelechia, the World-Soul.[32] Once this was accomplished, "the totality of created life unfolded in ordered progression from the nurturing womb of Silva" (I.ii.75), a totality Bernardus celebrates in a long poem on the order and plentitude of life. The second part of the poem, *Microcosmos*, describes the creation of man in a similar way. This time Noys delegates her authority: to Urania is assigned the composition of the soul; to Physis, the creation of the body; to Nature, the union of the two contraries. Since Physis must work with the dregs of chaos left over from the creation of the universe, she approaches her task with considerable fear and trembling, doubting her ability to harmonize its discord. Knowing, however, that "she would not go astray in creating the lesser universe of man if she took as her example the pattern of the greater universe" (II.xiii.121), she creates the four humors as Noys had the elements and arranges them suitably. Thus, she forms the body a microcosmic harmony of contraries. *Microcosmos* ends as *Megacosmos* had, with a poem, this one celebrating man. It focuses on the physical body, not the soul it houses, and it culminates in a celebration of the two genii whose task it is to "fight unconquered against death with their life-giving weapons, renew our nature, and perpetuate our kind" (II.xiv.126).

Taken literally, Bernardus's account of creation presents serious doctrinal difficulties, especially in its seemingly radical Platonic dualism and in its presentation of matter as fundamentally malignant, as incapable of being perfectly ordered. While it seems to me highly likely that the work is to be read as an allegorical fable, as Silverstein and Wetherbee have both persuasively argued, it is not necessary for our purpose to argue the issue.[33] Certainly, the idea that man is destined to die because he is made of contraries incapable of permanent reconciliation is a commonplace, however much it may ignore the doctrine of the Fall.[34] At times this would seem to be but another example of the imperfect adjustment of classical thought to Christian dogma so common in the Middle Ages; at times, as with Bernardus, it would seem to be a poetic way of depicting the human condition, a metaphor for the effects of the Fall. There is in the *Cosmographia* considerable ambiguity in the way man is treated, as Bernardus simultaneously stresses man's limitations due to his creation from discordant elements and celebrates the glory of that creation.[35]

The unity of contrary elements in microcosm and macrocosm is also elaborately presented in Alain de Lille's *Complaint of Nature*, a work modeled on the *Consolation of Philosophy* and substantially indebted to the *Cosmographia*. Though its subject is not the creation of the universe but the reformation of man, it presents a vision of universal order much like that in Bernardus's epic. It begins with the narrator complaining about the perversions of love which afflict the world, until the goddess Nature appears to instruct and console him, as well as to shed a few tears of her own for wayward man. She is crowned with a diadem and dressed in garments which together symbolize the totality of Nature's domain, the physical universe. The diadem contains twelve fiery jewels representing the zodiac and seven additional gems signifying the planets. Her diadem represents the firmament and the heavens, the fiery part of the universe. Her garments have three parts, hierarchically arranged, one part representing the air and full of birds, one part representing the water and full of fish, one part representing the earth and full—once again hierarchically arranged—of representations of men, animals, trees, herbs, and flowers. The variety and plenitude of life is stressed, as is the orderliness and harmony of all, save where man has created discord and division by not following Nature's laws.[36] All of nature greets the goddess's arrival by bursting from winter into spring and pays her homage except the poet, who is overcome with grief, and thus reveals, like Boethius at the opening of the *Consolation*, the lack of harmony within himself. The goddess undertakes his cure by reminding him both of who he is and who she is. She, "Vicegerent of God the Creator," formed his body from primordial matter that it might be a suitable spouse for the spirit; she is also responsible for dissolving the same bond. She goes on to explain that she formed him a microcosm: "I am she who has fashioned the form and eminence of man into the likeness of the original mundane mechanism, that in him, as in a mirror of the world itself, combined nature may appear. For just as, of the four elements, the concordant discord, the single plurality, the dissonant consonance, the dissenting agreement, produce the structures of the palace of earth, so, of four ingredients, the similar unsimilarity, the unequal equality, the unformed conformity, the separate identity, firmly erect the building of the human body. And those qualities which come together as mediators among the elements—these establish a firm peace among the four humors" (*pr.iii.26*). Once again we see both hierarchy and contraries harmonized. However, though the humors are here presented as reconciled in the same manner as the elements, through the mediation of their shared qualities, the firm peace established between the humors was not traditionally envisioned hierarchically as it was with the elements. In the case of the humors, what is desired is a harmonious balance, a well-tempered mixture in which none predominates.[37] The psychology of the humors tended to produce a morality based upon temperance, on "measure," where extremes of any kind are to be avoided. This, too, is in part a transmission of classical thought into the medieval world, one not always easily reconciled with Christianity's quest for perfection, with either the *contemptus mundi* asceticism of the monastic ideal or the Franciscan ideal of giving up all to follow Christ. Other aspects of the doctrine of contraries produce a different conception of morality, however, one of a more radical, absolute kind, as we shall see.

With the physiological psychology of the humors we move beyond the merely physical to the moral and spiritual world, for if man's temperament is an index to his physical constitution, it also indicates dimensions of his character. Though the humors, like the stars which influence man through the humors, may predispose, orthodoxy never allows them to dictate. Morally man remains free to choose, and the choice is typically characterized in terms of contraries, the straight and narrow, the broad and the crooked, contraries which are part of God's total harmonious order but which are not to be temperately mixed by man. The choice is complicated by the fact that man is divided against himself. Since the Fall man has been out of tune with the rest of the universe, where contraries are harmonized with love. Thus, in the *Complaint*, for instance, Nature's garment is torn where man should have been depicted, "but elsewhere its parts were united in unbroken eloquence, and suffered no discord nor division" (*pr.*i.15). Thus, the goddess's complaint, a complaint Jean de Meun's Nature will reiterate with even more vigor, is against man, who, alone of all her creatures, does not follow her laws.[38] The fact that man is divided against himself is no more central to the literary tradition we are examining than the question of how harmony is to be restored in man. Is the *opus restaurationis* solely the work of Christ or must man himself contribute to it? If man must at least in part reform himself, which great lady shall he follow, Reason, Nature, Philosophy, Theology, or should he follow the god of Love? Though none of these works, not even the *Consolation,* can be called a ringing affirmation of man's ability to save himself, the seriousness and boldness with which these works confront the question reveal that man and his work were being assigned a dignity and worth which rightly entitles this literature to be called humanistic. A recognition of the seriousness with which such philosophical poems as the *Complaint*

and the *Roman* examine how man is to be reformed should go
a long way to dispel the notion that the only concern of "courtly
love" literature is to denounce sin.

One common representation of this battle of contraries for
dominion in man can be seen in the vast literature treating the
vices and virtues. Usually, they are treated as opposing pairs;
frequently, they are pictured as trees, having their roots respectively in *cupiditas* and *caritas* and historical counterparts
in Adams' tree and Christ's cross.[39] The whole psychomachia
tradition presents in externalized, personified abstractions and
in the chronological order necessary for narrative the mind at
war with itself, the mind simultaneously compelled in contrary
directions. Prudentius's *Psychomachia*, to which C. S. Lewis
rather too generously attributed the invention of the genre of
psychological allegory,[40] seems the appropriate illustration. It
presents in the manner of a battle poem each of the virtues at
war with its opposing vice and ends the description of the triumph of the virtues over the vices with a summary characterization of the struggle it has just dramatized by means of personified abstractions: "How often, when the plaguing sins
have been driven away, have we felt the soul aglow with the
presence of God, how often, after these pure joys, felt our
heavenly natures grow cool and yield to foul desire! Savage
war rages hotly, rages within our bones, and man's two-sided
nature is in an uproar of rebellion; for the flesh that was formed
of clay bears down upon the spirit, but the spirit that issued
from the pure breath of God is hot within the dark prison-house
of the heart, and even in its close bondage rejects the body's
filth. Light and darkness with their opposing spirits are at
war, and our two-fold being inspires powers at variance with
each other, until Christ comes to our aid."[41]

In this passage we find a traditional association of the moral
and spiritual division in man with a fundamental division in
his composition, with the contraries body and soul, flesh and
spirit. Though these contraries may have beeen harmonized in
man prior to the Fall, since, they have been at war with one
another. Their opposition, as much as anything else, defines
the human condition for medieval man. The generally Platonic
nature of the characterization of the dualism here is worth
noting, especially in the picture of the flesh as the "prison-

house" of the spirit, as though the incarnation of the soul in
the flesh were the Fall.

The union in man of the heavenly and the earthly—of form
and matter, soul and body, spirit and flesh—requires examination here, however great a commonplace it may be. It will
become clear as we progress that this union was also understood as a hierarchy and as a *concordia discors*. This duality
in man is, of course, another aspect of his microcosmic nature.
Since man's body was vivified with a soul, to follow strictly
the theory of man the microcosm was to assign the world's
body a vivifying soul, as Plato had done. Given the doctrinal
difficulties the concept of the World-Soul created, however,
such an obvious and seemingly necessary parallel was seldom
asserted, though we have seen Bernardus employ it. It was
much more common to express this particular correspondence
between macrocosm and microcosm generally, to assert, for
instance, that just as the universe was comprised of the stable
and permanent heavens and the mutable and transitory sublunar world so man was formed of the eternal and the temporal.
The conviction that the movements of the heavenly bodies
exhibited a regularity indicative of rationality and that the
planets and the stars had their own intelligences strengthened
such a parallel, making it something more than metaphorical.
Since macrocosm and microcosm share the same nature and
order, they were understood to be the consequence of a similar
creative process. In their philosophic understanding and their
poetic representation of this union of contraries in man, the
poets in the tradition we have been examining turned once
again to their Platonic inheritance. Just as they had used the
cosmology of the *Timeaus* to understand the creation of the
universe and its order, they used aspects of another Platonic
myth to express the divine origin and nature of the soul and
its union with the body, the myth of the cosmic cycle of the
soul.

The myth of the cycle of the soul was handed down to the
high Middle Ages in considerable detail by Macrobius in his
Commentary on the Dream of Scipio, where it culminates a
series of ideas Macrobius presents about the origin and nature
of the soul and its union with the flesh. Though he allows
that the association of the soul with the whole of the super-

lunar world, the body with the sublunar world, has some merit, he prefers those "Platonists" who divide the universe into two distinct parts, "the fixed stars, as one part, the seven so-called errant spheres and what is between them and the earth, and the earth itself, as the second part."[42] He continues, "according to this sect, which is more devoted to reason, the blessed souls, free from all bodily contamination, possess the sky; but the soul that from its lofty pinnacle of perpetual radiance disdains to grasp after a body and this thing that we on earth call life, but yet allows a secret yearning for it to creep into its thoughts, gradually steps down to the lower realms because of the very weight of its earthly thoughts. It does not suddenly assume a defiled body out of a state of complete incorporeality, but, gradually sustaining imperceptible losses and departing further from its simple and absolutely pure state, swells out with certain increases of a planetary body: in each of the spheres that lie below the sky it puts on another ethereal envelopment, so that by these steps it is gradually prepared for assuming this earthly dress. Thus by as many deaths as it passes through spheres, it reaches the stage which on earth is called life."[43] After this life, the worthy soul returns to its place of origin, its star in the sphere of the fixed stars. Macrobius follows this general description of the descent of the soul with an explanation that the circle of the zodiac and the circle of the Milky Way intersect at Cancer and Capricorn and that Cancer is the portal of souls descending, Capricorn the portal of souls returning to the company of the gods. In addition, he supplies a planet-by-planet enumeration of the attributes the soul acquires from each planet as it descends. From Saturn, for instance, it obtains "reason and understanding"; from Venus, "the impulse of passion"; from the Moon, "the function of molding and increasing bodies."[44]

Though medieval orthodoxy could not accept the myth of the cosmic cycle of the soul literally, somewhat generalized, it was a useful fable to represent the divine nature of the soul with its half-remembered intimations of its own immortality and its vague desires to return to its source, and to characterize the ambiguity of its life in this world. This myth is suggested with varying degrees of elaboration, for instance, in Boethius's *Consolation*, Bernardus's *Cosmographia*, and both of Alain's fables. The journey of man to the Creator through the created, the central theme of the literature associated with the school of Chartres, is repeatedly characterized as a return.[45] A brief consideration of Bernardus's account of the creation of man in the *Cosmographia* and Alain's picture of Nature's efforts to create a new and perfect man in the *Anticlaudian* will demonstrate the utility of this myth in representing the union of the heavenly and the earthly as a *concordia discors*.

In the second book of the *Cosmographia*, Noys, after celebrating the beauty, order, and harmony of the universe she has created in response to Nature's prayer, declares her intention to complete her work with "a worthy consummation," the creation of man the microcosm. To accomplish this, she delegates her authority: to Urania is assigned the composition of the soul; to Physis, the formation of the body; to Nature, the union of the two. She then dispatches Nature "to seek out the dwelling places of Urania and Physis" (II.iii.94). In her quest to find Urania, to be found "in close attendance" on Noys's throne, Nature journeys upward through the heavens until she reaches the sphere of the fixed stars. In her ascent, she observed "a numberless throng of souls clustered about the abode of Cancer." They were weeping, for they were "destined to descend, pure as they were, and simple, from splendor into shadow, from heaven to the kingdom of Pluto, from eternal life to that of the body" and were struck with terror "at the clumsy and blind fleshly habitation which they saw prepared for them" (II.iii.95–96). Upon locating Urania in the firmament, which is distinguished from the rest of the created universe in that it alone is made of the quintessence, Nature encounters a similar reluctance. Urania does not wish to leave the delights of her abode, recognizing that a descent to "base earth" will mar her brillance, but she submits to the divine will, which she declares before Nature can say anything: "God's will is that man be formed; his body will issue from the depths of chaos and his spirit from the powers above. Let the whole be perfect, let his beauty consist in the joining of his parts; it is God's will that nothing be lacking in his composition. It is God's will that the mixture be balanced, that the balance effect a bond, that the divine bond bestow harmonious relation, lest it disgust the mind to dwell in shadowy blindness and suffer the forced hospitality of the body, lest the spirit have cause to complain of the flesh that it is too much subject to its dictates, that the concord of unlike powers may come about peaceably" (II.iv.97).

After passing briefly out of the created universe to pray to the Trinity for success in their undertaking, Nature and Urania descend to earth together. They pass through each of the planetary spheres, and Bernardus characterizes the influence of each on earthly life. Though the descent is not pictured explicitly as a gradual incarnation but as an education of the soul into the order of the universe and the laws of fate, it is clearly indebted to Macrobius in general conception and occasional detail. The fact that the first of the planets encountered, Saturn, is identified as the father of time and is characterized as hostile to life indicates abruptly that the descent from the firmament is a fall. The intermediary position of the planets between the immutable sphere of the fixed stars and this sublunar world of turbulent change is matched by at least two intermediate functions. They operate as agents of Fate, insuring that the changes which occur in this world conform to divine providence. Though Saturn's malevolence might cause us to question the wisdom of that providence, Jupiter, the next encountered, is pictured with a scale representing justice. With the aid of Clotho, who unfolds in time whatever he weighs out, he insures that all is just. The planets have a second intermediate function. Bernardus would seem to associate a Usiarch or Genius with each planet, though he does not mention one in every case.[46] The function of each is presumably related to that of the Usiarch we meet in the sphere of the fixed stars, who is "devoted to the art and office of delineating and giving shape to the forms of things" (II.iii.96). That is, they would seem to function as intermediaries between the forms and this world, insuring that the things of this world conform to their archetypal exemplars. By having Noys instruct Nature to join the soul to the body "through emulation of the order of the heavens" (II. ii.114), Bernardus establishes another parallel between macrocosm and microcosm. Just as the planets join the firmament to this sublunar world, their order joins the soul, which originates in the firmament, to the body, born of earth. Though Bernardus insists that it is God's will that the soul and the

flesh be joined and that this union is harmonious, his characterization of the malignancy of matter and the frequently destructive nature of the influence of the intermediary planets
which join soul to body suggest the inevitability of discord
and division in man.

Once Nature and Urania join Physis, Noys appears to give
her final instructions: "That this sensible universe, the image
of an ideal model, may be able to attain fullness in every part,
man must be made, his form closely akin to the divine. . . . He
will derive his understanding from the heavens, his body from
the elements, so that while his body sojourns on earth his
mind may dwell far above. His mind and body, though of
diverse natures, will be joined into one, such that a mysterious
union will render the work harmonious. He shall be both divine
and earthly, comprehend the universe about him through
knowledge, and commune in worship with the gods. Thus he
will be able to conform to his two natures, and remain in
harmony with the dual principles of his existence" (II.x.113).
She concludes much more in the same vein by asserting that
"when at last the tottering structure of his bodily dwelling
falls, its binding harmony dissolved, man will ascend the heavens, no longer an unacknowledged guest, to assume the place
assigned him among the stars" (II.x.114).

We find a related drama in Alain de Lille's *Anticlaudian*, a
poem about Nature's efforts to create a new and perfect man. It
is not an epic of creation but of re-creation, of reconstruction,
in which Nature and God collaborate in the restoration of man
to his prelapsarian perfection. In this allegory, it is Prudence,
assisted by the seven liberal arts among other things, who
must journey to the uppermost reaches of the universe in quest
of a soul. The planets and their mixed and multiple effects are
described during the ascending journey. To secure the necessary soul, Prudence must leave the created to ascend, guided
by faith, to the godhead. God himself provides the soul by
summoning Noys, "which prepares for Him an exemplar of
Deity, the idea of the human mind" (VI.viii.127). It is then
anointed with "a celestial moisture" which protects it from
the influences of the planets as Prudence descends with it.
After Nature forms the body of the four elements, "Concord
leagues soul to flesh, connects the dissonant with a steadfast

knot, by a close joining, adjusts with slender bonds the absolute to the compounded, the delicate to the gross, binds in a favorable compact, marries the divine to the flesh. Thus she ties light to darkness, and ether to earth: thus the different keep peace, thus the disagreeing lay aside their own strife, nor does the flesh now threaten wars, yielding to the spirit, but not without much murmur" (VII.ii.130). That the soul is ultimately to return to its place of origin has already been indicated in Alain's celebration of heaven when Prudence first entered it as the ultimate abode of those who triumph over the flesh.

In both these works we see aspects of the myth of the cosmic cycle of the soul being used to dramatize the creation of man and to understand his nature and the conditions of his life as a *concordia discors*. Central to these allegories are the figures who seek out the contraries and unite them in man. In Bernardus's work, Nature has both functions, questor and uniter. In Alain's *Anticlaudian*, Prudence seeks; Concord joins. That Bernardus incorporates a journey through the cosmos in his allegory of creation, that he makes that journey an essential part of the creation of man, demonstrates, at least with the logic of art, that man is a microcosm. The order of the macrocosm is the order of the microcosm; to know the one is to know the other. Thus, the intellectual journey through the cosmos is also a journey through the self. That Alain incorporates a similar quest into his allegory of re-creation demonstrates that the restoration of harmony in man is a return to his prelapsarian state, a recovery of his original harmony. It suggests that if one understands and imitates the harmony of the cosmos, one can harmonize the discordant in oneself. The regaining of Eden for Alain, as for Dante, is a consequence of a simultaneous exploration of the world without and the world within.[47] Though this journey cannot be made without God's help, natural justice, the order of the created, can guide one, like Virgil in the *Commedia*, much of the way.

By having Nature function as both questor and uniter, Bernardus can employ the quest as a dramatization of the intermediary function of the powers that unite contraries, for it is a commonplace of the *concordia discors* tradition that an intermediary is necessary to join opposites, an intermediary sharing in the two natures that he joins. Thus, for instance, in the theory of the four elements, each element is seen as an intermediary linking the two adjoining it, sharing one of its qualities with each. Thus, Augustine can argue that the only true intermediary between man and God is Christ, for only Christ shares equally in God's and man's nature.[48] In the poetic tradition we have been examining, a number of familiar figures have this function. One such figure is Genius, who is pictured in the *Cosmographia* as assigning "the forms of all creatures" and in the *Complaint* as forming men true copies of their exemplar when he draws with his right hand, distorted ones when he uses his left.[49] It is the intermediary function of Genius which accounts in part for his being cast in the role of Nature's priest in the *Complaint* and the *Roman*. The most important such figure is Nature herself. In the complex of works we are examining, Nature signifies many things and has many functions.[50] She is at times the whole of the created universe, at times the order of that whole, a surrogate for the World-Soul, at times the archetypal exemplar of that order, another name for the divine mind itself.[51] She is also the generative force in the universe, that force which insures that the universe and all witin it will, once created, perpetuate itself. Her totality includes both the heavenly and the earthly, the superlunar and sublunar worlds. These halves were at times distinguished in medieval thought by identifying the superlunar world as Nature, the sublunar as the work of Nature.[52] Such a distinction helps clarify her intermediary function, revealing that she, like Fate, which was also associated with the heavens, joins this world to the mind of God and helps insure that it conforms to the ideas in that mind. She is, as it were, a cosmic go-between. The ambiguities of the term "go-between" are appropriate; for if this function can be viewed as priestly, it can also be seen, especially given Nature's identification as the generative power of the created, as having a pander dimension as well. The persistent suspicion that Nature herself was fallen insured some ambiguity in her characterization by even her greatest enthusiasts. This ambiguity is fully and delightfully exploited by Jean de Meun, as he now praises her as the indescribably beautiful vicar-general of God, now denigrates her as God's chambermaid.[53] The possibility always existed that she, as intermediate creator, would deform man when she joined together in him the contraries which comprise him.[54]

One more such intermediary figure requires at least mention, the god of Love. Given the repeated insistence in the Middle Ages that it was love which bound together the contraries of macrocosm and microcosm, it was perhaps inevitable that the courtly god of Love would be transformed into a similar intermediary. Given the medieval distrust of the passions, it was also inevitable that he would perform this function even more ambiguously than Nature. Indeed, in Alain's *Complaint*, though Cupid and Venus were originally assigned part of Nature's intermediary harmonizing function by Nature herself, they have become such sources of discord and division that they are conspicuously absent from the restoration of Nature that climaxes the poem.[55]

The dualistic analysis of man into soul and body is frequently paralleled in medieval thought by a similar division of the soul itself into its rational and irrational faculties. One form such a dyadic conception of the soul often took, the form most significant for the *concordia discors* vision of universal order, can be seen in a significant passage in the *Complaint*. Though its analysis of the contrary powers of the soul may be less familiar to the modern reader than the division of man into spirit and flesh, it is scarcely less traditional.[56] After the goddess Nature explains to the dreamer that she formed man through the marriage of the spirit and the flesh, she proceeds to characterize the results of that union as a microcosm in a number of ways. First, as we have seen, she gives us her version of the harmony of the elements and the humors. She then characterizes another microcosmic aspect of man.

And just as the army of the planets opposes with contrary motion the fixed rolling of the firmament, so in man is found a continual hostility between lust and reason. For the activity of reason, taking its rise from a celestial source, passes through the lower levels of the earth, and, watchful of heavenly things, turns again to heaven. The activities of lust, on the other hand, wandering waywardly and contrary to the firmament of reason, turn and slip down into the decline of things of earth. Now the latter, lust, leads the human mind into the ruin of the vices, so that it perishes; the former, reason, bids it, as it rises, to ascend to the serenity of virtue. The one dishonors man, and changes him to a beast; the other mightily transfigures him into a god. Reason illuminates the darkness of the brain by the light of contemplation; lust extinguishes the radiance of the mind by the night of desire. Reason makes man to talk with angels; lust forces him to wanton with brutes. Reason teaches man to find in exile a home; lust forces him in his home to be an exile. And in this, man's nature cannot reproach me for my ordering and management. For, out of the council of wisdom, I have set such a war of opposition between these antagonists that if, in this strife, reason bend down lust to defeat, the victory will not be without its following reward. (*Pr.* iii.26)

Though now the villain is a motion of the soul, "lust," not the flesh, much in this passage—for instance, the association of reason with divinity, light, and virtue, of lust with beastiality, darkness, and vice—differs little from Prudentius's characterization of the dual nature of man. One significant difference deserves consideration, however, namely the association of this duality in man the microcosm with a division in the superlunar world in a way which recalls aspects of the myth of the cosmic cycle of the soul and its use by Bernardus and Alain to dramatize the creation of man from contraries. To understand this passage we must return once more to the *Timaeus*. There Plato pictures the World-Soul as two circles turning in opposite directions, the circle of the Same (the fixed stars) turning to the right and the circle of the Different, subdivided into seven unequal circles (the planets), turning to the left.[57] Man's soul, he asserted, contained the same two divine revolutions.[58] However Plato may have understood these movements in the World-Soul and in man's soul, his followers and commentators consistently associated the circle of the Same with reason, the contrary movement of the Different with irrationality, with the passions. In the World-Soul, the opposite revolutions are harmonized in that the movement of the firmament dominates the contrary motion of the erratic planets as it turns them with it in its daily revolution of the earth. While Alain's passage is silent on the World-Soul, he does associate human reason with the sphere of the fixed stars, the passions which destroy man by moving him downward into darkness and beastiality with the contrary motion of the planets. Though the motion of reason here recalls the theory of the cycle of the soul, as it takes "its rise from a celestial source, passes through the lower levels of the earth, and, watchful of heavenly things, turns again to heaven," Alain is not depicting its life cycle but its proper mental activity.[59] The order which should govern the mind at all times is the order governing its creation and its final resolution. Similarly, the association of the activities of lust with the wayward planets recalls their malefic activities, which in the myth take one from one's true life in the firmament to the death and darkness which is this world. The analysis of psychic life here presented by Alain is succinctly stated in *The Sphere of Sacrobosco*, which Thorndike calls "the most used textbook in astronomy and cosmography from the thirteenth to the sixteenth century."[60] After associating the motion of reason in the microcosm with the movement of the firmament and irrationality in man with the movement of the planets, Holywood adds "rational motion in the microcosm" is found when "thought goes from the Creator through creatures to the Creator and there rests." The contrary, irrational movement in the microcosm is "from things corruptible to the Creator and back again to things corruptible."[61]

The contrary circular movements of the heavenly bodies are related to other significant contraries in terms of which medieval man ordered his world under the influence of the *concordia discors* model. Though Aristotle rejected the concept of the World-Soul, he saw, as did the Middle Ages, evidence of the "divinity" of the heavens in their diurnal movement in a perfect circle.[62] In the contrary motion of the planets and particularly the sun, he saw the source of earthly mutability. The second motion accounted for the fact that all things come to be and pass away.[63] This commonplace is represented by Bernardus in the *Cosmographia* by picturing "the 'Helian highway' in which the sun is borne on its annual journey" as "four diversely colored segments" (II.v.103). Each quarter of the circle equals one of the seasons. All things in this world are influenced by and take part in both the divine cycle of the heavens and the contrary and wayward cycle which accounts for their generation and corruption.

The association of rationality and irrationality in the microcosm with the contrary heavenly movements in the macrocosm helps explain why Lady Philosophy can characterize Boethius's sickness in the *Consolation* both as a failure to remain watchful of the heavens and as ignorance of the true na-

ture of the self. Boethius's lack of self-knowledge is apparent
when he admits that though he knows his origin, he does not
know his end. Lady Philosophy's cure is in large part a demon-
stration that his source is his goal. Indeed, she explains that the
order of all things is a circle which unites beginning and end:[64]
"Alle thynges seken ayen to hir propre cours, and alle thynges
rejoysen hem of hir retornynge ayen to hir nature. Ne noon
ordenaunce is bytaken to thynges but that that hath joyned
the endynge to the bygynnynge and hath maked the cours of
itself stable" (III.*m*.ii.39–46). The source of the stability of
this circle, its stable center, is, of course, God. Though Boethius does not explicitly say so, he would seem to have in mind
two contrary circles which perhaps can be best characterized
as tragic and comic circles.

The tragic pattern is exemplified by Dame Fortune's wheel.
Sitting at its stable center, Fortune spins it, raising those who
serve her gifts aloft only to cast them down. The same pattern
characterizes Nature and her gifts. It is evident in the cycles of
the year, rising from the dead winter through an awakening
spring into the glory of summer, only to return through fall to
winter. The same order is also evident in man's natural life,
with its return at the end to a second childhood. Thus, Bernardus adds to his characterization of the "Helian highway"
of the sun as four segments signifying the seasons a picture of
the sun itself progressing from youth to age "through a four-
fold change of countenance" (II.v.102). The pattern of ascending to descend is the pattern of sin, of man's first disobedience
and his subsequent wayward thoughts and deeds.[65] The cycles
of Fortune and Nature are, of course, the consequence of
Adam's first assertion of self in contempt of God. This is the
pattern of all things which are born to die, even of the world
itself, which, whether by fire or ice, will ultimately return to
the chaos from which it arose.

Opposed to the tragic pattern of all things natural is the
comic pattern of all things divine. This is not the order of
nature but the order of grace, of that love and light which
descend from God to man and lead him back to his creator. We
can see it exemplified in Christ's three advents, his initial descent into the flesh and hell to redeem, his final descent to
judge, and in his repeated descents into the soul of man as

grace.[66] This pattern is the order of the soul's history and of the mind in search of God, as the soul returns again to its source. This is the descent in humility which is actually an ascension. We can recognize it, for instance, in Augustine's adjuration to man to seek true life: "Even now after the descent of Life to you, will ye not ascend and live? But whither ascend ye, when ye are on high, and *set your mouth against the heavens?* Descend, that ye may ascend, and ascend to God. For ye have fallen, by ascending against Him."[67] Christ in his descent and ascension has shown the way, just as Dante shows it in his descent through hell which is at the same time an ascension. The comic cycle of the divine contains and governs the tragic cycle of the natural, just as the diurnal revolution of the fixed stars contains and orders the contrary movement of the wayward planets. Though the natural cycle is contrary to the divine cycle, it is part of God's total order, an order in which such contraries are harmonized. If the demands of justice require that all things which are born must die, the mercy of God insures that the soul, which was not born to die, may live, that it may return to its source by passing through nature's tragedy.

The war within divided man is only part of a struggle being waged throughout the cosmos between the contraries good and evil, a struggle which progresses, of course, toward the ultimate triumph of the good, though, paradoxically, only the good can be said to have any essential existence. Though evil was considered to exist only as a privation, a deficiency in something good, it was also considered contrary to good. Speaking in this for the whole Middle Ages, Augustine tells us that "to that nature which supremely is, and which created all else that exists, no nature is contrary save that which does not exist. For nonentity is the contrary of that which is. And thus there is no being contrary to God, the Supreme Being, and Author of all beings whatsoever."[68] He goes on to assert a few lines later that "it is not nature, therefore, but vice, which is contrary to God. For that which is evil is contrary to the good. And who will deny that God is the supreme good? Vice, therefore, is contrary to God, as evil to good. Further, the nature it vitiates is a good, and therefore to this good also it is contrary. But while it is contrary to God only as evil is contrary to good, it is contrary to the nature which it vitiates, both as evil and as hurtful. For to God no evils are hurtful."[69] Indeed, evil can only exist in conjunction with its contrary, good, for it has itself no being and consequently can only exist in things good in themselves, but vitiated by it.

The cosmic struggle between good and evil began with the fall of the angels, which created, Augustine argues, "two angelic communities," communities "dissimilar and contrary to one another, one both by nature good and by will upright, the other also good by nature but by will depraved, . . . spoken of in this book of Genesis under the names of light and darkness."[70] With the Fall, the family of man is similarly divided into two contrary cities which become allied with the two angelic communities. Augustine describes the qualities of these two cities as contraries: "Humility is specially recommended to the city of God as it sojourns in this world, and is specially exhibited in the city of God, and in the person of Christ its King; while the contrary vice of pride, according to the testimony of sacred writings, specially rules his adversary the devil. And certainly this is the great difference which distinguishes the two cities of which we speak, the one being the society of the godly men, the other of the ungodly, each associated with the angels that adhere to their party, and the one guided and fashioned by love of self, the other by love of God."[71] Augustine's vision of the war between the city of *caritas* and the city of *cupiditas* is simultaneously a vision of history and a vision of every man's spiritual life. Though the good is destined to win this conflict, only in the fullness of time in macrocosm and microcosm will God be all in all. The conflict of *caritas* and *cupiditas* in man is not simply analogous to the warfare of the two cities; it is part of it and one with it.

Before closing this discussion of the *concordia discors* model of cosmic order with an examination of number as the principle which harmonizes the diverse and the discordant, I should like to examine Chaucer's use of *concordia discors* in *The Knight's Tale*. Such an examination should consolidate much that we have explored and suggest much that we might have explored "had we but world enough and time," for the close correspondence and interaction of the contraries at war within man and those ordering the cosmos is nowhere more evident than in *The Knight's Tale.*

The Knight's Tale opens with a picture of Theseus returning in triumph from a war with the Amazons. It is a picture of harmony restored through Theseus's conquest of "al the regne of Femenye" and his marriage to its Queen, Ypolita. Male and female are united. War has produced love. This concord is almost immediately destroyed, however, as Theseus encounters a company of ladies who have lost their husbands in a war. Those blessed by Fortune meet those cursed by her. Explaining that the Theban tyrant Creon refuses to bury their husbands, the ladies ask for mercy. Theseus promises vengeance, and immediately marches to Thebes, levels it, and slays Creon. In the process, he captures two Thebans, Palamon and Arcite, and returns once more in triumph to Athens, where Palamon and Arcite are imprisoned for life. In spite of all Theseus's chivalry, nothing fundamental seems to have changed: "wele" still confronts woe.

The juxtaposition of contraries continues, as we next watch Palamon and Arcite fall in love with Emelye, Ypolita's sister, as she does her observance to May in the garden adjacent to the prison. She is weaving a garland out of flowers white and red, and is herself the fairest flower in the garden. More accurately, she unites two flowers, the white lily and the red rose. Straightway the two blood brothers are transformed to mortal foes for the love of Emelye: Love produces war. Eventually, Arcite is released from prison and banished to Thebes through the intercession of a friend The first part of the poem ends with both lovers in sorrow, each envying the lot of the other.

Part II begins with Arcite, who has been turned "up so doun" by love, returning to Athens in disguise. The royal Theban has become a servant. When Palamon escapes prison and encounters Arcite doing observance to May in a grove, they agree to fight to the death the next day for sole claim to Emelye. Their fight is interrupted, however, by Theseus, who discovers them while hunting with all his retinue, ladies of the court included. Palamon confesses all and demands that both he and Arcite be slain in the name of justice. Theseus is willing to oblige, but the ladies plead for mercy, so that Theseus, his

reason overcoming his ire, forgives them. To settle their conflicting claims to Emelye, he decrees that each shall gather a
force of one hundred knights and return a year hence to win
her in mortal combat in a tournament. Part II ends with the
formerly sorrowful lovers rejoicing.

Such a rehearsal of plot reveals that *The Knight's Tale* pervasively pictures life in terms of contraries. Virtually everything is viewed as united opposites or as capable of being transformed into its opposite. Everywhere the contraries seem in
conflict. This picture of a world of warring contraries is transformed in the third section into an image of a universe seemingly hopelessly torn by contrary forces.

Part III begins with a description of the "lists" Theseus
builds to hold the battle royal which is to bring peace and secure love. The circular theatre with its temples in the East to
Venus, in the West to Mars, in the North to Diana reveals the
contrary nature and influence of these classical deities and
their respective planets. Though Theseus liked the theatre
"wonder weel," it should give the reader pause, for as an
image of macrocosm and microcosm, it is an image of contraries unharmonized.[72] When each of the principals in the
human triangle goes to pray to one of the deities in the cosmic triangle—Palamon to Venus, Arcite to Mars, Emelye to
Diana—and both Venus and Mars promise success, the human
triangle is subsumed under the cosmic one, so that man appears little more than a manifestation of these cosmic forces,
mere puppets in their warfare. Cosmic necessity seems to have
totally eliminated its contrary, human freedom. The fact that
Saturn, who describes himself as the most malefic of the planets and the most powerful, since his course through the heavens is the widest, promises to make peace between Venus and
Mars is cold consolation, for Saturn is a principle of vengeance, death, and destruction.[73] The parallel established between the human and the cosmic triangle establishes a parallel between Theseus and Saturn, for Theseus seeks to order
the human world just as Saturn promises to order the cosmic
one. The solution both would seem to have in mind at this
point is the same, death. Thus, the third section leaves us with
a picture of universal discord, of a macrocosm of contrary
forces dominated by the god of death and destruction, of man

the microcosm similarly torn by Venus, Mars, and Diana, with only his own destructive impulses able to make a peace.

Part IV of *The Knight's Tale* corrects, as it were, the limited vision of Part III. Though Saturn does resolve the conflict by slaying Arcite as soon as he has won the combat, thus giving Mars his due, yet leaving Emelye for Venus's devotee, Jupiter emerges as the ultimate harmonizer of these warring contraries. We learn that Jupiter rules the universe by binding contraries together,

> For with that faire cheyne of love he bond
> The fyr, the eyr, the water, and the lond
> In certeyn boundes, that they may nat flee.
>
> (I.2991–93)

The appeal to the hierarchical principle of the fair chain of love does not negate the image of a cosmos of contraries, but completes it, for hierarchy is one of the ways God harmonizes contraries into a stable order which converts "al unto his propre welle/ From which it is dirryved" (I.3037–38). Just as Jove emerges over Saturn in the macrocosm so the Jove in Theseus triumphs over the Saturn in him, as Theseus changes the conditions of the tournament in the hope of preventing any loss of life. Once again his reason has triumphed over his bloodlust.

Though Theseus lectures Palamon and Emelye on making a "vertu of necessitee," his actual behavior suggests human freedom is consistent with divine necessity, however contrary the two may seem.[74] That Arcite is reconciled with Palamon on his death bed and recommends him to Emelye and that Theseus solidifies the peace between Athens and Thebes and insures the continuation of the human species by marrying Palamon and Emelye suggest that, however powerful the forces which tear man asunder, he is capable of rational choice and a limited measure of freedom. Though the stars influence, they would not seem to decree.

The work ends with a funeral juxtaposed to a marriage. The tragic cycle of all things born to die is enclosed within a comic cycle which ends the poem where it began, with a marriage, that archetypal image in the *concordia discors* tradition of love's power to bind together contraries into a harmonious

order.[75] Jove's order contains Saturn in macrocosm and microcosm, but Saturn does not rule in the one and need not rule in
the other, if man can triumph over his own passions, if he can
let the spirit of mercy within him triumph over the spirit of
vengeance and destruction.

Harmony in the macrocosm and microcosm was also considered a consequence of number and proportion. The medieval
world inherited a rich theory of numbers from the classical
world. Two aspects of this theory concern us, the idea that
numbers are forms and that harmony is the consequence of
numerical proportions. For the Pythagoreans, from whom
Plato apparently derived his theory of numbers, a number is
a form determined by an arrangement of points. As Copelston
explains, "One is a point, two is a line, three is a surface, four
is a solid."[76] Though numbers define portions of space and
impose shape upon matter, they are themselves abstract ideas.
Macrobius, for instance, tells us that "the attribute of perfection is common to all numbers, for in the progress of our
thought from our own plane to that of the gods they present
the first example of perfect abstraction."[77] The creation of the
universe out of contraries was dependent upon number. After
explaining in the *Timaeus* that the element fire is necessary that
things be visible and the element earth that things be tangible,
Plato goes on to explain the necessity that there be two means
linking them together: "Now if it had been required that the
body of the universe should be a plane surface with no depth,
a single mean would have been enough to connect its companion and itself; but in fact the world was to be solid in form,
and solids are always conjoined, not by one means, but by
two. Accordingly the god set water and air between fire and
earth, and made them, so far as possible, proportional to one
another, so that as fire is to air, so is air to water, and as air
is to water, so is water to earth, and thus he bound the frame
of a world visible and tangible."[78] Though one can see in
Plato's explanation of the creation of the universe the Pytha-
gorean theory that four points are necessary to define a solid,
his own conception is more complex. It is not the number four
but four numbers in geometrical progression which are necessary to create the world. The four elements must be united in
the created in the proper proportions.

Though it is doubtful that the Middle Ages properly understood Platonic number theory, one repeatedly encounters safely vague assertions that the ideas are numbers and that the harmony of the created is a consequence of proportion. The following, for instance, is from St. Bonaventure's *The Mind's Road to God:* "Since, therefore, all things are beautiful and in some way delightful, and beauty and delight do not exist apart from proportion, and proportion is primarily in number, its needs must be that all things are full of numbers (*numerosa*). And for this reason number is the outstanding exemplar in the mind of the Maker, and in all things it is the outstanding trace leading to wisdom."[79] Just as all numbers are ultimately derived from and united in the number one, which is both odd and even, male and female, so all things, which have form and proportion, derive from God the Monad and are united in Him.[80] History, in its totality another image of God, is similarly based on number, on proportional and harmonious sequences of time, and has its beginning, its Alpha, and its end, its Omega, in God.[81]

Just as the harmony of things and history is dependent upon number, so music and poetry, classed with music by Augustine, are dependent upon number.[82] Medieval musical theory is a theory of mathematical ratios and proportions. Harmonious chords are defined by the numerical ratios of the lengths of the strings producing them, and poetic meter by the ratio of the length of the accented and unaccented syllables in the various metrical feet. The musical scale itself, the diapason, is first a series of numerical proportions understood by the intelligence, though its number can be heard by the senses. The same proportions governing the diapason governed the harmony of created things. Thus, music is more than the ultimate metaphor for the divine harmony in all things; it is a revelation of it. The same mathematical laws which govern music govern creation and make it harmonious.

Boethius distinguishes three kinds of music: *musica mundana, musica humana,* and *musica instrumentalis. Musica mundana* is a consequence of the harmonious proportions of all of God's creation. He tells us that "the music of the universe is especially to be studied in those things which are observed in the combining of the elements, the variety of the seasons and the sky itself. How indeed could the swift mechanism of the sky move silently in its course? . . . Unless a certain harmony united the differences and the contrary powers of the four elements, how could they form a single body and mechanism? But all this diversity produces the variety of the seasons and fruits, and thereby makes a unity of the year."[83] Man is also musically ordered: "What human music is, anyone may understand by examining his own nature. For what is that which unites the incorporal activity of the reason with the body, unless it is a certain mutual adaptation and as it were a tempering of low and high sounds into a single consonance."[84]

Hugh of St. Victor, no doubt following Boethius in part, distinguishes the same three varieties of music, and tells us that "of the music of the universe, some is characteristic of the elements, some of the planets, some of the seasons: of the elements in their mass, number and volume; of the planets in their situation, motion, and nature; of the seasons in days (in the alternation of day and night), in months (in the waxing and waning of the moons), and in years (in the succession of spring, summer, autumn, and winter)."[85] That the harmony of the universe results from the concord of discordant and contrary things is especially apparent in Hugh's description of the music characteristic of the seasons. Concerning human music, Hugh informs us that "some is characteristic of the body, some of the soul, and some of the bond between the two."[86] Among those things indicating the music of the body, Hugh notes "those fluids or humors through the mixture or complexion of which the human body subsists—a type of mixture belonging to all sensate beings."[87] We have already seen the importance of contraries in the theory of the bodily humors. Hugh continues: "Music is characteristic of the soul partly in its virtues, like justice, piety, and temperance; and partly in its powers, like reason, wrath, and concupiscence. The music between the body and soul is that natural friendship by which the soul is leagued to the body, not in physical bonds, but in certain sympathetic relationships for the purpose of imparting motion and sensation to the body. Because of this friendship, it is written, 'No man hates his own flesh [Eph.5:29].' This music consists in loving one's flesh, but one's spirit more; in cherishing one's body, but not destroying one's virtue."[88] Such is the harmony of man, a harmony, like that of the universe, the result in large measure of the concord of contrary things.

One frequently encounters in the Middle Ages the idea that the whole universe is a vast musical instrument.[89] Honorius of Autun expresses the traditional ideas in the following manner: "The supreme artisan made the universe like a great zither upon which he placed strings to yield a variety of sounds, for he divided his work in two—into two parts antithetical [*contraria*] to each other. Spirit and matter, antithetical in nature yet consonant in existence, resemble a choir of men and boys blending their bass and treble voices. . . . Material things similarly imitate the distinction of choral parts, divided as things into genera, species, individuals, forms, and numbers; all of these blend harmoniously as they observe with due measure the law implanted within them and so, as it were, emit their proper sound. A harmonious chord is sounded by spirit and body, angel and devil, heaven and hell, fire and water, air and earth, sweet and bitter, soft and hard, and so all things are harmonized."[90]

Since the music of all things is based upon the same numerical principles, principles originating with and abiding in God, both music itself and the music in created things can lead to God, though Augustine, consistent with his whole attitude toward the world, finds it more of an impediment to the soul's hearing the music which is God than traces leading back to Him.[91] For one more inclined to view the world's beauty as a reflection of God capable of leading to Him, like many men in the later Middle Ages who developed a new appreciation of the literal and the visible, the writing of poetry could be a deeply religious and highly serious task, for all its ultimate vanity, an effort to mirror in poetry the number and proportion of all things and thereby restore in man the harmony which unites him with God. For medieval man, to assert that "music has charms to soothe a savage breast" or that it is "the food of love" is to state fact. In the *Dream of Scipio*, after Africanus has described the music of the spheres, he tells Scipio that "gifted men, imitating this harmony on stringed instru-

ments and in singing, have gained for themselves a return to
this region."[92] Certainly a Christian poet could similarly hope
to advance his soul.

Just as the universe can be viewed as harmonious music, as
a grand symphony, so it can be considered a poem, a poem
whose author and maker is God. Augustine presents this idea
at length.

> For God would never have created any, I do not say angel, but
> even man, whose future wickedness He foreknew, unless He had
> equally known to what uses in behalf of the good He could turn
> him, thus embellishing the course of the ages, as it were an exquisite
> poem set off with antitheses. For what are called antitheses are
> among the most elegant of the ornaments of speech. They might be
> called in Latin "oppositions," or, to speak more accurately, "con-
> trapositions;" but this word is not in common use among us, though
> the Latin, and indeed the languages of all nations, avail themselves
> of the same ornaments of style. In the Second Epistle to the
> Corinthians the Apostle Paul also makes a graceful use of antithesis,
> in that place where he says, "By the armour of righteousness on the
> right hand and on the left, by honour and dishonour, by evil report
> and good report: as deceivers, and yet true; as unknown, and yet
> well known; as dying, and, behold, we live; as chastened, and not
> killed; as sorrowful yet always rejoicing; as poor, yet making many
> rich; as having nothing, and yet possessing all things." As, then,
> these oppositions of contraries lend beauty to the language, so the
> beauty of the course of this world is achieved by the opposition of
> contraries, arranged, as it were, by an eloquence not of words, but
> of things. This is quite plainly stated in the Book of Ecclesiasticus, in
> this way: "Good is set against evil, and life against death: so is the
> sinner against the godly. So look upon all the works of the Most
> High, and these are two and two, one against another."[93]

Since *Troilus and Criseyde* is a poem about a universe which
is itself a poem of united contraries, it should hardly surprise
us if the *Troilus* is itself a harmony of contraries. When Troilus
is translated to the heavens at the end of the poem, he hears
the music of the spheres, that traditional image of the harmony
of all in and through God. The question of whether or not the
harmony he experienced in this world with Criseyde was a
snare and an impediment keeping him from this heavenly
music or an echo of divine harmony intended to lead him to
this his true home must also be asked of the poem itself. Is it

merely cursed pagan poetry or can its harmonies, provided no careless scribe "mysmetre" them, lead us to God? Such questions cannot be answered until we have considered the whole of the poem, of course, but they are among the questions the *concordia discors* tradition insists that we ask.

The influence of the *concordia discors* tradition on the *Troilus* is evident in such passages as Troilus's song on the paradoxes of love, Pandarus's argument that two contraries make "o lore" and his characterization of life as juxtaposed opposites, and, most notably, Troilus's song at the end of Book III on the binding power of love, all passages Chaucer added to Boccaccio's *Il Filostrato*.[94] This study is not primarily concerned with what the poem's characters conceive the order of the created to be, but with the poem's order and the possibility that its order imitates the *concordia discors* conception of the cosmos. Let me avoid being disingenuous: it is the basic conclusion of this study that Chaucer imitated the *concordia discors* conception of universal order in forming *Troilus and Criseyde* from the matter of Boccaccio's *Il Filostrato*. The remainder of this chapter is limited to an examination of the influence of this model upon the structure, content, and style of the first three books of the *Troilus*. In a sense, it seeks to demonstrate that Troilus's song at the end of Book III on how love binds together contraries characterizes the order of the poem as well as the order of the world as Chaucer represents it in the *Troilus*.

Sanford Meech has stressed the balancing of "significant oppositions" in the poem, especially among the characters.[95] Though easy generalizations oversimplify the complexity of the characters, none of whom is one-dimensional, it is true that contrast is a controlling principle of characterization in the poem. For instance, beside Troilus's idealism stands Pandarus's realism; beside his considerable sincerity, Diomede's opportunism; beside his truth of a kind in loving and his relative selflessness, Criseyde's infidelity and truth to self. Muscatine, Meech, and Payne have all stressed, in varying degrees and from varying perspectives, that significant differences in the characters are revealed not only by their actions but also by the general level of style associated with them.[96] Though inadequate, as we shall see, Muscatine's formulation seems the most widely accepted. To Troilus belongs the high, nonrepresentational style of romance; to Pandarus, the lower, more realistic style of the bourgeois tradition; to Criseyde, a mixed style, one fluctuating between the styles of Troilus and Pandarus.

Although Criseyde makes a brief appearance in Book I and Pandarus an extended one, Book I primarily depicts Troilus and the effects of love upon him. When we first meet him he is footloose and fancy-free, a typically proud mocker of love, one every bit as trite as such phraseology. After Cupid smites him, he is transformed into an equally typical lover—provided, that is, one takes one's conception of typicality from the tradition of the courtly romance. As Muscatine has demonstrated, Troilus "is conceived and constructed almost exclusively according to the stylistic conventions of the courtly tradition."[97] What individuality Troilus possesses seems largely a product of the extreme degree to which he satisfies the requirements of the courtly lover. He is simultaneously epitome and caricature of the conventional hero of the courtly romance; indeed, he comes to represent the tradition from which he derives, reflecting all the glories and limitations of the idealistic view of life.[98] Presented in the style of the romance, he also embodies its metaphysics, an idealism, generally Platonic in character, which sees this world not as isolated and discrete but as a continuation and incarnation of the transcending Beautiful and True. Thus, for Troilus the gods control events, and Criseyde seems as much goddess as woman.

Just as *Troilus and Criseyde* combines distinctive styles, it unites, as Muscatine indicates, different generic characteristics; it is a *sui generis* combination of the qualities of the romance and those we have come to associate with the novel. Certainly Book I is almost straight romance, as it is dominated by idealism and the high style, by the lyric rhapsodies, the complaints, and the nonrepresentational dialogue in which Troilus pours forth his soul. The lyric mode in the poem is almost exclusively Troilus's: Robert Payne has counted ten lyrics in the poem, eight of which are spoken by Troilus; Muscatine, understanding lyric somewhat more broadly, attributes "thirty-odd lyric monologues" to Troilus.[99] Though Chaucer is equally interested in Criseyde's psychology, she, significantly, does not express herself in lyrics very often. Even when Toilus is not expressing his joy in songs of praise, or his sorrow in laments, but merely talking with Pandarus or Criseyde, his conversation is presented in a highly stylized form; it seldom is made to appear realistic. Clearly Chaucer has chosen to present Troilus in this fashion partly at least because of what Troilus is. He cannot indulge in everyday conversation, in give-and-take and witty repartee, because he is always true to himself, to his total commitment to love and the passion and exaltation within him. It is significant that Book I, after Troilus has fallen in love, takes place entirely inside Troilus's bedroom, though we are told that he goes forth to the battlefield from time to time. In the first book we are taken inside Troilus, into the private world of his thoughts and emotions. As a whole, Book I is unconcerned with the mundane, with the bodily; it presents internal spiritual experience, the life of the soul externalized through speech. Such a subject matter is not particularly susceptible to realistic treatment. The reality of Book I is the spiritual world because that is the only world which has much reality to Troilus. Once awakened to love, he is concerned with spiritual experience, not persons, places, and things.

If Troilus impresses us with his idealism, we are also struck by his earnestness and his sincerity. He is painfully earnest and almost boorishly sincere. In Book I, things seem to be exactly what they appear to be. We must be careful not to oversimplify, however. In the midst of the scene between Troilus and Pandarus when Pandarus thinks Troilus may die or fall "in frensie" and thus cries "Awake" loudly, the narrator tells us Troilus's thoughts and suggests that his behavior is not without art. For instance, Troilus thought that "som tyme it is a craft to seme fle/ Fro thyng which in effect men hunte faste." Similarly, when Pandarus tells Criseyde in Book II about how he learned that Troilus was in love by overhearing him in a garden—if we assume that this indeed happened— we are forced to reassess the simplicity and sincerity of Book I. Perhaps neither Troilus's nor Pandarus's behavior was as simple, direct, and honest, as spontaneous, as it seemed. How relatively straightforward everything is in Book I is apparent, however, when we compare it to Book II, where almost nothing is what it seems. There Pandarus and Criseyde almost always speak for effect; the calculated remark and response is everywhere present. Though Chaucer may tell us that Troilus calculates, his calculating is seldom evident, not because he is a more artful calculator than Pandarus or Criseyde, but because there is less of that in him than in anyone else in the poem. Unlike both Criseyde and Pandarus, he is not related to Calchas. Though he will prove capable of duplicity, in Book I, and indeed throughout the poem, he is, in comparison with Criseyde and Pandarus, remarkably true to himself, remarkably consistent in his commitment to love and what he understands that to entail, however mistaken a commitment that may be.

It is true, as Muscatine argues, that Pandarus has a leveling effect upon Troilus, though he is unable to keep Troilus's feet planted firmly on the ground for long. Pandarus's presence does create a double perspective on what takes place, so that we are forced to judge it both from the perspective of his own relative realism and that of Troilus's idealism, with each perspective revealing the limitations in the other. It seems to me, however, that the range of Pandarus's character and the style in which it is expressed are greater than Muscatine allows. Though Muscatine judges Pandarus's style the most realistic in the poem, Payne characterizes it as sententious.[100] Such differing evaluations of Pandarus's style are the consequence of whether one focuses upon him when he is with Criseyde, when he is realistic in manner, or with Troilus, when he is sententious. The following is perhaps typical of Pandarus and Criseyde together.

> "As evere thrive I," quod this Pandarus,
> "Yet koude I telle a thyng to doon yow pleye."
> "Now, uncle deere," quod she, "telle it us
> For Goddes love; is than th'assege aweye?
> I am of Grekes so fered that I deye."
> "Nay, nay," quod he, "as evere mote I thryve,
> It is a thing wel bet than swyche fyve."
>
> "Ye, holy God," quod she, "what thyng is that?
> What! bet than swyche fyve? I! nay, ywys!
> For al this world ne kan I reden what
> It sholde ben; some jape, I trowe, is this;
> And but youreselven telle us what it is,

> My wit is for t'arede it al to leene.
> As help me God, I not nat what ye meene."
>
> "And I youre borugh, ne nevere shal, for me
> This thyng be told to yow, as mote I thryve!"
> "And whi so, uncle myn? whi so?" quod she.
> "By God," quod he, "that wol I telle as blyve!
> For proudder womman is ther noon on lyve,
> And ye it wist, in al the town of Troye.
> I jape nought, as evere have I joye!"
>
>   (II.120–40)

This is colloquial conversation from the real world, though perhaps somewhat exaggerated. When Pandarus and Criseyde are together, they are, for the most part, stylistically indistinguishable. When he talks to Troilus, we rarely hear such tit-for-tat dialogue; then even Pandarus's speeches, and they are rightly termed "speeches," are as much a monologue as part of a dialogue. The following is characteristic of Pandarus when he is talking to Troilus. It is in response to one of Troilus's few colloquial moments—"How devel maistow brynge me to blisse?"

> "Ye, Troilus, now herke," quod Pandare;
> "Though I be nyce, it happeth often so,
> Than oon that excesse doth ful yvele fare
> By good counseil kan kepe his frend therfro.
> I have myself ek seyn a blynd man goo
> Ther as he fel that couthe loken wide;
> A fool may ek a wis-man ofte gide.
>
> "A wheston is no kervyng instrument,
> But yet it maketh sharppe kervyng tolis.
> And there thow woost that I have aught myswent,
> Eschuw thow that, for swich thing to the scole is;
> Thus often wise men ben war by foolys.
> If thow do so, thi wit is wel bewared;
> By his contrarie is every thyng declared."
>
>   (I.624–37)

He goes on for nearly three more stanzas before Troilus gets a line, and then launches into another speech, with another appeal to Troilus to "herkne," this one lasting nine stanzas. Such sententiousness must be judged every bit as artifically stylized and hence nonrepresentational as a Troilus lament.

Though Pandarus is endlessly proverbial, he is almost never as sententious with Criseyde as he is with Troilus.[101] When talking with Troilus, as we have just seen, he pontificates, especially in the first book; when talking with Criseyde, he usually japes and playacts, though in Book IV her very real sorrow renders Pandarus somber. When he is with Troilus, we sometimes laugh at him; when he is with Criseyde, we usually laugh with him. Pandarus's different manner and style with Troilus and Criseyde are partly the result of art. One recalls Pandarus's condescending concern that he not make his "tale" to Criseyde too difficult, "for tendre wittes wenen al be wyle/ Theras thei kan nought pleynly understonde" (II.271–72), and his advice to Troilus not to make his "argumentes tough" when writing to Criseyde. Both Troilus's idealistic, earnest nature and his captivated conditions require one kind of art, just as Criseyde's practical, almost Epicurean nature and her free condition demand another. Just as Pandarus's art allows him to play different parts, so his own nature makes him eminently qualified for the role of intermediary, since he himself shares characteristics with both Troilus and Criseyde. Being a bit like both of them, he often knows them better than they know themselves. He knows, for instance, that Troilus's love is not as pure and ethereal as Troilus supposes it, that Troilus will go along with the Horaste story, and that Criseyde, once she leaves Troy, will never return, something Criseyde herself does not know. According to medieval psychology, one can only know something one is in some measure like, hence the necessity that man be an image of God that he may know Him. Similarly, according to the doctrine of contraries, the mean links the extremes by partial participation in their nature.

With Troilus, Pandarus is usually serious and idealistic, though less so in Book II than in Book I. Though Pandarus begins almost every one of his appearances with a jape, when he is with Troilus he does not persist in his japing, but inevitably becomes serious. In Books II and III, once he has begun to succeed in his endeavors to get Criseyde for Troilus, overcome by high spirits and a sense of mastery, he allows himself a certain "familiarity" with Troilus; he chides and mocks and introduces a note of realism concerning what love is about, but he is never able to sustain this manner with Troilus for long simply because Troilus does not respond in kind. In Book I there is even less of this quality. Troilus brings out the best in Pandarus. His love of Troilus is genuine and unqualified: "I have, and shal, for trewe or fals report,/ In wrong and right iloved the al my lyve" (I.593–94). He is at least capable of sharing Troilus's exalted view of love: "And thynk it is a guerdon, hire to serve" (I.818). This is hardly the bourgeois tradition! He has himself, it would seem, served long and faithfully. When he recommends in Book IV that Troilus get another girl, Troilus reminds him that he, Pandarus, has been unable to love another.

Understanding Pandarus's mixed nature and many-sided art is important to understanding Book I, for though his realism creates a double perspective in Book I, his own idealism, his genuine concern for Troilus, and his own variety of high style keep the book by and large in the province of romance. The dialogue does become comically contentious and stichomythic at times. Significantly, this quality is most pronounced in the middle of the scene, when Troilus breaks down, comes out of himself and down to earth enough to tell Pandarus the cause of his sorrow. Before it, Pandarus had been earnestly pleading his friendship and seriously arguing that he can help. After it, though he japes a bit at Troilus's former mocking of love, Pandarus is again sententious: love is a good thing; Criseyde is virtuous and must not be brought to shame; all things are created to love. Troilus is seriously repentant and intent on doing only what is good. The book ends very much in the province of the high style of romance. Troilus is on his knees rhapsodizing.

> Now, Pandare, I kan na more seye,
> But, thow wis, thow woost, thow maist, thow art al!
> My lif, my deth, hol in thyn hond I leye.
> Help now!
>
> (I.1051–54)

Pandarus swears his truth and goes forth thinking on this matter, dignified by Chaucer's picture of him as a man preparing to build a house and taking thought before sending forth his "hertes line" to achieve his purpose: "Al this Pandare in his

herte thoughte,/ And caste his werk ful wisely or he wroughte"
(I.1070–71). The book ends focusing upon Troilus, now the
perfect romance hero.

> For he bicom the friendlieste wight,
> The gentilest, and ek the mooste fre,
> The thriftiest and oon the beste knyght,
> That in his tyme was or myghte be.
> Dede were his japes and his cruelte,
> His heighe port and his manere estraunge,
> And ecch of tho gan for a vertu chaunge.
>
> (I.1079–85)

Though the reader has occasion to laugh at the human
comedy, Book I remains romance, as it is dominated by the
lyrical and idealistic Troilus and the sententious and earnest
Pandarus.

How true this is is readily apparent when we enter the second book and discover a new and different world, one which
contrasts sharply with that of the first book. Left behind is the
inner world of Troilus's idealism and the privacy of his bedroom for the public world of sophisticated society, the drawing
room, where ladies collectively read romances and conversation is above all else witty. D. W. Robertson has aptly termed
Book II "the first comedy of manners in English."[102] We have
now moved to what was to become in time the world of the
novel. It is a world where people speak in "ambages," words
"with two visages"; thus, it is appropriate that the narrator
invokes Janus, the god with two faces, to guide Pandarus.
Pandarus enters japing, and finds in Criseyde a near match for
his wit. When he asks if the book she and her companions are
reading is about love and that she teach him something good,
she responds, "Uncle, youre maistresse is nat here." When he
suggests dancing and doing observance to May, she answers
with at least partially-mock horror.

> "I? God forbede!" quod she, "be ye mad?
> Is that a widewes lif, so God yow save?
> By God, ye maken me ryght soore adrad!
> Ye ben so wylde, it semeth as ye rave.
> It sate me wel bet ay in a cave
> To bidde and rede on holy seyntes lyves;
> Lat maydens gon to daunce, and yonge wyves."
>
> (II.113–19)

She has, after all, been reading a romance, not a saint's life, and is too perceptive, to aware of who she is and what she is doing for this to be simply irony at her expense. Criseyde seldom lacks substantial control over her words and actions.

This scene between Pandarus and Criseyde is over five hundred lines long, nearly as long as that in Book I between Pandarus and Troilus, and is very much the contrary of that scene. It sets the tone for the whole book and is perhaps best characterized by the word "game," in sharp contrast to the "ernest" of Book I. It is full of japing and comedy, and has all the artificiality of the social world, as she and Pandarus play verbally with each other according to the rules of polite society. In such a world no one states the naked truth; one clothes one's meaning in artful words. When Pandarus says that he knows something to make her five times as happy as an end to the siege of Troy would, she says that this must be "som jape" and that she does not know what he means. Such avowals of ignorance become a *leit motif* for Criseyde, as she repeatedly insists that she does not understand, while all the while understanding a great deal. The narrator tells us that she never wished to know anything so much in her life and that she said, "Now, uncle myn, I nyl yow nought displese,/ Nor axen more that may do yow disese" (II.146–47). Sometimes it is indeed a "craft to seme fle/ Fro thynge which in effect men hunte faste." Criseyde reveals all the art she is here using in a single gesture, "and down hire eyghen caste." Though this may seem a sign of submission, Criseyde is not submitting; she is artfully employing the manners and mannerism of polite society. Variations of this image appear throughout the poem and reach their culmination in Book V, when Diomede, who knows "more than the crede" of the craft of false seeming in love, swears his love of Criseyde and asserts his own worth, "and caste asyde a litel wight his hed." Later, when Pandarus, without having revealed his little secret, announces that it is time for him to go, Criseyde restrains him with a jape—"What aileth yow to be thus wery soone,/ And namelich of wommen?" —and a request for some serious "business" conversation, for some advice. It is in such a mixed atmosphere of mutual confidence and mutual wariness that Pandarus insists that she is the woman he loves best excepting "paramours"; and she, that he is the man she most loves and trusts. Pandarus and Troilus

exchanged similar testimonies of friendship in Book I. There
we believed them; here we also do, but we understand that
here such assertions of devotions do not really mean very
much. After this exchange, Pandarus asks her to take for good
what he will say, and "she gan hire eighen down to caste," and
he "to coghe gan a lite," all the while protesting that he uses
no art. When he finally announces that Troilus loves her and
requests that she befriend him, her immediate reaction is to
think, "I shal felen what he meneth, ywis." Her second reaction
is to burst into tears and lament her unfortunate lot. Here,
obviously, almost nothing is simply what it seems, as everything that is said or done is for calculated effects.

Nevertheless, just as there are touches of realism in the first
book, so there are moments of romance here, most noticeably
when Chaucer focuses upon Troilus and Criseyde's reaction
to him. The picture of Troilus riding by in arms on wounded
horse is sheer romance. Similarly of the world of romance is
the scene in the garden, where Antigone sings of love, the description of the descent of night, the song of the nightingale,
and Criseyde's dream, according to Muscatine, "the sequence
in which the poem comes closest to pure romance."[103] Before
long, however, we are back in a naturalistic world, one where
Pandarus can thrust a letter in Criseyde's bosom and displays
his best japes, japes he would never waste on Troilus. Just as
the realism of Book I is surrounded by romance, so the romance
elements in Book II are enclosed and dominated by its naturalistic style and content. It ends as it began, in the public world
of high society with the games people play, as Pandarus
gathers a large part of the better half of Troy at Deiphebus's
house, where all, with varying degrees of feigning, act out
Pandarus's grand charade.

This scene links the end of Book II with its beginning and
culminates the characterization of its world. When Pandarus
first came to visit Criseyde, he almost immediately began to
praise Troilus as a second Hector. Criseyde responds to this
with the observation that she believes it, for he is much talked
of. Indeed, she says, "alle pris hath he/ Of hem that me were
levest preysed be" (II.188–89). The final scene of the book is a
picture of all the right people, even Helen of Troy herself,
praising Troilus.

> After compleynte, hym gonnen they to preyse,
> As folk don yet, whan som wight hath bygonne
> To preise a man, and up with pris hym reise
> A thousand fold yet heigher than the sonne:
> "He is, he kan, that fewe lordes konne."
> And Pandarus, of that they wolde afferme,
> He naught forgat hire preisynge to conferme.
>
> (II.1583–89)

The narrator tells us that Criseyde heard all this and noted every word, so that her heart laughed, "For who is that ne wolde hire glorifie,/ To mowen swich a knyght don lyve or dye?" (II.1593–94). How well Chaucer understood the effect on mere mortals of the flattery of the great! Nonetheless, Criseyde maintains a "sobre cheere," as social tact requires, just as when they were complaining of Troilus's illness, she thought, but did not say, "Best koud I yet ben his leche." Even the narrator is apparently taken in by the two faces of this social world, for he repeatedly insists that Criseyde is "innocent" of all that is taking place. Thus, just as Book I has a circular shape, beginning with romance, descending to realism and then returning to romance, so Book II begins realistically, ascends to romance in the middle only to descend again to the world of the comedy of manners. Both are in a sense circular; however, they are contrary circles, one descending to ascend, the other ascending to descend.

That Book II is dominated by the realistic vein is not surprising. Much of it is of necessity given over to the machinations of Pandarus. Even more important in establishing its characteristics than Pandarus's ubiquitousness is Criseyde's nature. Pandarus suits his style of wooing to Criseyde, becoming in her presence wholly the half of him that is like his niece. The occasional moments when Criseyde seems like a romance heroine are all moments when she is under the influence of Troilus and the transforming power of love. On her own, free from the influence of Troilus and love, she is ever down to earth and practical, desiring her independence and freedom, wanting pleasure but pragmatically fearing pain, laughing, japing, and debating, now tending this way, now that.

Just as the spiritual world of Book I requires a nonrepresentational style, the social world of Book II demands a realistic one. Its realistic mode is ideally suited for treating people who are "realistic," who submit their own desires and aspirations to considerations of what society allows and approves. Troilus tends to consider the world to be what he wishes it to be; he subordinates it to his own vision and his own feelings. Thus, for him Criseyde is what he assumes her to be. Criseyde, on the contrary, conforms her private world, her own inner life, to the demands and expectations of the public world.[104] Considerations of estate, reputation, name form her. She worries about what people think and what they will say. We have just seen that Troilus's foremost virtue in her mind is that he is praised by all the people she would willingly be praised by. Even when she is alone, she thinks in public terms, as when she debates the pros and cons of loving Troilus. If Troilus falls in love with her by seeing her apart in a corner, she falls in love with Troilus when he rides by to the cheers of the public world. In Book II we see her primarily in social settings because she is primarily a social person; she does not have an overpowering inner life and no transforming imagination, but she does have a strong sense of the realities of everyday life and by and large conforms herself to them. Finally, Book II is as much her book as Book I is Troilus's. It is in Book II that we learn who and what Criseyde is, and however much she may become like Troilus, she remains true throughout the poem to the temporizing self we meet here in Book II.

The differences in tone and style between the first two books are precisely what we would expect given their respective proems. The narrator of Book I is himself full of sorrow, a "sorwful instrument," far from the god of Love's help "in derknesse," reminding us of Boethius in prison at the opening of the *Consolation* or of Dante in the dark wood at the beginning of the *Divine Comedy*. He invokes as his muse, perhaps under the influence of Dante, Tisiphone, the suffering "goddesse of torment." Whatever the cause of the narrator's own sorrows, whether they derive from lack of success in love or from the human condition in general, he clearly has little difficulty throughout the book in empathizing with his hero. The narrator's attitude in Book II contrasts sharply with this attitude. Now he is only a translator, writing without feeling and without the need for any art save that of the historian. Reason, not passion, is now required. The only muse he invokes is Clio, the muse of history, for suddenly his matter is remote and foreign, not something touching him to the quick. If before he was singing of love and living in charity that he might advance his soul, now he refuses either praise or blame and seemingly continues only because he has begun. Now he speaks only as his author spoke before him. Such differing narrative stances are appropriate to the differing modes of the first two books; to depict idealism and sorrow in the high style of romance requires inspiration, to present the world realistically requires only the techniques of the historian, no doubt a more mundane calling from the point of view of a poet. Indeed, a large part of the invocation of Book I is a bidding prayer by the narrator, as he, speaking for himself, adopts one form, the prayer, of Troilus's characteristic style. The central portion of the invocation to Book II, on the other hand, is a dispassionate reflection on the pastness of the past, reminding us of the analytical Criseyde. Like the poem's other artist, Pandarus, the narrator adapts his style and point of view to the subject at hand. Apparently the principle of decorum announced in the proem to the first book—

> For wel sit it, the sothe for to seyne,
> A woful wight to han a drery feere,
> And to a sorwful tale, a sory chere.—
>
> (I.12–14)

is still operative; its fulfillment merely requires an antithetical narrative pose.

Just as both the first two books contain elements of their opposite, however, so the narrator at times, in both books, forgets his pose. However involved he may be in Book I, for instance, he is distant enough from Troilus to somewhat haughtily mock him for haughtily mocking lovers Similarly in Book II, however distant he may be from Criseyde, when she first "sees" Troilus and asks "Who yaf me drynke?" he is emotionally involved enough in his subject to insist, somewhat gratuitously, that this was not a sudden love. Significantly, both interruptions come precisely at the same point in the structure of the two books, after each has first "seen" the other, and reveal conflicts within the narrator's value system.

At first, love seemed both "a law of kynde" and "vertuous in kynde," something to exult over; now it seems something to be apologized for. If love is good, it remains good in spite of Criseyde's failure to be true; if it is bad, Troilus's fidelity will not justify it. Whatever the wisdom of the narrator's varying response to his subject, however, it seems true that the basically opposing attitudes he takes toward his material in Books I and II are a consequence both of the differences in the two characters upon which each book focuses in turn, Troilus and then Criseyde, and of the difference in the nature of the love each character experiences.

The interpretation that Chaucer has organized and structured his material to present in differing styles two contrary worlds, one associated with Troilus and represented by the first book, the other associated with Criseyde and represented by the second book, is supported by a comparison of the structures of *Troilus and Criseyde* and its main source, *Il Filostrato*. Boccaccio ends his first part with Troilo in love, but prior to the appearance of Pandaro. Part II presents both Pandaro's initial encounter with Troilo and his subsequent interviews with Criseyde and Troilo in turn. By moving Pandaro's first scene with Troilo into Book I, Chaucer is able to devote the first book almost exclusively to Troilus and the second book, save for Pandarus's necessary returns to Troilus, almost exclusively to Criseyde. In Boccaccio, it is the entrance into the poem and the activity of Pandaro which accounts for the shape of Part II. Chaucer's Pandarus is active in both Books I and II; in Book II, Criseyde is the main focus of attention and the main reason for its separation from Book I and its form and style. The distribution of Pandarus between the two books is, of course, one of the ways Chaucer indicates his intermediate nature, as is his differing style in the two books.

Book III, the center of the poem, narrates the union of the lovers, though it is a center that will not hold. With laborious help from Pandarus, love, that force which unites contraries, brings these two contrary individuals together both physically and spiritually. By the end of the book, their union seems complete and perfect; they seem to have but one will, as "ech of hem gan otheres lust obeye." Indeed, love so unites them that they seem nearly undistinguishable. One recalls Macrobius's contention, one common in the tradition, that contraries are capable of union because of fundamental similarities underlying their differences. This union elevates and spiritualizes Criseyde, degrades and sullies Troilus through contact with the real and mundane. Now Criseyde can for the moment sing a lyric, her *aube* regretting the passing of night, and talk with Pandarus in a nonrepresentational form, her soliloquy, aimed vaguely at Pandarus, on the imperfection of worldly happiness. Troilus can play games, can employ false seeming, as he accepts and carries through the ruse of the Horaste story; he even refers to that fiction as a "game," though he blames it on Pandarus. In their union, though they ultimately retain their own natures, they become to a considerable degree alike and harmonious.

Book III begins with the first private meeting of the lovers, if a meeting with Pandarus present can be considered private. Chaucer ends Book II with Pandarus and Criseyde on the threshhold of the room where Troilus lies sick in bed, so that his proem to Book III functions both as an interruption in the events he is narrating and as a prayer for the success of what is to come. There are, no doubt, several reasons why Chaucer chose to end Book II where he did. Thus interrupting the scene creates suspense. Ending the second book with Pandarus about to bring Criseyde in to Troilus neatly answers the ending of Book I, where we see him set forth to get her. Now we see him return with her: Mission accomplished. Chaucer also ends Book II here, that he may delay even the mere physical union of Troilus and Criseyde in the same place until Book III; indeed, its primary purpose is structural, for Book III relates the union of the lovers and itself unites Books I and II, wedding significant of their disparate qualities into a union.

Though apparently unaware of its structural significance, when Muscatine seeks to illustrate the full mixture of the qualities of romance and realism in the poem, he turns to the third book.[105] Books I and II occasionally admit elements of their opposite for brief periods, but it is only in Book III that we find simultaneously present the high style of the romance and the more realistic style and perspective of the bourgeois tradition. In both the major scenes of Book III in which the lovers are together we are more conscious than ever before of a dou-

ble perspective. It is as though Chaucer were trying to unite—
to present simultaneously—the world view of *The Knight's
Tale* and *The Miller's Tale*.

Since Criseyde has been in some measure transformed by the
power of love, Pandarus is the primary character by which the
realistic perspective is incorporated into Book III. Criseyde
does remain true enough to her own nature to function in this
way at times. When Troilus swoons in the consummation
scene, for instance, she asks, "Is this a mannes game?" When
he is fervently thanking the gods for their grace in bringing
Criseyde and him together, she reminds him that she is lying
there naked beside him. She seems every bit as impatient as
Pandarus with Troilus's tendency to spiritualize his love. Significantly, when Pandarus forces a realistic view of what is
happening upon us, he does so as much by being comically
idealistic and overly enthusiastic as by being himself realistic
about it. He is certainly being realistic when he tells the praying Troilus before the consummation scene that he need not
fear that Criseyde will bite him. The comedy and absurdity is
unintentional on his part, however, when he responds to the
first kiss Criseyde gives Troilus by falling on his knees, thanking Cupid and Venus, and announcing that he hears each bell
in town ringing "withouten hand." Indeed, here he is adopting
precisely Troilus's mode. Such extreme behavior parodies itself
and indeed the whole scene, and reminds us of just what a kiss
amounts to. It ought also to remind us, however, that when
contraries are united, the result is a harmonious music.
Whether or not the bells are ringing, Venus is making "melo-
die." Throughout the book, Troilus prays and rejoices more
fervently than ever; Pandarus japes and leaps and helps with
even greater vigor. When Troilus swoons in fear of Criseyde's
displeasure, Pandarus, "For this or that, he into bed hym
caste." We may be in the private territory of Troilus, the bedroom, but Pandarus and Criseyde have brought the real world
into it with a vengeance. The ridiculousness of farce and the
sublime of romance are one.

The union of contrary styles and forms of behavior in Book
III and the intermediate nature of Pandarus is perfectly cap-
tured, for instance, when he is urging Criseyde, in the first
scene of the book, to accept Troilus as her lover.

> Therwith his manly sorwe to biholde,
> It myghte han mad an herte of stoon to rewe;
> And Pandare wep as he to water wolde,
> And poked evere his nece new and newe,
> And seyde, "Wo bygon ben hertes trewe!
> For love of God, make of this thing an ende,
> Or sle us both at ones, er ye wende."
>
> (III.114–19)

Only Pandarus could genuinely weep and poke his niece at the same time, and perhaps only Chaucer in the history of English literature could so completely interweave elements from the high and the low style. The "manly sorwe" of romance causes Pandarus to weep, as men do only in romance, but to weep "as he to water wolde." Though the sentiment that they will die if she is pitiless is straight from the lexicon of courtly love romance, "make of this thing an ende" has all the abruptness of his repeated poking.

When we are not simultaneously living in both worlds, we are rapidly traveling back and forth between them. After managing to bring Troilus and Criseyde together for the first time, for instance, Pandarus finally has doubts about the game he has been playing, fearing that he has been a bawd. His doubts, however, are not even as strong as his enthusiasm for the game, much less for Troilus's rarified interpretation of his behavior as "gentilesse,/ Compassioun, and felawship, and trist." Similarly, the central scene of the book, the night at Pandarus's house, begins as sheer comedy of manners, as we watch Pandarus and Criseyde fence about whether Troilus is present, about whether Criseyde will spend the night, about whether she will comfort Troilus at once or tomorrow. Immediately following the consummation scene, we are back in the real world, as Pandarus pays Criseyde a morning-after visit and japes with her about the rain keeping people awake all night and giving them headaches. She responds by calling him a fox and pulling the sheet over her head. His response, one of the moments in the poem most reminiscent of the fabliau, makes us face squarely what has happened and the part he has played in it: He simply pries under the sheet, puts his arm under her neck and kisses her. The impulse to see more sex here than mere kissing does not misread entirely the spirit of this scene, however much it misrepresents what actually takes place. From this, we go immediately with Pandarus to Troilus and watch Troilus throw himself passionately on his knees before Pandarus and express his ecstatic gratitude, one of the few scenes to this point in the poem which Pandarus has entered without japing, as he greets Troilus "ful sobrely."

That Book III unites contraries other than Troilus the man and Criseyde the woman and the characteristics of the romance and the novel will be apparent when we examine it more fully later, after we have studied Troilus, Criseyde, and Pandarus to understand better who they are and what they represent. The above should be sufficient to demonstrate that the basic pattern of the first three books is to establish two contrary worlds, that of the first and that of the second book, and to unite them in Book III. The idea of contraries relates significantly to the structure of the last two books and of the poem as a whole— the basic pattern of the poem is from woe to "wele" to woe under the influence of that contrarious lady, Dame Fortune, and the epilogue seems to contradict all that has preceded it— but such considerations are best left until we have comprehended more fully the actors in our drama, the contraries they represent, and the significance of their union.

2

Psychological and
Sacramental Characterization

No aspect of *Troilus and Criseyde* has received more critical attention than its characterization. Its chief characters have been so thoroughly examined that one hesitates to begin another inspection of them, lest the reader despair and the author unwittingly plagiarize, since life is too short and criticism too long for even the professional Chaucerian to have read all that has been said about them.[1] Criseyde has proved especially fascinating, nearly as fascinating to the critics as to Troilus, though for different reasons. Indeed, it is the radical difference between what critics see in Criseyde and what Troilus sees that has persuaded me that the poem's characterization can benefit from further speculation. What has for the most part fascinated the critics of the poem's characters is their complex psychology and the realism with which Chaucer has portrayed them, as though in its characterization the poem were only the prototype of the psychological novel. Their representational quality, their symbolic significance, has been generally ignored, in spite of the nearly universal recognition that medieval art is symbolic art and in spite of the fact that Troilus himself sees something transcendent in Criseyde.[2] While Troilus has no doubt been blinded by love, we have Pandarus's authority that a blind man can sometimes walk "ther as he fel that couthe loken wide." Before we can explore the contrary nature and significance of the hero and heroine and the intermediate character of Pandarus, additional general observations about the nature of Chaucer's art and its union of contraries are necessary, for to assert that Chaucer's characterization is both psychological and sacramental is to insist upon the necessity of reading Chaucer in contrary ways, as a realist and as a symbolist. This chapter seeks to demonstrate not only that the characters can be profitably studied in terms of their contrary

natures but also that Chaucer's art harmonizes *historia* and
allegoria, "solace" and "sentence," the flesh and the Word.
It is true that in all the arts the later Middle Ages revealed a
heightened interest in the realistic representation of this world,
no doubt ultimately the result of the gradual transformation of
consciousness we somewhat narrowly call the twelfth-century
renaissance. It is also true that the progress of Chaucer's art is
in general from conventionalism to realism, from French
medieval to early Italian Renaissance models. Nonetheless,
though fourteenth-century artists had learned to represent the
world more realistically than their medieval predecessors, they
still saw, for all the warts with tufts of hair now visible, the
transcendent in the here and now. The world remained for
them a complex set of interlocking symbols, revealing divine
truth in its parts and in its whole The commonplace that
Chaucer showed an increasing interest in the physical and
psychological as he matured as an artist is no doubt as true as
most such generalizations generally are; it is a fallacy, however, to conclude that the greater his interest in realistic appearance the less his interest in allegorical significance. Even
in his most realistic art, Chaucer never abandoned the essential understanding of the world which is the basis of allegory—
that the world is and means, that things are both things and
signs[3] Though *Troilus and Criseyde* looks like Boccaccio's *Il
Filostrato*, in important ways it means like the *Roman de la
rose* and the *Complaint of Nature*.

On the other hand, though we must recognize that the universe as Chaucer understood it and reproduced it in his art was
a symbolic one, we cannot ignore the increasing frequency and
skill with which he represented it realistically. We must abandon the effort to view his art either as simply literal and realistic or as simply allegorical.[4] If it is wrong to read the *Canterbury Tales*, for instance, as a psychological and sociological
study of life in medieval England in the waning years of the
fourteenth century, it is equally wrong to consider it a thinly
veiled theological treatise in which the literal exists only as a
springboard to the allegorical, a husk to be cast away once one
has penetrated to the kernel. The fiction that *Troilus and
Criseyde* is a history or that the pilgrimage to Canterbury was
an actual pilgrimage which Chaucer is merely reporting is the

first thing we must accept as true when we willingly suspend our disbelief, for though Chaucer was concerned with Christian truth as he understood it, his objective as an artist was, as we shall see, to reveal how the Word manifested itself in concrete times and places, whether the then of ancient Troy or the now of fourteenth-century England.

While I am not convinced that broad generalizations about biblical exegesis are the best tools for understanding Chaucer's art, the relationship between *historia* and *allegoria* as it was understood in the later Middle Ages supports such an assertion. By Chaucer's time students of the Bible understood clearly the importance of the literal-historical level.[5] In those places where the literal level of the Bible recounted historical events, they found the allegory in the historical events themselves and considered these events important not only for the spiritual truths they manifested but also as events revealing the hand of God in history. God redeemed men through history. The crossing of the Red Sea was just as important as part of the historical sequence of events preparing for Christ as it was significant as a type of baptism. What Singleton has demonstrated for the *Divine Comedy*—that if we define the "allegory of the poets" as an allegory in which the literal level exists only for the sake of the allegorical, a "this for that," then we must consider the allegory of the *Comedy* the "allegory of the theologians," in which both the literal and the allegorical are essential, a "this and that"—is equally true for *Troilus and Criseyde* and much of the *Canterbury Tales*.[6] The history of Troy reveals both the spiritual condition and the possibilities of man prior to Christ and is part of the historical means by which God redeems man. The fall of Troy requires and leads to the founding of Rome both historically and allegorically.

Adding to our confusion about the nature of Chaucer's art and its allegorical dimensions is a common misunderstanding about the nature of symbolism in the later Middle Ages, a misunderstanding in part the result, perhaps, of too great a reliance upon the Augustine of *On Christian Doctrine*. In discussing "the symbolic method" of the later Middle Ages, M. D. Chenu has demonstrated that the Pseudo-Dionysian conception of symbolism made substantial inroads upon the Augustinian conception.[7] Both see the things of the world as both

things and signs, but for Augustine there is no *essential* connection between what a thing is and what it signifies. While
one cannot say with Augustine that the connection between
the thing itself and that which it signifies is arbitrary—God intended the signification—the connection between the thing
and what it signifies is in no way dependent upon the essential
nature of the thing itself. The signified is completely detach-
able from the thing itself, and that is precisely what the mind
should do, detach itself from the thing and flee to the spiritual
truth signified.

The Pseudo-Dionysian view of the universe as symbol is
rather different. For Dionysius, the whole created universe, the
immaterial as well as the material, is an emanation from God,
an outpouring from God which is both of God and other than
God. The universe is a vast hierarchy which manifests the divine at every level according to the capacity of that level of
being. Though God remains transcendent and unknowable,
best approached only negatively, in terms of what he is not,
everything participates in the One, reflects It, and makes It
known according to its capacity to do so. One of his metaphors
for this is the archetypal seal and the multiple impressions it
makes, each of which will resemble the archetype, each of
which will be different, depending upon the relative ability of
the material stamped to receive a clear impression.[8] In short,
what a thing is determines its ability to reflect the One. Chenu
calls this innate capacity one of the "laws of symbolic value":
the "values emerge only in proportion as the *res* retains its
integrity while functioning as a *signum*."[9] It is this conception
of symbolism which informs *Troilus and Criseyde*. Troilus and
Criseyde are first and last Troilus and Criseyde, but like all
things, they mirror the transcendent to the degree that their
own natures permit. Only by understanding their individuality
can we understand their symbolic value, for the one determines
the other.

Another of the important "laws of symbolism," one also deriving from Pseudo-Dionysius, is the law of "dissimilar similitude." All things are like to God, yet unlike Him, however
paradoxical it may be, "for the same things are both similar
and dissimilar to God: the likeness being in the measure of
their imitation of the inimitable; the dissimilarity being pro-

portional to the disparity between the effects and the Cause and the infinitely immeasurable degree of their inferiority."[10] Both similarity and dissimilarity are necessary, for the one allows us to know God, insofar as He can be known at all, through his creatures, the other prevents us from mistaking the likeness, the image, for God Himself. Richard of St. Victor expresses this idea quite clearly: "Every figure demonstrates the truth more clearly in proportion as by dissimilar similitude it figures that it is itself the truth and does not prove the truth; in so doing, dissimilar similtude leads the mind closer to the truth by not allowing the mind to rest in the similitude alone."[11] Man's tendency to "rest in the similitude alone" accounts for the fact that the world is a perilous mirror; it also caused Dionysius and those influenced by him to prefer the crudest possible symbols, the likenesses with the greatest dissimilarity, since this prevents one from seeing only the likeness.[12] Though Chenu finds little evidence that the idea of "dissimilar similitude" made much headway among twelfth-century poets, given their enthusiasm for personification allegory, in the thirteenth-century *Roman de la rose* the symbolism struggling for life among the petrified abstractions is precisely of this kind.

Though Christ and the Bible remain the preeminent revelations of the godhead for Dionysius, as for all medieval Christians, the whole universe so viewed becomes a revelation of the transcendent and triunal One. All things are incarnations of the Word and the Light, and, however profane, sacred. Such a conception of the universe as total symbol is often called a sacramental one, and the term is well chosen, for a sacrament is both a symbol and a vessel of grace, just as for Dionysius the whole universe is both revelation of its Maker and an outpouring of His Love and Light.[13] All things mediate between man and God. All things receive Life, Light, and Love from the One and reflect It, becoming means by which man can know and ascend to God.[14] Such a conception of the things of the world as simultaneously profane and sacred was necessary before Dante could envision Beatrice, a daughter of Eve, as a possible way to God, or Jean de Meun could use the rose as the crudest of possible "dissimilar similitudes."

Though Chaucer may not have been directly acquainted with theoretical discussions of such concepts as "dissimilar similitude," however commonplace they may have been, he must have been thoroughly acquainted with the basic concept from the *Roman de la rose*, for Jean de Meun represents the universe in his portion of the poem as just such a mirror of God. The world's "dissimilar similitude" to Truth is especially apparent in the comparison of the garden of Delight, in which the Lover's quest of the rose takes place, and the park of the Shepherd, God's eternal paradise.[15] Though Genius stresses the dissimilarity, insisting that the Lover's garden is "nothing in comparison with" Christ's, just as Troilus at the end of *Troilus and Criseyde* judges the world a vanity "To respect of the pleyn felicite/ That is in hevene above," the Lover's garden has a fundamental likeness to that paradise. Genius presents the two gardens through point by point comparison of their similarities, that he may indicate their differences. Both have walls depicting on the outside what is excluded from the gardens, though pointedly those things presumably excluded from the garden of Delight, such as poverty (Friend) and old age (Duenna), prove to be in it. Both have a central fountain containing crystals with trees towering by them. The Lover's fountain is a "perilous mirror," however, and its beauty is not its own: "N'est nule chose qu'ele tiegne/ Qui trestout d'ailleurs ne li viegne" (V.20429–30). Even the two crystals within it are "dull and cloudy," for they "leur clarte d'ailleurs aquierent" (V.20457). The Shepherd's fountain, on the other hand, "proceeds from itself," is triunal, and contains a carbuncle whose three facets shine with their own light; it is the sun of this garden and produces eternal day. This is the fountain of life; the Lover's fountain is the fountain of death. Though it is a misleading copy, a parody, as C. S. Lewis has termed it, the Lover's garden remains a copy, however distorted.[16] All the brightness and beauty of the Lover's garden comes ultimately from this garden and its God.

We should remember that in Jean's portion of the poem, the garden of Delight is no longer simply a poetic image of a young man's fantasy but an image of nature. The comparison of the garden and the park is a comparison of this world and the next. The fountain at the center of the garden reflects the whole garden, indeed is, in a sense, the whole garden, for it is in it that the lover sees the roses and falls in love. Nature for Jean is just such a fountain. Jean confesses his inability to describe Nature; in fact, he says, no one except God can adequately describe her.

> Car Deus, li beaus outre mesure,
> Quant il beaute mist en Nature,
> Il en i fist une fontaine
> Toujourz courant e toujourz pleine,
> De cui toute beaute desrive;
> Mais nus n'en set ne fonz ne rive.
>
> (IV.16233–38)

He concludes that "her beauty and her value cannot be understood by men." The relationship between Nature and God is clarified in another passage by Jean, though one must remember the partisan character of the speaker, Genius. Speaking of God, the "maistre" of Nature and the salvation of body and soul, Genius says,

> C'est li beaus miroers ma dame.
> Ja ma dame riens ne seust
> Se ce bel miroer n'eust.
> Cil la gouverne, cil la regle;
> Ma dame n'a point d'autre regle.
>
> (V.19900–4)

The beauty of Nature, like everything in this Dionysian universe, comes from God; indeed, Nature proves to be only a copy of the archetype of her existing in the mind of God. For Jean this world is nothing but a vast mirror manifesting God, but it is a perilous, dark mirror, one capable of leading man from God as well as to Him. One sees through it but darkly.

Jean's conception of the world is illuminated by the discussion of mirrors which he assigns to Nature, a digression she gets into by talking of the love of Mars and Venus for each other and the trap set for them by Vulcan with his net. She laments their capture and regrets that they did not have a mirror by which they might have seen the net and avoided capture and exposure. She then goes on to talk about the properties of mirrors, which can both help us see and deceive us.[17] The mirror of the world is, of course, just such a mirror, for it can help us see its Creator or lead us astray. She observes that mirrors can make one thing seem many and many things seem one. This, indeed, ought to remind us of the world as mirror as the symbolists understand it, for it is precisely through a series of emanating reflections that the One generates the plenitude of Nature. Nature is she who at her forge shapes the "common form," the archetypal *idea* in the mind of God, into individuals. Similarly, God as mirror of Nature unites in Himself in one image all the plenitude of Nature.

We should be careful not to oversimplify Jean's conception of Nature, for if he is struck with awe and a sense of inadequacy before the beauty and plenitude of such a lady, he makes it clear that she too has suffered the effects of the Fall. Thus in his symbolic representation of her, she is "dark and cloudy," nothing compared to God. Thus also in his representation of her as a personified abstraction, she often acts more like the "chambermaid" of God than the "vicar." Though she is described as sublime, and indeed still is in spite of the Fall, her behavior and her reasoning are often comically ridiculous. Though she argues at some length and with some difficulty man's freedom, she cannot understand why he, unlike all the rest of nature, which operates of necessity, often errs.[18] She rebukes man, the summit of her creation, for not being natural, yet admits that man's noblest attribute, his reason, was not given him by her and that he should follow his reason.[19] If she does not understand reason, she does not understand love either, for she repents of having made man and promises to vilify him as never before, "so help me God the crucified." God, in His love, of course, did not repent of making man, but redeemed him by taking on the flesh (by being born of a Virgin, something Nature also admits she cannot understand), and dying on the cross that man might live. Not understanding divine love, she can only scorn virginity, urge man to reproduce, and repent herself of having made man. But then even Reason, whom Jean characterizes as the likeness of God in man, cannot understand the mysteries of divine love. Jean associates Reason with pagan wisdom; her heroes are such men as Socrates and Plato. Plato, Nature tells us, knew that reason was not of nature, for it is immortal and she creates only the corruptible, but, she also tells us, he did not comprehend the incarnation and the mysteries of the Trinity.[20] Certainly Jean de Meun loved nothing better than dramatizing the

irrationality of man the reasoner, in "wandering mazes lost."
Thus both nature and reason remain highly hazardous guides
to truth.

All this has important implications for art, a human activity
which Jean sees as an imitation of nature, an exercise in reason,
and a consequence of love. Just as the universe is a mirror of
love, so Jean's poem, itself commanded by the god of Love, is
a "Mirror for Lovers." It is itself a highly complex and distorted mirror, very much a maze and an enigma, but one in
which we are to seek and find the truth. Though we have
been looking at the poem's symbolism, its most striking characteristic is its personified abstractions. That personification
allegory is radically different from symbolism has been clear to
modern critics of medieval literature at least since Helen Dunbar's *Symbolism in Medieval Thought* and C. S. Lewis's *Allegory of Love*, where similar distinctions are made between the
two.[21] Personification allegory begins with the abstract, the
idea, and renders it concrete, putting sensible flesh on the idea
by personifying it. Symbolism begins with the particular and
concrete and sees through it to the general and abstract. Allegory confronts the reader with the world as it is understood by
man's intelligence, in the abstract categories in which the intelligence finds the meaning and order of life. Symbolism confronts the reader with the world as it appears to the senses,
though in a way which leads him to see behind the *naturalia*
the transcendent. Their differences as poetic techniques reflect
both differing habits of mind, differing forms of thought, and
differing conceptions of how the world reveals its meaning—or
such, at least, was the assumption of the later Middle Ages.
These differences will be clearer if we sketch briefly a portion
of the intellectual history behind the *Roman de la rose*, a poem
rich, as we have seen, both in personification and symbolism.

Though personification is an ancient poetic technique and
habit of mind, the ideas made flesh in two, at least, of Jean's
more important personifications derive from the school of
Chartres, that twelfth-century center of Platonic philosophical
speculation.[22] Similarly, though symbolism is also ages old, the
kind of symbolism we have seen in the *Roman* suggests another intellectual center of the twelfth century, the abbey at
St. Victor. The Victorines were in the twelfth century the great

defenders of the symbolic universe and the foremost opponents of the rationalists. For the students of the *Timaeus* at Chartres, the natural world was above all else rational, the product of laws comprehensible to the inquiring mind. Like the modern physicist, for whom nature is mathematical law, they understood the created universe through categories invented by the human mind. Their nature was the four elements, elements which, once created, become themselves the means of subsequent creation. Though they thought of nature as independent of its Creator, as self-maintaining, they did not divorce it from its Creator, but rather viewed its order as evidence of the wisdom of the divine mind. Its order, proportion, and harmony are analogous to the order, proportion, and harmony of God. Symbolists see the universe as revealing its Creator in a radically different way. Though they too could see God's harmony in the world's, for them every individual thing is a unique manifestation of the transcendent and unknowable. Everything mirrors in its own way its Maker and Sustainer; indeed, for such a radical symbolist as Dionysius, a thing is its capacity to manifest God. The Victorines considered the efforts of the rational mind to understand God through the workings of nature a hazardous, indeed hopeless and presumptuous, task. To seek truth in nature through reason was to wander in mazes lost, since it was to ignore both the consequences of the Fall and the incomprehensible miracle of the Incarnation.

The confidence we find at Chartres in the ability of the mind to understand the world and its Creator is paralleled by a similar confidence in poetry. Even pagan poetry can be an important source of truth, since a good deal of the truth can be comprehended by reason alone. Poetry for them is an exercise in logic embellished by the "colors of rhetoric." Such a conception of the universe gives rise, logically enough, to a poetry of personified abstractions, to a poetry which confronts directly the abstract categories in which the mind understands the universe by the metaphoric process of personification. Thus Jean de Meun brings Nature, that grand collectivity of laws, on stage and has her explain herself; she describes the four elements, the operations of the heavens, the qualities of mirrors, and so forth. Jean, however, also shared the Victorines' distrust of reason and their consequent distrust of poetry. All of his "characters" are reasoners, and nearly all of them hopelessly contradict themselves. In creating his *Roman de la rose*, Jean was not content merely to follow and show the limitations of the conception of the universe and the kind of poetry deriving from the school of Chartres. He also, as we have seen, incorporates into his poem the symbolic conception of the universe deriving in part from Dionysius and popular among the Victorines and reveals its limitations as well. He finds it as hazardous to try to see the transcendent as the immanent as it is to seek to understand creation, for the mirror of the world in which one sees God is a dark and murky mirror, one which both distorts and by its beauty seduces the viewer. Jean insists on both ways of approaching the transcendent and upon the limitations of both.

Jean's discussion of the poet as imitator of nature occurs in connection with his picture of nature as creator at war with death.[23] Nature shapes the "common form" into individuals through generation. Though death can destroy individuals, it cannot destroy the common form of the individuals, the species. It is through nature that the form of a thing, the archetypal model of which, no doubt, resides in the mind of God in this Neoplatonic world of mirrors, is united with matter to create new life. One recalls that Alain de Lille's goddess Nature describes herself as that which unites body and soul and recognizes at least in Jean's description of generative creation the idea that, once created, nature maintains itself, ever stamping out new copies of its forms. When Jean speaks of the poet as imitating nature, it is clear that he is not thinking about imitation as realism, as an effort to produce photographic copies of the end products of nature's creative act. The poet watches Nature at work in her forge; what he imitates is the creative act itself, the practice of creating individual instances of the common form, though he concedes nature's superiority because its individuals live. The poet, then, imitates nature's activity. He creates by an analogous process an analogous world. Imitating nature, and indeed ultimately God, the poet creates a *heterocosmos,* another world, not one that necessarily looks like God's world, nature, but one formed and ordered according to the same principles.[24] Thus, for instance, Jean joins the idea with the flesh of metaphor to create his personified characters, just as nature unites form and matter to create individuals. Thus, Chaucer creates the poetic universe of *Troilus and Criseyde* out of contrary characters, themes, and styles, just as God made the universe out of contraries. Just as the world which God created and nature maintains is a sacramental one, itself a vast allegory, an incarnation of the Word, so the poet's analogous creation, his poem, seeks to be sacramental, itself an allegory incarnating the Word, whether through personification or symbolism, for however different the two poetic techniques, both are ways of clothing truth in poetic fiction.

If Chaucer is seeking in *Troilus and Criseyde* to make the Word flesh, to incarnate truth in the sensible images of poetry, his method is not only the structural one we briefly examined in the previous chapter but the symbolic one as well. He confronts the reader (by means of words) with things, *naturalia*, which are themselves intended as signs, as manifestations, of truth. The great model for such poetry, apart from the world itself, a divine allegory full of signs, is of course Scripture, where behind the things described the medieval mind endlessly discovered divine revelation. Though perhaps the most common explanation for God's veiling of the truth was that it protected sacred truth, keeping it from the undeserving, more affirmative reasons were also offered. One offered by Augustine is explained by D. W. Robertson in the following way: "In one of his letters (55.11.21), Augustine asserts that those things which are said figuratively in the Scriptures move and inflame love more than those things which are said literally. When the mind is immersed in terrestrial things, it is slow to be ignited with the fire of divine love, but when it is directed toward similitude based on corporal things and thence referred to those spiritual things figured in the similitudes, it is excited by the transition from one to the other so that it is carried with a more ardent love toward the peace it seeks. In other words, a figurative expression offers an opportunity to discern the *invisibilia Dei* through 'the things that are made,' and it has the effect of stimulating love for the *invisibilia*."[25]

One finds a similar conception of how enigmas based upon worldly things move a man to love what he does not know, what, given his fallen condition, he has difficulty loving directly, in St. Gregory's *Super cantica canticorum expositio*.[26] Neither explanation is far from one implicit in Pseudo-Dionysius, for whom both Scripture and reality function as means for man's illumination, as we have seen. For Dionysius all such illuminations are in a sense accommodations to man's limited ability to know the Unknowable. Everything participates in and reveals the Unknowable, shedding illumination upon the mind of man: "Yet the Good is not wholly unshared by any of the things that are, for it lovingly tempers to all things Its super-essential Ray, firmly rooted in Itself, by illuminations adapted to the nature of each, and thus draws up into such contemplation, communion and similitude as is fitting to them, the holy minds which strive after it with all their powers."[27] The illumination which is the things of the world themselves and which is Scripture moves a man to love, drawing him up toward that love which continually descends to him through and in all things. Man can only understand the divine if it is accommodated to him in the sensible things of the world and in the sensible symbols of Scripture.

We can see a related idea in St. Bernard's treatment of carnal love, of man's love of things and the self.[28] For St. Bernard, the beginning of all human love is carnal, a love which can lead to sin or be a first step in a "Platonic" ascent from the sensible to the insensible. Indeed, St. Bernard argues that one of the reasons for the Incarnation was man's limited ability to love.[29] Since many men can only love carnally, Christ took on the flesh that man might love Him. Inasmuch as all things are sensible incarnations of the Truth, they can all similarly inspire a love which leads to Truth, but unlike Christ, they are perilous mirrors, for though they "demonstrate the truth," they are not the Truth.

It is, I believe, such a conception of the nature and function of the created that informs the *Troilus*. Its imitation of the world reveals that Chaucer understood the created as sacramental and as intended to lead man back to God, though capable of leading him away from God. Since it mirrors a sacramental world, the world created in the *Troilus*—its persons, places, things, and acts—is itself sacramental and the drama which is its principal concern is, as we shall see, the soul's journey through the perilous mirror of this world to its Creator.

The place to begin a discussion of Chaucer's psychological and sacramental characterization in *Troilus and Criseyde* is with the poem's two major characters and their most fundamental difference: Troilus is male; Criseyde, female. Just as the World-Soul is constituted of odd and even numbers, male and female, so the world, the copy of the World-Soul, is full of things male and female.[30] This is, of course, one of the basic pairs of contraries in God's harmonious order—God created man male and female—and one of the basic principles by which the plenitude and harmony of creation is maintained. Chaucer stresses Criseyde's femininity, telling us that never was there a creature "lasse mannyssh in semynge" (I.284). He also stresses Troilus's masculinity.[31] When Troilus rides by Criseyde's house, for instance, we are told that he looked like Mars, "that god is of bataille" and that he was such a man and such a knight that "It was an heven upon hym for to see" (II.637). Nonetheless, Chaucer's characterization of them frequently frustrates at least our contemporary expectations of what is masculine, what feminine.[32] However aggressive Troilus may be on the battlefield, he seems impossibly hesitant in the bedroom. However innocent and fearful Criseyde may be, she repeatedly startles us with her self-assurance and her command of difficult situations. For instance, when she first enters the room in Deiphebus's house where Troilus lies feigning illness and he asks who is there, it is she, not Pandarus, though he has just led her in "by the lappe," who answers. While Chaucer probably intended certain of their differences to reflect what he considered fundamental differences in the two sexes, he individualizes each, so that their differing responses to love seem a consequence of their past experiences, their present circumstances, their individual natures, and their innate capacities to love.

When we first meet Troilus, he is a proud, young peacock strutting about the temple of the goddess of wisdom, Pallas Athena. Though he echoes the words of the wise in his contempt for the young lovers in his company, there is no wisdom in him, only an exaggerated sense of his own superiority. This love of self to the contempt of nearly everyone else is perfectly expressed in the highly superior tone in which he mocks lovers as fools. Even if one is not so convinced as the narrator that

love of "kynde" is a good thing and makes men virtuous, one
feels compelled by Troilus's "surquidrie" to second the narrator's mockery of him. Looking "now here, now there," now
"on this lady, and now on that," but impressed only with himself, Troilus is another Narcissus. His japing both expresses
and fittingly represents this love of self. If Troilus's sudden
love is a fall destined to produce the tragedy inherent in all
false loves, his spiritual condition prior to it certainly suggests
it may be a fortunate fall.

Chaucer uses Cupid to dramatize the inexplicable mystery of
why men fall in love when they do and with whom they do,
telling us that the god of Love "shop for to be wroken."
Troilus's overweening pride and the narrator's insistence that
love is a law of nature suggest that there is another god of love,
the author of nature, who may also be taking his revenge.
Troilus's love is as sudden and as absolute as it is mysterious.
In the midst of his playing, as he looks now at this, now at that
lady, he sees Criseyde and his wandering eye stops—"and ther
it stente." Never again in this world, not even after Criseyde
leaves and Pandarus takes Troilus to Sarpedoun's house where
there is an incomparable company of fair ladies, will he look
even for a moment elsewhere. Whatever god of love is taking
his revenge and however ambiguous the effects of that revenge
may be, once again it is hard not to approve the narrator's
sentiments—"Blissed be Love, that kan thus folk converte!"
(I.308).

The fact that Chaucer has Troilus fall in love with Criseyde
simply by seeing her is important, however commonplace the
idea that love dwells in the eye, the gateway to the soul. For
such a mystic as St. Bonaventure as for any radical symbolist,
the ultimate act of knowing is simply a question of seeing.[33]
One sees the transcendent as immanent; all things reveal God.
Though Troilus is hardly a mystic, his sight is insight, vision.
Thus, in Book I he thinks Criseyde is a goddess and in Book III
he tells Pandarus that no one ever saw such "inly" beauty. He
sees and praises in her the love which creates and sustains the
universe. Though Criseyde may be just another woman to the
rest of the world, for Troilus she is the one incarnation of the
Good, the Beautiful, and the True. She is his Beatrice. As he
tells us when he learns that she must leave and imagines him-

self living in darkness without her, like Oedipus, she is the light by which he sees. To recognize that Criseyde is something less than Troilus thinks she is, is not to negate his vision. It is only to insist upon the dissimilitude accompanying her similitude to the transcendent. Troilus's notorious passivity as a lover is certainly as much a consequence of what he sees, or at least believes he sees, in Criseyde as it is the result of any innocence and naïveté. One does not call a goddess up on the phone to ask for a Saturday night date. Troilus's tendency to see the transcendent in this world accounts in part for his fatalism as well. His sudden and overwhelming experience of love and his perception of its power and beauty in and through Criseyde persuade him that this world is obedient to a will not his own. Thus, though he takes "purpose loves craft to suwe" and ponders how "to arten hire to love" immediately upon returning to his room, shortly he delivers his spirit into the hands of the god of Love.

Troilus characterizes love and its effects upon him in the song quoted at the beginning of this study. Though this song is based upon a sonnet of Petrarch, *S'amor non è*, it is far from a literal translation. The *Canticus Troili* opens by asking whether or not love exists, and if it does, what kind of thing it is.[34] As Wilkens has pointed out, Petrarch's sonnet focuses on the lover-narrator's experience, asking what is this thing I am feeling if it is not love. Similarly, as Wilkens also observes, when Petrarch questions whether it is good or bad, he would seem to be referring to the lover's experience, not to the nature of love. Chaucer has generalized Petrarch's sonnet to make it an analysis of both the lover's psychic state and the general nature of love. Chaucer also intensifies the oxymoronic quality of the song, especially by translating Petrarch's final line, *e tremo a mezza state, ardento il verno* (I tremble with cold in midsummer, I burn in winter), as "For hete of cold, for cold of hete, I dye" (I.420).

The characterization of love and its effects by means of contraries is, of course, commonplace. Though Chaucer heightens this quality in Petrarch's sonnet, his use of oxymoron is decidedly restrained in comparison to the descriptions of love we find in the *Roman de la rose* and the *Complaint of Nature*.[35] In the *Complaint*, asked by the dreamer to define Cupid, the goddess Nature, after telling him that he has asked for an "explanation of the inexplicable," lists literally dozens of oxymorons to characterize love. Alain's whole treatment of Cupid is highly ambiguous. Though the goddess urges the lovers to flee Cupid and admits that she has interspersed "slight signs of blame" in her portrait of him, she also insists on "the essential nature of love's honorableness if it is checked by the bridle of moderation." The characterization of love by oxymorons in the *Complaint* represents not only the irrationality and the inexplicable mystery of love but also its similarity to that love which created the universe by binding together contraries. Alain makes Cupid the legitimate son of Hymen and Venus prior to her corruption, of that Venus who is the *musica mundana*, the harmony of the created. Jocus, sport, is the child of the adultery of Venus fallen and Antigamus; he, not Cupid, represents totally illegitimate love.[36] The "slight signs of blame" in the portrait suggest the effects of the Fall upon Cupid. Though the Fall did not completely obliterate the honorableness of love and its procreative function, it has insured that Cupid works for ill as well as for good. Cupid's ambiguity is evident in the goddess's characterization of love's effects upon man in response to her own rhetorical question, "Does not Cupid, working many miracles by changing things into their opposites, transform the whole race of men?" If Cupid causes Scylla to lay aside her fury, he causes "the good Aeneas . . . to be a Nero" (*m.v.*47).

Love certainly transforms Troilus. Though the narrator unequivocally approves of this transformation, Chaucer's characterization of Troilus once he falls in love is every bit as ambiguous and nearly as oxymoronic as Alain's description of love. The proud young prince becomes a humble servant, resigning his "estat roial" into Criseyde's hands and becoming "with full humble cheere . . . hir man." Loving Criseyde with an almost religious awe, he cannot imagine that she could love such a wretch as he. Similarly transformed is his motive for warring on the Greeks.

> But for non hate he to the Grekes hadde,
> Ne also for the rescous of the town,
> Ne made hym thus in armes for to madde,

But only, lo, for this conclusioun:
To liken hire the bet for his renoun.

(I.477–81)

He makes war for love, becoming a *miles Criseydae* in an effort
to prove himself worthy of her. In the process, he does bridle
in significant measure his passion and become a model of at
least the courtly virtues. Though Cupid's transformation of
Troilus does not produce *caritas*, "the love of God even to the
contempt of self," it does eradicate much of Troilus's original
"love of self even to the contempt of God."[37] The japing
mockery we hear in the temple, a mockery which perfectly
expresses his arrogance and self-satisfaction, stops.

The effects of love upon Troilus in Book I are presented in a
number of ambiguous images. He is caught in a trap. Like a
bird, his feathers are limed, for instance. His love is a sickness,
a raging fever. We are repeatedly told that he burns with the
hot fire of love. However traditional such images may be in
courtly love poetry, we cannot deny their substantial negative
connotation. The world, the flesh, and the devil were all com-
monly pictured as snares. When love is characterized as a
burning fire, it is often lust that is being described. One thinks,
for instance, of the fire of love raging in Dido, a burning easily
identifiable as lust even without the help of the medieval commentators on Virgil's *Aeneid*. The idea that love ensnares has
affirmative connotations as well, however, for the love which
created and sustains the universe, the love "that al maist circumscrive," is repeatedly represented in the poem as a love
which binds. Similarly, there are affirmative aspects to the fire
of love. Chenu has noted that traditionally in the Middle Ages,
"the symbol was seen as ambiguous; Fire warms, casts light,
purifies, burns, regenerates, consumes; it symbolized the Holy
Spirit or concupiscence equally well."[38] Dante used fire in the
Purgatorio both as a symbol of the sin of lust and as a means
by which the lustful are cleansed of their sin.[39] The pilgrim
Dante must pass through flames that he may come to Beatrice
and regain Eden. Once he has done so, Virgil declares him master of himself, since the process of rectifying the will by ascending the purgatorial mountain is now complete. Chaucer's use of
fire is similarly ambiguous. It represents both Troilus's sexual

passion and the torment and suffering which gradually cleanse and purify him of much of his love of self.[40] One of the reasons he repeatedly calls on death is that a part of him is dying to be reborn. Now that he loves Criseyde more than himself, he dies to himself and lives in Criseyde; she becomes his life. He does experience something related to the death of self necessary for true spiritual life.

When Alain de Lille's goddess Nature is characterizing Cupid's effects on man by means of contraries, she tells the dreamer that "When the monk and the adulterer have both been foreign to a man, he [Cupid] compels these two to possess and dwell in him at the same time" (*m.v.*47). Troilus is such a man. Though we are told that he occasionally ventures forth in Book I to make war on the Greeks for love of Criseyde and to catch a glimpse of her, the only scenes Chaucer dramatizes in the first book after Troilus has fallen in love take place within the walls of Troilus's bedroom. We see him cloistered in his room, where he fasts and prays, prays and fasts. He repents of his sins and sings hymns in praise of both Cupid and Criseyde. He contemplates his goddess Criseyde, and calls on her to save him, all the while mortifying the self. When he rises up and goes forth at the end of the book, dignified with some magnificent poetry, we are told that he has become "oon the beste knyght,/ That in his tyme was or myghte be." In spite of the fact that Troilus goes forth to commit something akin to adultery, the narrator's assessment of the beneficient effects of love upon Troilus is at least as true as it is ironic. Many, if not all, of his vices have become virtues and his "japes" are dead.

We need not take the narrator's word for it, however, since Criseyde has another lover with whom Troilus can be compared, Diomede. Indeed, Chaucer forces us to compare the two by having Diomede's courtship virtually duplicate Troilus's. Pointing out this parallelism, Ida Gordon suggests that its purpose is to make us recognize how like Diomede Troilus really is, questioning whether or not it makes much difference that Pandarus does the dirty work for Troilus that Diomede does for himself.[41] While one must admit that there are more similarities than have sometimes been recognized, Troilus will not reduce to Diomede.[42] Troilus employs Pandarus precisely because he cannot speak for himself, because he is too full of awe and too aware of his own worthlessness. Diomede feels no such reverence and has no such doubts as to his own worth: "I am, al be it yow no joie,/ As gentil man as any wight in Troie" (V.930–31). Similarly, though the vows of devotion Diomede utters to Criseyde echo Troilus's, he thinks in his heart,

> Happe how happe may,
> Al sholde I dye, I wol hire herte seche!
> I shal namore lesen but my speche.
>
> (V.796–98)

Though we may doubt that Troilus actually will die if Criseyde rejects his love, we never doubt that he believes he will. He does have more to lose than his speech. The difference, of course, is that Diomede never really falls in love with Criseyde. Troilus cannot pursue the goal with "sodeyn" Diomede's directness both because he sees the goal differently—Criseyde is never just "queynte" for him—and because the love that impels him is radically different. Love has transformed him so that he does forget himself, something Diomede vows—and for once we believe him—he will never do. Part of Criseyde's tragedy is not to see the difference between Troilus and Diomede. Critics need not make the same mistake.

The ambiguous nature of love and its effects on Troilus are most significantly revealed through the poem's treatment of ravishing. Chaucer makes ravishing the original sin of the poem's world, the cause of the war and the ultimate reason Troy is destined to fall. It is the poem's archetypal image of *cupiditas*, of the love of the things of the world for their own sake, a love ultimately of the self "even to the contempt of God." Though Troilus and Pandarus do not literally ravish Criseyde, their seduction of her has similarities to ravishing. Pandarus makes his first visit to Criseyde after being awakened by "a sorowful lay" of "the swalowe Proigne" about "whi she forshapen was." The day of Pandarus's first visit draws to a close with Criseyde in bed listening to the song of a nightingale, perhaps, we are told, "a lay of love." However traditional and romantic such imagery, by enclosing the fateful day in allusions to the fate of Procne and Philomela, one of literature's

most grotesque tales of ravishing, Chaucer raises serious questions about the moral significance of what is taking place.
However honorable Troilus's intentions, he at least half feigns
his illness at Deiphebus's house when he first speaks of his love
to Criseyde. Helen's role in that scene is no doubt intended to
remind us of her ravishing by another of Troilus's brothers,
Paris. Similarly, in the consummation scene, Troilus repeats,
however reluctantly, the Horaste lie, and once he and Criseyde
are alone together, suddenly demands that she yield, "for other
bote is non!" Criseyde's response—I wouldn't be here if I
hadn't already yielded—does not alter the questionable intention in that demand.

Troilus is not another Paris, however, any more than he is
another Diomede. When it is decreed by the Trojan council
that Criseyde is to be given to the Greeks in exchange for
Antenor, Pandarus urges Troilus to prevent the exchange by
force, to show himself a man and a Trojan by ravishing Criseyde. He reminds Troilus that his brother Paris has his love.
Though Pandarus is able to persuade Troilus to forget all the
noble reasons Troilus advanced against ravishing, he cannot get
him to agree to ravish her unless she is willing. He will not impose his will upon Criseyde. Richard Green has pointed out
that Helen in the *Complaint of Nature* "is a figure of the beauty
of created things which may be loved and desired as means or
abused as substitutes for the true object of love which they
represent."[43] Criseyde has a similar function in the *Troilus*.
Though Troilus may be guilty of loving her more as an end
than as a means, when he must either ravish her or forget himself, he forgets himself. Love does so transform him that he
will sacrifice himself rather than serve himself against Criseyde's will. His refusal to sacrifice Criseyde to his desires indicates that the love he experiences does restore in him something of man's original prelapsarian perfection.

Though it may seem peculiar to characterize Troilus by
characterizing the nature of love and its effects upon him,
Troilus is largely an embodiment of the love which possesses
him. He is "Cupides son." For all the ambiguity with which
Chaucer depicts Troilus as lover, he is radically one. Once he
falls in love with Criseyde, his love of her motivates his every
act. Though his love of her is false, a feigned love, both in the

sense that it is capable of deception and in the sense that it is directed toward a partial, and hence false, good, it is true in the sense that it never changes. However mistaken this love may be, he is remarkably faithful to it. Though Chaucer characterizes love in terms of contraries, they are contraries bound together and made one. The unifying effect of love on Troilus accounts in part for his fatalism and his fidelity. Just as God's goodness and love make the creation of the universe necessary, though God is free, so Troilus's love makes his fidelity necessary, though presumably he is also free. Though Chaucer urges us at the end of the poem to love Christ, who "nyl falsen no wight," Troilus's unity and constancy make him a mirror of the divine, though a distorted one. It is this oneness which ultimately accounts for Chaucer's characterization of him by means of lyric monologues.

In a very real sense, Troilus is simply the human spirit giving expression to the joy and sorrow of life in this world. In his room pouring forth his soul in song, he is, in a sense, disembodied, representing the soul and its immortal longings. His lyric monologues are the song of the soul. Though Troilus, like Boethius at the beginning of the *Consolation*, has forgotten who he is and where his true home is, the desire Criseyde awakens in him is the soul's desire to return to its true home. Moved by love, he seeks that perfect bliss which he was created to enjoy. Created in the image of God, the soul reflects God's unity and perfection. It was, of course, created to love and sing; it journeys through this world in order to tune its song that it may sing to God in the next world. The disorder in Troilus's love—he loves and sings the world, not God—is evident in the fact that his songs are secular love lyrics; that his love of Criseyde is not simply a perversion is evident in the religious quality of his songs; for when he sings, he praises both Criseyde and the God who made her, celebrating in her the love which binds together the universe harmoniously. The very fact that he sings is significant, for in the *concordia discors* tradition song is both an expression and a reflection of the harmony of God and His creation. Troilus's songs express his harmony and reveal that it is a reflection of God's harmony, soul mirroring Soul; mind, Mind; spirit, the Spirit.

Chaucer's characterization of Criseyde reveals that she is in many ways Troilus's opposite. If Troilus typically expresses himself in lyric monologues, an indication of his unity and constancy, Criseyde, except for parts of the consummation scene, seems to be endlessly debating. Her characterization by *débat*, whether a witty one with Pandarus or a more formal internal one with herself, indicates her duality and inconstancy.[44] When Troilus first sees Criseyde and falls in love, he immediatey goes home to sing about how love has united contraries within him, so that he is dying for "hete of cold, for cold of hete." At the same point in Book II, Criseyde's book, when she first sees Troilus and returns to be alone, she debates between contraries. She is "now hot, now cold." This fatal ability to change is both a consequence of her own nature and the nature of the love which moves her.

If Troilus is an idealist, Criseyde is a realist. She does not see in this world evidence of the transcendent. She is not guided by intimations of eternity but by a clear perception of the here and now of this world. Thus, for instance, in spite of all of Pandarus's efforts to manipulate her and the even more potent control of events by fate, as when Troilus rides by the day before Pandarus arranges for him to do so, she is convinced that she is free, that she is the master of her own destiny. Though she is aware that the world is one of false appearances, where one prepares a face to meet prepared faces and seeks that honor which is finally only reputation, she lives by its values. Her argument that her love of Troilus is not subject to change because what she loves is not subject to time and fortune, Troilus's "moral vertu, grounded upon trouthe," suggests that since her love does change, what she loved was not Troilus's "trouthe" but what she pondered after she first saw him:

> his excellent prowesse,
> And his estat, and also his renown,
> His wit, his shap, and ek his gentillesse.
>
> (II.660–62)

Though she may well recognize the radical difference between Troilus and Diomede, she can love Diomede because in outward appearance, to the world's eyes, they are similar.

Similarly, if Troilus is idealistic, Criseyde is pragmatic. She

is ever able and ultimately ready to accommodate herself to
the realities of the moment. In her endless debates we see her
art, as she calculates what to seem. Thus, when everyone is
praising Troilus at Deiphebus's house and she is thinking "who
is that ne wolde hire glorifie,/ To mowen swich a knyght don
lyve or dye" (II.1593–94), she maintains a "sobre cheere,"
though "hire herte lough." She can appear just as reluctant to
her uncle when he is urging her to have mercy on Troilus now
as enthusiastic to Troilus when minutes later the two are alone
together. Abandoned by her father to an uncertain fate in Troy
and by the Trojans to an equally uncertain one in the Greek
camp, she must fend for herself, depending on her wit and her
beauty. Though no doubt Pandarus is partly correct when he
insists to Troilus that her pity will move her to love Troilus,
her love of Troilus, as of Diomede, is also the consequence of
considerable debate concerning the advantages and disadvan-
tages. Significantly, while Troilus falls in love at first sight,
with Criseyde words precede sight—the public word of Troilus's reputation, Pandarus's many words of ravishing praise,
and her own. In a sense, Criseyde reasons herself into love,
persuading herself that there is little to be lost, especially since
Troilus is secretive, and much to be gained.[45] With some help
from Diomede, she will also reason herself out of it.

As a pragmatic realist inhabiting a social world, Criseyde
views life as essentially a game, a game whose rules she has
mastered well. When Pandarus enters this world of calculated
appearances guided by Janus, the god with two faces, he meets
a match in Criseyde. In sharp contrast with the ever earnest
Troilus, she even considers love a game. When Troilus and
Criseyde are about to part after this first night together, she
assures him that the "game" has now gone so far that he will
never leave her heart. In a game, of course, if one loses today,
one can always play again tomorrow: "To Diomede algate I
wol be trewe" (V.1071). Through her characterization by
game, Chaucer associates her love with Jocus. Her inability to
make a total commitment should not surprise us. Given her
perception of reality and her sense of what is valuable, it makes
little sense to abandon forever one's freedom, to lay one's all
on a single cast of the dice. When trying to persuade Troilus
to get another love after learning that Criseyde must leave
Troy, Pandarus exclaims,

> What! God forbede alwey that ech plesaunce
> In o thyng were, and in non other wight!
> If oon kan synge, an other kan wel daunce;
> If this be goodly, she is glad and light;
> And this is fair, and that kan good aright.
>
>   (IV.407–11)

Though Troilus cannot love another, Criseyde can, in part because what she loves are the pleasures of the world, song and dance.

Ultimately Criseyde cannot commit herself totally to another because she is committed to herself. When Pandarus first praises Troilus to her, she asserts that she believes in his worthiness for "alle pris hath he/ Of hem that me were levest preysed be." When she first sees him, significantly as he rides by to the cheers of the crowd, and asks "who yaf me drynke?" we are told that "moost hir favour was, for his distresse/ Was al for hire." Unlike Troilus, she never doubts her own worth. She accepts her role as master and superior in their relationship—indeed, insists upon it—as easily and naturally as Troilus accepts his role as servant. She is ever highly conscious of her worth, even delightfully so—

> Ne me to love, a wonder is it nought;
> For wel woot I myself, so God me spede,
> Al wolde I that noon wiste of this thought,
> I am oon the faireste, out of drede,
> And goodlieste, whoso taketh hede,
> And so men seyn, in al the town of Troie.
> What wonder is though he of me have joye?
>
>   (II.743–49)

Love of self—*cupiditas*—never appeared more charming in another. Though we may admire her ability in difficult situations to look out for herself, we should never forget that that is precisely what she does. It is a talent her father had before her. In a world dominated by time and "remuable Fortune," anyone committed to self and place in the world must change. When Criseyde must choose between her love of Troilus and her public image, the only image she has of herself, she remains true to her love of her own image. Unlike Troilus, she can never quite forget herself. Love does not transform her.

Though Troilus characterizes his love of Criseyde in terms borrowed from Christianity, Criseyde borrows her metaphors to describe love from nature. In both cases Chaucer is making the word cousin to the deed. Once in love, for instance, she tells Troilus that the game is so far gone

> That first shal Phebus fallen fro his spere,
> And everich egle ben the dowves feere,
> And everi roche out of his place sterte,
> Er Troilus out of Criseydes herte.
>
> (III.1495–98)

She believes it is as contrary to her nature to stop loving Troilus as it is contrary to the immutable laws of nature for the sun to fall from its sphere or the eagle to love his contrary, the dove, or a rock to acquire motion. Later, when she and Troilus must part, she again draws her comparisons from nature. Fearing that she cannot live without Troilus, she asks, "How sholde a fissh withouten water dure?" and "How sholde a plaunte or lyves creature/ Lyve withouten his kynde noriture?" (IV.767–68). Here again she finds her love as binding as a law of nature. She forgets that the principal law of nature is change. In Book I, Pandarus consoles the woeful Troilus with the Boethian wisdom that Fortune is true by ever changing: "For if hire whiel stynte any thyng to torne,/ Than cessed she Fortune anon to be" (I.848–49). The same thing, of course, is true of nature, where all things endure only for their appointed seasons. Nature's is a mutable world. Criseyde is true to her divided nature, to the hot and cold alternating within her, like nature and fortune, by changing. Her circular course from widow's weeds to Troilus's arms to widow's weeds and, finally, to Diomede's arms is the recurrent cycle of all things in sublunar nature. She finally represents sublunar nature; that is, she is in her essence similar to it, for in her "now hot, now cold" changeability we see the union and dissolution of the things of the world due to the warring impulses of their contrary content. Though nature harmonizes these, as Criseyde will be harmonized by love in Book III, nature's harmony does not last; only heavenly harmony, the music of the spheres, continues without change. When Pandarus is persuading Troilus to have hope, he tells him that everyone is apt to suffer love's heat, either "love celestial or elles love of kynde." Love is the force that ends the discord and division within, bringing one into harmony with universal harmony. "Love of kynde," however, only unites contraries for a time; love celestial unites the contraries in man forever, leading him to the harmony of heaven. Troilus's love lasts, unlike Criseyde's, because it contains something of that perfect and lasting love, that true harmony, while hers is only of "kynde."

The *débat* form of Book II is precisely suited to its content and its main character, Criseyde. As we have seen, Chaucer invokes Janus, the god of two faces, to guide Pandarus in the world of Book II; he does so because it is the world with two faces. In its social world everyone speaks in "ambages," words with "two visages." Criseyde herself is of two minds, now this, now that, now hot, now cold. She is ever in Book II "at dulcarnoun." Her ambiguity is the duality of this world, of nature, with its summer and winter, its day and night, and of fortune.[46] As we shall see when we examine Book III in detail, Chaucer presents Venus, Fortune, and Criseyde as ladies with two faces, a bright face and a dark one. Psychologically, Criseyde is divided against herself, caught in a love of self which is discord and which her nature cannot transcend. Thus she is incapable morally and spiritually of making a sustained and total commitment, of being one as Troilus is one. There is always a half of her urging her the other way, so that she cannot truly sing. Metaphysically, she exists while unharmonized by love more in potentiality than in act. If love creates and perfects by uniting contraries, she is as yet not fully created, a chaos of contraries unharmonized by that love which binds together hot and cold.[47] As Pandarus says to Troilus when he urges him to be patient and persevere, "he that parted is in everi place/ Is nowher hol" (I.960–61). Her psychological character is indeed the key to her symbolic import. In Book II we see in her chaotic matter prior to the descent of the love which creates, primordial chaos not yet ornamented with order. She is body awaiting the unifying form of soul.

We should not leave Criseyde on such a negative note, however, for in the Christian scheme of things even mere matter is good, as are passing flowers, however soon they may fade. Though she is in one sense only a "worldly vanitee," her paradox is the paradox of all worldly vanities—they are not in vain. When we first meet Criseyde, she is introduced through her

father Calkas, traitor to Troy. Meeting her through Calkas and
having already been told in the proem that she forsook Troilus
before he died, we conclude like father, like daughter, that she
is heir to his original sin, treason. Simultaneously, however,
we are told that she at least seems to have quite different
origins.

> As to my doom, in al Troies cite
> Nas non so fair, for passynge every wight
> So aungelik was hir natif beaute,
> That lik a thing inmortal semed she,
> As doth an hevenyssh perfit creature,
> That down were sent in scornynge of nature.
>
> (I.100–105)

The irony of these lines is obvious, as she proves far less
"hevenyssh" and "perfit" than she seemed. She does inherit
her family sin.

One recalls that when Pandarus expressed his fears that he
had been a bawd, Troilus insisted upon the necessity of being
able to distinguish between things seemingly alike, an intellectual exercise as important in reading this poem and understanding the world as seeing the union of contraries.

> Departe it so, for wyde-wher is wist
> How that ther is diversite requered
> Bytwixen thynges like, as I have lered.
>
> (III.404–6)

Criseyde does seem like a "hevenyssh, perfit creature"; she
also seems in Books III and IV very like Troilus. We should
not, like Troilus, fail to see that she is not what she seems. But
this is true of both ways we are invited to see her; she is neither
a perfect creature nor simply a traitor. If she is not the goddess
Troilus thinks she is but a woman "slyding of corage," she
nonetheless is a mirror, a distant and quite distorted one, of the
heavenly and perfect. Like all beautiful things, Criseyde, as
microcosm of the beauty of all things in God's creation, contains traces of divinity. Troilus sees the similitude—witness
his song in Book III on the binding power of love—but misses
the dissimilarity. Not only Criseyde's beauty but even her
falseness ultimately mirror, however darkly, the goodness and
beauty of God, for her falseness ultimately serves a good pur-

pose, revealing the insufficiency of created things, and the fact that Venus, Nature, and Fortune are all part of God's order, an order which leads man away from God only to return him to God. The paradox of Criseyde—and of the world—is reiterated, apparently quite unconsciously, by the narrator at the end of the poem. There he urges us to reject the world and love God in words which affirm the ultimate value and goodness of the world.

> Repeyreth hom fro worldly vanyte,
> And of youre herte up casteth the visage
> To thilke God *that after his ymage*
> *Yow made,* and thynketh al nys but a faire
> This world, that passeth soone as floures faire.
>
> (V.1837–41; emphasis added)

Criseyde is a passing flower but one who images forth her Creator and who, in incarnating the way of the world, incarnates the divine order of things. Her paradox is that though she is herself insufficient, she participates in and mirrors the sufficient. Like all the world, she is a perilous mirror, having, even as has matter and body, a "dissimilar similitude" to God.

Before examining the union of contraries in Book III, we should consider in greater detail the principal human architect of that heaven, Pandarus. As an intermediary, it is appropriate, even necessary, that he be like both the extremes between which he goes. We have already discussed some ways in which Pandarus falls between Troilus and Criseyde, both in terms of character and style. These can be best summed up by calling him a realistic lover: like Criseyde, he is a sophisticated citizen of the world and a pragmatic realist; like Troilus, he is a devoted lover, having served long and faithfully.[48] He is no more able to love another than Troilus is. Muscatine mentions in passing his androgynous character, referring apparently both to the fact that many of his literary ancestors have been female matchmakers, and to the ease with which he moves in both Troilus's male world and Criseyde's female one.[49] If anything, he is more familiar with Criseyde than with Troilus. The contraries which meet in him and link him with both extremes are most evident when he begins to doubt the game he has been playing.

That is to seye, for the am I bicomen,
Bitwixen game and ernest, swich a meene
As maken wommen unto men to comen.

(III.253-55)

By "bitwixen game and ernest" he refers, of course, to the fact
that he has been carrying out his efforts to join Troilus and
Criseyde half in earnest, half in play. This indeed places him
in the middle, a mean between extremes, for we repeatedly
watch him go between the earnest Troilus and the "japing,"
playful Criseyde, and be earnest with Troilus and playful with
Criseyde.

Other things besides his role as go-between and his intermediate nature place him in the middle. Indeed, given his relationship to Troilus—friend—and his relationship to Criseyde
—uncle and guardian—he is caught in the middle. As he understands the responsibilities each relationship confers upon him,
his position is indeed delicate, inasmuch as a friend helps a
friend and an uncle protects his niece. Though he seems more
vigorous helping Troilus, he does seek to protect Criseyde's
honor, or rather her reputation, having no more success than
Criseyde at distinguishing between the two. Thus, for instance,
he lectures Troilus on not being a braggart and on being artful
enough to keep the world ignorant. Even when he is having
doubts about the role he is playing, he seems most concerned
with what people would say if they knew and persuades himself to go on with the game even before Troilus assures him
that what he has been doing is not "bauderye," but "gentilesse,/ Compassioun, and felawship, and trist."

Though he unquestionably carries friendship too far, like
one of his prototypes, Friend in the Roman de la rose, he has
a high ideal of friendship. Here is no fair-weather friend! He
believes that friends should share each other's joys and sorrows, and he certainly shares both: He divides Troilus's sorrow
with him and weeps many a genuine, as well as many an artful,
tear on his behalf, and he participates in as much of Troilus's
joy as he can, as he reluctantly leaves the bedroom the night
of the consummation and hastens back the next morning. He
also believes that a friend should ever remain a friend—"I have,
and shal, for trewe or fals report,/ In wrong and right iloved
the al my lyve" (I.593-94)—though he misinterprets what

such a friendship entails. Indeed, in some ways his love of Troilus proves more lasting than Criseyde's. When he advises Troilus to ravish Criseyde, he promises to assist him at whatever cost to himself. Unlike Criseyde, he is prepared to sacrifice his reputation for Troilus. Such a love reminds one of God's love of man, which continued in right and wrong, whatever the suffering and sacrifice it may entail. One must admit that the "dissimilitude" is greater than the "similitude," however, for God through His love seeks to correct man's sins, not to indulge him in them. He does believe that love is a good thing, though the goodness he sees in it is different from what Troilus sees, and he commits himself totally to it. When Criseyde finally betrays Troilus, he too feels betrayed; having been intimate with Troilus throughout the whole affair, sharing through empathy both his sorrows and his joys, he is in a sense one with him, so that he too is betrayed. To a considerable degree he is merely a victim of his own love of love, not a fate likely to befall a person who is only a pragmatic realist.

However, if it is too easy to be cynical about Pandarus, it is too easy to be sentimental as well. His perversion of friendship cannot be taken lightly. He is ever ready to employ false seeming, for instance, and in spite of the fact that he shares some of Troilus's idealism, he never manages to see his function for long as much more than to get the two in bed together. The limitations of his conception of love find perfect representation in his act of boosting Troilus into bed with Criseyde. Though he sometimes can see higher than that, he does not fully understand the quality of Troilus's love. He is the worldly-wise man, full of wit and proverbial wisdom, and not the holy fool. His own earnestness is always adulterated with game. Older and more experienced than Troilus, he is confident of his knowledge of human nature and the way of the world, and indeed he is quite successful for a time at manipulating Criseyde, in turning the world to Troilus's and his own advantage. He is a master of psychology and of the uses of time, or rather of certain uses of time, since he understands little about using time to gain eternity. He knows how to make a time of sorrow pass quickly, though his methods do not work very well with the unworldly Troilus. He knows how, like Harry Bailly, to shorten the way to the shrine and how to find a time and a place for pleasure. His art is the art of enjoying the world—not that of using it to enjoy God. He repeatedly speaks "for the nones," as, for instance, when he persuades Troilus that since he is down Fortune will be his friend, conveniently forgetting to mention that Fortune's friendship will not last. Once again like the worldly-wise man, he is certain that the end justifies the means, almost any means, even the total lie.

It is when we look at him in terms of his relationship with Criseyde that he looks the least attractive. Especially with Calkas departed, as her uncle and guardian, he ought, as she says, to have more concern for her honor than for Troilus's pleasure. Given his enthusiasm for love and his belief that it is a good thing, he usually manages to avoid seeing anything wrong. If we accept Troilus's conception of love as a sacred thing, we may be inclined to think him a priest, mediating between a man and his god. If we accept his own conception of love in his less idealistic moments, we are more likely to conclude that he is a bawd. However willing Criseyde may be, he must answer for his own intentions and must bear much of the responsibility for what happens. Though there are redeeming qualities in Troilus's love of Criseyde, Pandarus shares too little of these aspects of his love, too many of those which pervert the proper end of love and serve the self. Just as the function of a priest is separate from the man himself, remaining sacred however much the man may be a "whiskey priest," so with Pandarus we must distinguish between the man and the function. If love is good, his function is good, however base his motives and though he himself will have to answer for his intentions; if sexual love is bad, his function is bad, however noble his motives. However much one loves Pandarus, one must finally judge him severely. His personal failure inescapably confronts us in his response to Criseyde's betrayal— hatred. If he is judged as he judges, his own betrayal of Criseyde can find little forgiveness.

Though a descendant of a long line of literary matchmakers, Pandarus has other, more impressive literary forebears who help define his character, function, and intermediate position. His efforts to reason Criseyde into love, to ravish her with his speech, make him a human equivalent of the god of Love. He, too, seeks to bind together contraries. Similarly, he recalls the traditional characterization of the goddess Nature in the *concordia discors* tradition as intermediary between God and this world. The heavens, through which Fate orders the sublunar world of Providence, cooperate with Pandarus in bringing Troilus and Criseyde together one dark, rainy night. As a priest of Venus, the deity who presides over the house that Pandarus builds, he recalls Nature's priest in the *Roman,* Genius, and Alain de Lille's prototype of Jean's character. In Alain and Jean he is a complex figure, both a cosmic force of generation uniting form and matter and the force, the genii, inhabiting the male genitals and responsible for "transmitting human form from one generation to another."[50] In both respects, his task is to transmit "Divine Wisdom into the sphere of Nature" and to administer "the 'mystical' union of form and matter" as Nature's priest. The effects of the Fall are evident in the traditional characterization of all these intermediaries. The god of Love, the goddess Nature, and the priest Genius are all ambiguous, capable of deforming as well as forming.

Pandarus's function as intermediary between Troilus and Criseyde duplicates on a human level the function of these cosmic forces, all of whom are traditionally pictured as agents which unite the contrary to help create this harmonious world. The degree to which Pandarus provides the impetus to get Troilus and Criseyde to bed together suggests the impetus to love provided by the *genitalia,* for instance. Without the aggression provided by Pandarus and necessary for the conquest of Criseyde—neither Troilus nor Criseyde seems quite able to get him off his knees beside her bed—the little world of love created in Book III would have remained uncreated. One recalls Reason's insistence in the *Roman* that the "cullions" are good and their function beneficial: they insure the continuation of God's creation.[51] If Pandarus's creative function is good, however, his repeated use of deception and false seeming reveals that he, too, has felt the effects of the Fall.

Besides being friend, guardian, bawd, and priest, Pandarus is also artist. If Troilus is in a sense love, then Pandarus is the art of love and would seem to demonstrate that, whatever the historical lines of transmission, the art of courtly love descends both from Plato and Ovid. For all the Ovidian slight of hand

Pandarus uses, Chaucer dignifies his artistic function when he
pictures him at the ending of Book I going forth to create a
"tyme" and a "place."

> For everi wight that hath an hous to founde
> Ne renneth naught the werk for to bygynne
> With rakel hond, but he wol bide a stounde,
> And sende his hertes line out fro withinne
> Aldirfirst his purpos for to wynne.
> Al this Pandare in his herte thoughte,
> And caste his werk ful wisely or he wroughte.
>
> (I.1065-71)

This passage is taken from Geoffrey de Vinsauf's *Poetria
nova.*[52] The picture it presents, minus the image of sending out
the "hertes line," is traditional and implies a traditional analogy between human and divine creativity. One creates the idea
of that which one wishes to make before making it. Two passages well known to Chaucer describing God's creation of the
universe, the first from the *Consolation*, the second from the
Complaint, will illuminate not only the conception of making
implicit in these lines but something of Pandarus's function in
the poem as well.

O thow Fadir, soowere and creatour of hevene and of erthes, . . . ne
foreyne causes necesseden the nevere to compoune werk of flo-
terynge matere, but oonly the forme of sovereyn good iset within
the withoute envye, that moevede the frely. Thow, that art althir-
fayrest, berynge the faire world in thy thought, formedest this
world to the lyknesse semblable of that faire world in thy thought.
Thou drawest alle thyng of thy sovereyn ensaumpler and comaund-
est that this world, parfytly ymakid, have frely and absolut his
parfyte parties. Thow byndest the elementis by nombres propor-
cionables, that the coolde thinges mowen accorde with the hote
thinges, and the drye thinges with the moyste; that the fyr, that
is purest, fle nat over-heye, ne that the hevynesse drawe nat adoun
over-lowe the erthes that ben ploungid in the watris. (III.*m*.ix.1–24)

When God wished to bring the creation of His worldly palace out
from the spiritual abode of His inner preconception into external
mold, and to express, as in a material world and by its very
existence, the mental world which He had conceived from the ever-
lasting foundation of the universe, like a splendid world's architect,
like a goldsmith working in gold, like a skilful artisan of a stupen-
dous production, like the industrious workman of a wonderful

work, He fashioned the marvelous form of His earthly palace, not with the laborious assistance of an exterior agency, nor by the help of material laying there at hand, nor because of any base need, but by the power of His sole independent will. Then God added to this worldly palace various kinds of things, and these, though separated by the strife of different natures, He governed with harmony of proper order, furnished with laws, and bound with ordinances. And thus He united with mutual and fraternal kisses things antagonistic from the opposition of their properties, between which the space had made its room from contraries, and He changed the strife of hatred into the peace of friendship. All things, then, agreeing through invisible bonds of union, plurality returned to unity, diversity to identity, dissonance to harmony, discord to concord in peaceful agreement. (*Pr.* iv.43)

Like God, Pandarus creates a time and a place and unites therein the contraries Troilus and Criseyde, as he gradually brings forth that which he first conceives in his mind, or as an agent for Troilus, that which is first conceived in Troilus's mind. Pandarus creates a little world of harmony by bringing together diversity, dissonance, and discord—but how ambiguous a maker and how ambiguous a product! For Troilus, the house that Pandarus builds is a palace, a sacred temple; time will prove it to be something of a house of ill repute as well, one built upon the sands of a love in many ways false. The house that Pandarus builds is, as we shall see in the next chapter, simultaneously sacred and profane.

The poem's ultimate artist is of course Chaucer. As an artist, he creates, as does Pandarus, in imitation of God's creative act as well as in imitation of the created. His poem is another cosmos, first conceived in the mind and then made by imposing form upon the matter of the *Filostrato.* We saw in the first chapter of this study that the structure of the first three books of the *Troilus* imitates the formation of the universe, bringing together the contraries of Book I and Book II to create Book III. I have been trying to demonstrate in this chapter that just as God, in creating, orders things which are themselves reflections of himself, so Chaucer's poem presents persons, places, things, and actions which mirror both nature and the Author of nature. Like the universe itself, Chaucer's poem seeks to incarnate the Word in the flesh of its poetry. The universe Chaucer creates in *Troilus and Criseyde* is thus a symbolic one both in its form and in its content.

3

The Marriage of
Heaven and Hell

Chaucer begins Book III with a proem in which he celebrates
Venus and her effects and invokes her assistance that he may
show the sweetness of love. Though the rhetoric of the proem
is unabashedly enthusiastic in its celebration of Venus's power
and goodness, the total picture that emerges is decidedly ambiguous. If it praises Venus as the force which created and
sustains the universe in language which recalls the Christian
conception of the Holy Spirit as the love which vivifies creation, it also pictures Venus as the force which moved Jove to
descend "in a thousand formes" to seize those Venus caused
him to desire.[1] Though such a description of Jove's descent in
love may well have been intended as a metaphor for the ravishing power of God's grace, the literal reference is, of course, to
Jove the ravisher of such "mortal thyng[s]" as Leda and
Europa. Similarly, though the assertion that Venus knows "al
thilke covered qualitee/ Of thynges," why, for instance, she
loves him or he loves her, may suggest God's omniscience and
even His predestination, the language "as whi this fissh, and
naught that, comth to were" suggest other more mundane
mysteries as well. In spite of the fact that the narrator appeals
to Venus's "benignite" in asking for inspiration, the proem's
characterization of the law she has set in the universe for man
implies that her effects are not always benign.

Venus is quite capable of bearing such a burden of ambiguity, since she was traditionally used, as we have noted, as
a representation both of celestial love and libidinous love.[2]
Bernardus Silvestris, for instance, distinguishes two Venuses
in his *Commentary on the Aeneid:* "We read that there are
two Venuses, a lawful goddess and a goddess of wantonness.
We call the lawful Venus cosmic harmony [*mundana musica*],
that is, the equal proportion of things in the cosmos, which

some call Astrea, others call natural justice. For she is in the elements, in the stars, in the seasons, and in living things. But the shameful Venus, the goddess of wantonness, is what we call concupiscence of the flesh, and she is the mother of all fornications."[3] The celestial Venus is that love which binds together the contraries of the universe in harmony. The wanton Venus is that force which moves man to ravishing. Though Bernardus is distinguishing between the two, the fact that they are both Venuses indicates that the latter is a corruption of the former. Bernardus makes Aeneas, the human spirit, the son of Anchises and the celestial Venus, but far from immune to the influence of Cupid and Jocus, the sons of Vulcan (natural heat) and that Venus who is "fleshly indulgence."[4] There is in the *Complaint of Nature* a related presentation of two Venuses, or rather of one Venus who has two aspects.[5] Venus married to Hymen is the harmony of the universe, the *musica mundana;* Venus committing adultery with Antigamus (antimarriage) is the wanton. From Venus legitimized by marriage is born Cupid; from Venus living in adultery comes Jocus (sport).[6] Alain's allegory of Venus and his picture of Hymen summoning Genius with "harmonious melody" to excommunicate the unnatural from Nature's company suggest that for Alain the sacrament of marriage could correct corrupted human nature, could transform Venus turned wanton into the harmonious Venus.

Though Chaucer does not invoke two Venuses, his invocation of her reveals the traditional duality. She has, as it were, two faces. Although the invocation to Book III is largely based upon a song Troilo sings in the *Filostrato*, it also recalls in general, though not in detail, Boethius's characterization of love as the force that orders the cosmos by binding together contraries.[7] Venus holds "regne and hous in unitee" and is the "sothfast cause of frendshipe." To say with F. N. Robinson that the love invoked here is "both sexual attraction and the cosmic love which binds together the universe" is to see only half the implications of the invocation, however;[8] for the ambiguity of Chaucer's characterization indicates that the effects of Venus on man are both celestial and wanton. Chaucer's invocation insists that human sexual love can partake of Venus's "benignite," can participate in that love which is the

musica mundana, for he pictures Venus as potentially en-
nobling. She appeases the ire of Mars and causes lovers to
resign their vices.[9] The reference to Jove the ravisher, however,
suggests the ease with which sexual love can be perverted from
its good and proper use. Ravishing is, after all, Paris's sin, as
well as Jove's, and he, like Jove, was moved to it by Venus.
Though Venus can ennoble man, she, at least as she is dis-
ordered by man, is also the cause of the discord of this world
figured in the image of besieged Troy. Love, it would seem, is
both the cause and the cure for the human condition.

Venus is not just a symbol for cosmic love and man's all-
too-frequent perversion of that love, for she is also informed
by Alain de Lille's and Jean de Meun's allegorical representations of nature. Influenced by the school of Chartres, according to which the universe maintains itself by natural laws
while God sustains it, Alain and Jean assign to Nature much of
the ordering and controlling function Boethius assigned to
love. Nature, as God's vicar, is both the order of created things
and the force which maintains and perpetuates that order.[10] As
the order of the universe, she is a mirror of the eternal archetypal pattern of all things in the mind of God, the Logos. Behind the conception of Nature in Alain and Jean as the force
which maintains the universe, we can see not only the love
which binds all things, the Holy Spirit, but also Bernardus
Silvestris's conception of Nature as the principle of generation which results from the fecundity of Noys.[11] Though
Nature reflects both divine order and divine love, she is now
a distorted mirror, having felt the effects of the Fall. Thus,
there is ambiguity in both Alain's and Jean's allegorical representation of nature.

Both the invocation of Venus beginning Book III and her
function throughout the poem indicate that Chaucer has ex-
panded her significance. In addition to reflecting the cosmic
love which creates Nature and the human sexual love which is
part of Nature's generative impulse, she represents the whole
of which the planet Venus is a part, nature itself. One of the
laws through which Nature operates as she expresses divine
wisdom and love is planetary influence. Jean de Meun, for instance, pictures Nature as shaping those things which she
makes through the agency of the planets, which, in their

circling course, bind together the contrary elements and make a peace among them.[12] The planets also insure that those things harmonized into being cease in due time. The planets are agents of both Nature and Fate in their related functions as intermediaries between God and man and his sublunar world. In *Troilus and Criseyde*, Venus's ambiguity presides over the duality of this world and she, as much as Fortune, accounts for the eternal pattern of all things in this world, the progress "fro wo to wele and after out of joie." The narrator accounts at the end of Book III for the fact that its "heaven" ends not only by telling us that Fortune turned her wheel but also by observing that Venus, Cupid, and the Muses "wol wende." By asserting that "man, brid, best, fissh, herbe, and grene tree/ Thee fele in tymes with vapour eterne" and that no creature "may endure" without love, Chaucer suggests the astrological influence of Venus and the intermediary function of Nature and Fate. Indeed, the term "vapour eterne," a translation of Boccaccio's "eterno vapor," suggests the whole Christianized Neoplatonic conception of this universe as an emanation hierarchically descending from God. More successfully than Alain or Jean, Chaucer unites the concept that love is the prime mover with the idea that the universe is ordered by natural laws which manifest their Creator and his will by using Venus as his representation of the love which manifests itself in and through the laws of nature. Rather than employing a personified abstraction, he employs symbolism, using a concrete part of the universe to represent the law of love of which it is in fact a product, a manifestation, and a transmitter. By making her ambiguous, he succinctly represents the paradoxical character of this glorious yet fallen world.

Chaucer indicates that he is thinking of the planet as well as the goddess by invoking Venus as the "blisful light" of "the thridde heven faire." He also refers to her light at the end of the third book when he addresses her as "lady bryght." She is not the only bright lady in the poem, however. Fortune is another; at the beginning of Book IV we are told that "From Troilus she gan hire brighte face/Awey to writhe." Thenceforth Fortune shows Troilus only the dark one of her two faces.[13] The principal bright lady of the poem is, of course, Criseyde. Chaucer indicates the essential oneness of these

three bright ladies by associating them in their brightness. They
are also all ladies with two faces, a bright and attractive one,
a dark and forbidding one. We have already touched upon the
ambiguity of Venus, and the double face of Fortune hardly
needs explicating. Criseyde, who is repeatedly associated with
light and brightness, who for Troilus always remains a blissful
light, undergoes a transformation in Book IV.

> She was right swich to seen in hire visage
> As is that wight that men on beere bynde;
> Hire face, lik of Paradys the ymage,
> Was al ychaunged in another kynde.
>
> (IV.862–65)

Now a purple ring encircles her eyes, the former seat of her
brightness, as she becomes an image not of paradise but of
death. This change indicates not only the very real suffering
she experiences, the hell into which she has fallen from the
heaven of Book III, but her basic duality as well, her contrary
nature. Janus, as we have seen, must be invoked to guide
Pandarus on his first visit to Criseyde, Janus, who, as Augustine explains, represents both the beginnings and the ends of
temporal things and by whom the pagans in their confusion
sometimes would seem to mean Jupiter, the World-Soul, sometimes the world's body.[14] The fact that Criseyde is transformed
in Book IV into a dark lady, a transformation which hardly
ought to surprise us, reveals both that "all human things are
subject to decay" and that she, when bright, shines with a
light not her own, like the Lover's pool in the *Roman de la rose*,
that her beauty is both transitory and only a reflection of a
beauty which does not change.

For Troilus, Criseyde is associated with light throughout the
poem. In Book III even her tears are bright. Ironically, Chaucer,
if anything, increases the frequency of Troilus's allusions to
her brightness in Books IV and V when the reader has seen her
lose her brightness and has realized that she was only bright as
a mirror is bright, by reflection. One thinks first of Troilus's
apostrophe to her empty house, a "paleys desolat" which is
now a lantern without light, a house no longer "Enlumyned
with sonne of alle blisse" (V.548). Similarly, when Troilus
learns that she is to leave, he imagines himself "Edippe,"

destined to live the rest of his life in darkness. He addresses his eyes, telling him that they are now of no worth since his whole joy was to see Criseyde's bright eyes, since the light, Criseyde, is quenched which was accustomed to illuminate them (IV.309–15). They are in vain because their "vertu is aweye." Thus Troilus reveals that Criseyde's brightness was both that which he joyed to see and that by which he was able to see. The irony of much of this is apparent: One recalls Boethius's insistence that the things of the world blind a man to the true light and realizes that Troilus was in some ways most blind when he thought he was seeing clearly, and that in Books IV and V when he considers himself blind, he is seeing some of the light of truth, that worldly beauty cannot bring true happiness. There is more than irony here, however, for he does manage to see a good deal by the light of Criseyde, as we will be able to see, if we examine some of the history of light imagery as Christianity employed it.[15]

In her brightness, Criseyde is associated with the "blisful" light of Venus—she is in a sense a mirror of that light. Both she and Venus reflect another light, however, the light of God. The association in Christianity of God with light rests upon biblical authority. To understand God, the church fathers eclectically appropriated the wisdom of the philosophers, a habit nowhere more evident than in their explication of the biblical references to the light of God. There was a wealth of philosophical thought about light to draw upon, for the Neoplatonists had evolved a metaphysics of light, a theory that ultimate reality was immaterial light and that the whole universe was a hierarchy of differing forms and varying degrees of light, all emanating with "vapour eterne" from the immaterial light of God. Indeed, the most famous of the biblical allusions to God as Light, the opening of the Gospel of St. John, was itself probably written under the influence of Neoplatonic thought. There Christ is both Word (Logos) and Light. St. Augustine credits Plotinus with sufficient wisdom to be in agreement with this portion of the Gospel of John, with understanding that the soul derives its happiness from the Light which created it and by whose "intelligible illumination" it understands things intelligible.[16] He also credited Socrates with seeking to purify the mind that it might "contemplate that

nature which is incorporeal and unchangeable light, where live
the causes of all created things."[17] The Neoplatonists, according to Mazzeo, derived their conception of light in part from
an analogy in Plato's *Republic* between the Good and sun.[18]
According to Plato, three things are necessary for sight: the
sense of sight, the objects of the sense, and light as a mediator
between vision and the visible. Likewise in the intelligible
world, the realm of the ideas, the Good, the sun of the intelligible world, mediates between the intelligence and intelligible
things. Both the basic analogy and subsequent Neoplatonic
thought had a profound influence upon Christianity, especially
upon Augustine, for whom "God is nothing other than intelligible light itself, by which all intelligible things shine in their
intelligibility."[19]

For a Christian, the ultimate mediator between man and God,
between the intelligence of the soul and the intelligible God, is
Christ, the God-man. He is the light by which we see the Light,
both the means and the end. However, though Christ is the
principal "divine illumination" by which we know God, he is
by no means the only mediator. All things can and do mediate
between man and God. This is nowhere clearer than in the
thought of Pseudo-Dionysius, whose thinking in this respect,
as in others, is clearly visible in dramatic form in both the
Divine Comedy and the *Roman de la rose*, whether directly or
secondhand.[20] Dionysius, perhaps the most Neoplatonic of
medieval Christians, also uses the Platonic analogy between
the Good and the Sun. "Just as our sun, not by deliberation of
choice, but by being what it is, enlightens all things which are
able to receive its light according to their own powers of participation, so also the Good, which is as far superior to the sun
as the transcendent archetype is superior to its faint image,
pours forth by its very Being the Rays of Its unitive Goodness
to all beings according to their respective capacity."[21] All
things manifest the Light according to their capacity to do so,
so that the universe is a vast hierarchy of degrees of light, and
all things desire the Goodness and Light which create them:[22]
"And all things seek it: the intellectual and rational by knowledge, lower things by sense perception, those of still lower order
through living movements, others through their properties of
matter or existence."[23] Ultimately for Dionysius, all reality, not

just Christ or the Scriptures or the angelic hierarchies, is divinely illuminated, for all sensible things reveal spiritual things, reveal through their form and shape the "Formless" and "Shapeless," through their light the Light. Indeed, for Dionysius things can almost be said to exist because of their desire to participate in God's emanating light, because of their love of that light.[24] No doubt, it was ultimately this idea—that created nature is a mirror and a manifestation of "that nature which is incorporeal and unchangeable light"—which caused Dante to link despising "natura" with blaspheming and denying God and to consign such violent souls to the seventh circle of hell.[25] Unqualified *contemptus mundi* apparently is as hazardous as unqualified love of the world.

Even such a brief background sketch illuminates Chaucer's use of metaphors of light. Just as *Troilus and Criseyde* imitates the divine order of things by harmonizing contraries, so in its symbolism it imitates the universe's symbolic revelation of the Light which is God. Chaucer's poem, like the universe, is filled with mirrors which reflect and distort the Light. The planet Venus is one such mirror of reflected light, manifesting the Light and mediating between It and this world. Fortune is another. The poem's most important symbolic light is, of course, Criseyde. Just as Venus can represent the sacred and the profane, cosmic love and sexual attraction, Criseyde is the daughter of Calkas and "hevenyssh," a bright star "under cloude blak," a divine soul in mortal flesh. Once again like Venus, she is an ambiguous light, having two faces, as she is now bright, now dark. We see in her two faces both her fatal ability to change and the fact that she is only reflected light. Her two faces, like the two faces of Venus and Fortune, indicate her "dissimilar similitude" to the Light. Criseyde, like Lady Philosophy for Boethius and Beatrice for Dante, is able to mediate between Troilus and God. The song which Troilus sings at the end of Book III about how love orders the universe is a song Lady Philosophy sings to Boethius. That Troilus sings it inspired by Criseyde's beauty demonstrates that she does reflect something of the light of true love and mediates between him and it. That Troilus can only see the similitude and mistakes it for identity should not lead us to suppose that Chaucer can only see and wants us to see only the dissimilitude. Our recognition that Criseyde is not the love which binds together the universe should not prevent our seeing that she mirrors that love at the same time that she distorts it. Criseyde is neither simply bright nor dark, nor is she simply now bright, now dark. She is simultaneously dark and bright.

Such is the perilous and ambiguous light of Venus. If it is a light which fallen man perverts into ravishing to cause the Trojan wars of this world, it is also the light which shines in all things, uniting the contraries within each thing and harmonizing the antithetical into a stable whole. Though it cannot produce in the sublunar world a harmony that lasts, it does insure the stable progression of change in this world, a stable change which mirrors the stability of the endlessly bright source of all things. It is thus that Venus, as vicar of God, holds "regne and hous in unitee," that she orders even the universe itself. Such is the force which moves all the poem's characters, not least of all Pandarus, who himself mediates between the lovers and helps unite them for a brief time in the house which he builds. It is to that house and its dark brightness that we must now turn. A careful reading of its heaven reveals it to be ambiguous precisely as the Venus who helps create it is ambiguous. Like the Lover's garden in the *Roman de la rose*, which contains all the qualities seemingly excluded from it by being pictured on its outer walls, and like the world of which it is a copy, this apparent heaven contains its contrary. It unites the sacred and the profane, *caritas* and *cupiditas*, heaven and hell.

The consummation scene is radically transformed from its original in Boccaccio.[26] Chaucer moves the scene to Pandarus's house, complicates the roles of the three main characters, and surrounds the whole with an aura of inevitability. In *Il Filostrato*, Pandaro, acting out Criseida's plan, merely sends for Troilo, who is at the battlefront.[27] Troilo returns and goes to Criseida's house, where she awaits him and sneaks him into the house. There is no doubt in anyone's mind as to what is to take place, and little or no pressure of circumstances. The whole scene is infinitely more complex in Chaucer. The psychological motivation and the moral responsibility become richly ambiguous. The movement of the scene to Pandarus's house is an especially significant alteration; like his presence throughout most of the scene, it reminds us of his instrumentality in bringing about the consummation of the love affair. Both Troilus and Criseyde are much more passive in Chaucer's version, and seem to the narrator—and to themselves at times—almost innocent, as though they were merely victims of fate and Pandarus's manipulation. If pressure from Pandarus is necessary to overcome Criseyde's fear for her honor, it seems equally necessary to overcome Troilus's fear—or rather awe—of Criseyde. All of Pandarus's machinations, even to the point of boosting Troilus into bed, and all the pressure of circumstance, even to the fortuitous rainstorm, cannot absolve Troilus and Criseyde of responsibility, however, for if Chaucer stresses the forces of necessity and the presence of mitigating circumstances, he also indicates his characters' freedom. Though divine providence insures their night together by means of a "smoky reyn," reminding us perhaps of Dido's and Aeneas's refuge in a cave one rainy day, there is no evidence that providence dictates what takes place in Pandarus's bedroom, any more than it dictated Aeneas's seduction of Dido in that "litel cave."[28] Chaucer's treatment of Criseyde's questions concerning the whereabouts of Troilus that night, for instance, leaves little reason for us to suppose she believed Pandarus's insistence that he was "out of towne." Though the narrator, protecting Criseyde as usual, takes refuge in the fact that his author does not say what "she thoughte when he seyde so," Criseyde's instructions to Pandarus—"Em, syn I most on yow triste,/ Loke al be wel, and do now as yow liste" (III.586–87)—leave little doubt as to what she thought, since they are superfluous if she did not suspect Troilus would be there. She herself admits, in a moment of candor, that if she had not earlier yielded she would not be there, though it baffles the reader to determine the precise point at which she did. This is not to say, of course, that she went to Pandarus's house intending to seduce or be seduced nor that she could have guessed he was in hiding.[29] Troilus, for all his fainting and praying, is able to seize the prize, and he does so with vigor once Pandarus leaves the room, and immediately after the narrator asks, "What myghte or may the sely larke seye,/ Whan that the sperhauk hath it in his foot?" (III.1191–92). Implications of ravishing are not far away.

The imperfections of Pandarus's paradise, its dark side, are also evident from the fact that it brings no real peace to Troilus. It is a night which affords no one any real rest. Indeed, it leaves Troilus more consumed than ever with desire—"I hadde it nevere half so hote as now" (III.1650). The "newe qualitee" which he feels, a quality he himself cannot identify, is not simply lust, as we shall see, but that is no doubt one aspect of it. The consummation scene is full of ambiguous imagery of binding. The "humble nettes" of his lady which bind him without bonds inevitably recall the invisible snares of cupidity. Though completely ensnared himself, he is still fearful that he may not be as firmly set in Criseyde's heart as she is in his. If their joys seem a heaven, the grief which accompanies the inevitable separation in the morning seems a hell. One need not reduce the poem to a piece of *contemptus mundi* moralization to recognize the inadequacy of trying to find a heaven in "sydes longe, flesshly, smothe, and white" and "brestes rounde and lite" (III.1250), or to recognize the bliss of ignorance in Troilus's assertion that God made him to serve Criseyde. Though Venus is invoked at the beginning of the book as light, one of the major attributes and perhaps even the essence of God, the consummation takes place on a dark, rainy night. Pandarus builds his paradise for a time "Right sone upon the chaungynge of the moone/ When lightles is the world a nyght or tweyne" (III.549–50). Were we to judge this paradise solely by the Boethian values Chaucer introduces into the scene in Criseyde's speech on the vanity of worldly happiness, we might conclude that all the participants in Book III, including the narrator, are hopelessly lost in the dark, blinded by thoughts of this world and that the only light in the house is the "darkness visible" of hell.

Just before committing herself completely to the worldly happiness of love, Criseyde proves in a Boethian lament that worldly happiness is false felicity.[30] Such happiness, she tells us, is imperfect because one either knows it cannot last, and hence cannot be happy in it, or is ignorant of its mutability, an "ignorance ay in derknesse" which also prevents complete happiness, for no true happiness can be based on ignorance. Though her speech is directed vaguely at Pandarus, who has been urging her to save Troilus now, and though Troilus no doubt overhears it, since he is in the room, all three manage to forget its inexorable logic and its bitter truth. Their paradise is only for "a time" and "a place," lacking both the eternity and the infinity of heaven. The sun, that ancient and pre-eminent symbol of the light of love and understanding which is God, is greeted with hostility by the lovers, for it signals their separation. The light of day is an enemy to their love, which can only thrive in the semidarkness of this world, and brings to a temporary end their paradise. It also forecasts their ultimate total separation and the hell of Books IV and V. This is especially evident in their matching *aubes*, passionate songs which, though they reveal their almost perfect harmony of thought and feeling, contain significant differences full of ironic references to the future.[31] Troilus curses the coming of the light of day into Troy, a curse in which we recognize his resistance to the truth of life in this world. Inevitably the light of truth, the fact of change, will enter Troy and Troilus with the departure of Criseyde, and cause him to wish he were blind and even dead. Criseyde's complaint is addressed to "blake nyght," created, she says, to hide this world. She regrets that it is hastening out of Troy and wishes that the laws of nature, the same laws which have brought them together, would be suspended that night might remain with them, as it did in one of Jove's amorous escapades. One is reminded that she will hasten all too soon out of Troy and end their joy permanently. In so doing, of course, she too is being true to the natural laws of change, laws which she in her blindness calls upon as evidence of the permanence of her love. The conclusion that she has much in common with the dark face of "blake nyght" is inescapable for all her associations with light. In her two faces we can see both the bright face of the day and the dark face of the night, two of the many contraries God's love harmonizes. When Troilus in his song at the end of Book III praises love for insuring that Phoebus brings forth the day and that the moon rules the night, he speaks truer than he knows, for if Criseyde's bright face insures his brief happiness, her dark face insures the night of his sorrow when, with the departure of Criseyde, the "Herynes, Nyghtes doughtren thre," will replace Venus as the ministers of destiny.

The very means necessary to build Pandarus's house insure

its participation in the fallen condition of this world, for one of its cornerstones is false seeming. One recalls that in the *Roman de la rose,* Friend advises the Lover to employ deception on the grounds that he will never win his rose without it, and that the god of Love accepts False Seeming, though reluctantly, into his company.[32] In the *Roman,* False Seeming represents the evil which is the consequence of the Fall, and the Lover's use of him to win his rose demonstrates his own fallen condition. Though the god of Love recognizes that False Seeming is evil, he accepts him because his followers require it, just as the Christian God accepts the evil man introduced into his creation. The allegory of the consequences of the Fall which Jean represents through the personified abstraction False Seeming, Chaucer dramatizes in Pandarus's and Troilus's use of a bit of false seeming, the Horaste fiction. Though Pandarus invents this fiction, finding it as necessary for the building of his house as Friend finds it to win the rose, Troilus, "Cupides sone," consents. When Criseyde asks him about it, he confirms the Horaste deception, rather than risking the hazards of telling the truth:

> And for the lasse harm, he moste feyne.
> He seyde hire, whan she was at swich a feste,
> She myght on hym han loked at the leste,—
> Noot I nought what, al deere ynough a rysshe,
> As he that nedes most a cause fisshe.
>
> (III.1158–62)

The narrator's almost careless attitude here ought not to be ours, for Troilus employs false seeming, like Cupid in the *Roman,* for reasons radically different from those for which God accepts evil. The Horaste fiction indicates Troilus's *cupiditas,* not his *caritas.* The effects of Venus upon Troilus are in some ways similar to her effects upon Jove. Indeed, the verbal force Pandarus employs—"If that ye suffre hym al nyght in this wo,/ God help me so, ye hadde hym nevere lief" (III.863–64)—reveals that there is too little difference between Jove's ravishing and Troilus's and Pandarus's seduction.

When Criseyde first accepted Troilus into her service in the first scene in Book III, the mutually accepted covenant between the lovers was based upon justice. Criseyde was to reward Troilus as he deserved.

> And I to han, right as yow list, comfort,
> Under yowre yerde, egal to myn offence,
> As deth, if that I breke youre defence.
>
> (III.136–38)

According to the law of justice, death is what he now deserves. Troilus's insistence that Criseyde's gift of herself to him is more than he deserves, is mercy, is correct. In the *Roman de la rose*, Venus is born when Jove ends the Golden Age by castrating Saturn, at the same time that Justice flees the universe.[33] Jean is here not simply allegorizing the Fall, for the Venus that is born is another two-faced Venus, signifying both the corrupted love which is the consequence of the Fall and something of the love which will redeem the fallen world, that love which in its mercy dies for the world rather than destroying it in satisfaction of justice. When Criseyde forgives Pandarus his deception the day after the consummation, the narrator observes, almost flippantly,

> What! God foryaf his deth, and she al so
> Foryaf, and with here uncle gan to pleye,
> For other cause was ther noon than so.
>
> (III.1577–79)

Though the narrator's reference to Christ's crucifixion may seem wildly inappropriate, we are witnessing mercy. Troilus's use of false seeming banishes justice from his relationship with Criseyde and makes mercy necessary. While Criseyde's mercy may seem little related to Christ's, in that it is at least partly self-serving, man's mercy is inevitably at best a distorted mirror of God's. The bright face of man's *caritas* is always clouded with *cupiditas*. Whether or not Criseyde is being merciful, God is, for even such a heaven as that enjoyed by Troilus and Criseyde in Book III is the consequence of God's love, of his continuous redemption of a world which man has filled with false seeming and which the requirements of justice alone would destroy.

Shortly after the description of the delights of Criseyde's body, we find Troilus praying: "O Love, O Charite!/ Thi moder ek, Citherea the swete" (III.1254–55). One laughs—perhaps too quickly—at Troilus's mouse's heart and at his apparent confusion of *cupiditas* and *caritas*. The pleasures of

Criseyde's body termed charity seem as misnamed as Cupid is here. There is more than irony here, however, for the fact that Troilus is forever forgetting to act and remembering to pray is a significant indication of the nature of his love, as well as of his psychology and his blindness. Criseyde moves him simultaneously to *caritas* and *cupiditas*. In an article on the *Roman de la rose* and medieval theories about love, Charles Dahlberg observes that St. Bernard constructed a "ladder" of love corresponding to a progression of the senses, one beginning at the bottom with natural, carnal love, signified in the sense of touch, and ascending up to the sense of sight, signifying the love of God aroused by the mystic vision of Him.[34] The ascent from touch to sight charts the growth, the way, of *caritas*. Though St. Bernard does not detail completely the contrary progression from sight to touch, he does imply, Dahlberg argues, that such is the progression of *cupiditas*, which begins in the sight of the beloved and seeks to end in the gratification of the sense of touch. Certainly, Troilus began by seeing Criseyde and has progressed to stroking her heavenly anatomy. It is equally certain that he repeatedly turns from that which he is touching to that which he sees in Criseyde. Book III ends, we recall, with a song in praise of the cosmic love he has seen in her, but even in the midst of the consummation scene, he turns from her to address the Love which she manifests. Whenever he encounters her beauty and brightness, he refers it to its source, toward the Beauty which it reflects and praises that Beauty, as well as hers. Perhaps we should also stop to remember that even the body, like night, is a gift of God and to recall the explanation of the goddess Nature in the *Complaint of Nature* that she made the body beautiful that the spirit would not reject it.[35] Thus, we find Troilus in bed with a naked Criseyde, in what is decidedly the traditional territory of *cupiditas,* and find him praising God and coming to the realization that "mercy passeth right."

So transported by love that he knows not what to do, he gives thanks to Cupid, Venus, Imeneus, and charity. He continues,

> Benigne Love, thow holy bond of thynges,
> Whoso wol grace, and list the nought honouren,
> Lo, his desir wol fle withouten wynges.

> For noldestow of bownte hem socouren
> That serven best and most alwey labouren,
> Yet were al lost, that dar I wel seyn certes,
> But if thi grace passed our desertes.
>
> And for thow me, that leest koude disserve
> Of hem that noumbred ben unto thi grace,
> Hast holpen, ther I likly was to sterve,
> And me bistowed in so heigh a place
> That thilke boundes may no blisse pace,
> I kan namore; but laude and reverence
> Be to thy bounte and thyn excellence!

                                                    (III.1261–74)

For one who knows not what to do, he has done rather well,
for though a pagan, he has discovered something of divine
charity. Though there are obvious ironies in this address to
"Benigne Love," given the speaker and the circumstances, the
heart of it remains true—praise is due to love for binding all
things with a holy bond. Without the grace of God, which
passes our deserts, however worthy we may be, no one would
come even to such a heaven as this, for however natural the
way there, nature itself is a product of "Benigne Love." At
this point, Troilus turns to Criseyde, kisses her, and expresses
again the feeling that he does not know what to do: "Now
wolde God I wiste,/ Myn herte swete, how I yow myght
plese!" (III.1277–78). Not knowing what to do, he goes on,
this time praising Criseyde in the same terms with which he
had just praised "Benigne Love." When he turns to her, he
sees mirrored in her a similar "benignite" and feels the same
unworthiness. That she, the fairest and best that he ever saw,
deigns rest her heart in him persuades him that "mercy passeth
right." Though such an evaluation of Criseyde reveals his
blindness, that very blindness contributes to his insight. Carnal
man can see truth only through distorted mirrors.

As has often been noted, this song in praise of "Benigne
Love" and the similar praise of Criseyde echo St. Bernard's
prayer to the Virgin in the *Paradiso*, a prayer which opens the
final canto of the *Divine Comedy* and prepares for the Beatific
Vision. That Chaucer is not simply being ironic in transferring
a portion of it to Troilus and having him address it to Criseyde
and the love he is experiencing through her is supported by a

careful reading of both the *Troilus* and Bernard's prayer.
Chaucer ends the *Troilus* with his own prayer to the Trinity
and the Virgin, a prayer which itself ends by characterizing the
Virgin as maid and mother "benigne." Thus, he associates the
love experienced here with the love manifested in Mary. That
Troilus can see in Criseyde something of what St. Bernard sees
in Mary should not surprise us, for Dante has St. Bernard
praise the Virgin Mary *as a creature.*

> In te misericordia, in te pietate,
>   in te magnificenza, in te s'aduna
>   quantunque in creatura e di bontate.[36]

She is simultaneously the humblest and the highest of created
things. It is she who so ennobled human nature that God did
not scorn to become a man. Though Criseyde does not unite
all the goodness in any creature, though she is neither a maid
nor a mother, she does manifest some of the same mercy, pity,
and bounty, some of the same "benignita," as Mary. Though
Mary is the flower of flowers, the summit of all creation, uniting in herself all the goodness and bounty of creation, even
such a flower as Criseyde can manifest God's boundless love,
for all of creation is good and is the product of God's
goodness.[37]

Whether or not Dronke is right that the words "O blisful
nyght" are intended to recall the Easter night service, he is
certainly right that throughout the scene recalls the Redemption.[38] The whole scene and the union it describes is based
upon the New Covenant, the new law of love and mercy which
completes the old law of justice. In Troilus's union with Criseyde, however parodoxical it may be, he is also united in ways
with God. There is something of a Beatific Vision even here.
What the Incarnation of the Word, Christ, reveals to all
Christians is revealed, however imperfectly, to Troilus through
Criseyde and their love. In and through her, he participates in
the Beauty, Light, and Truth of God's love, at however great
a remove. Though Troilus is enjoying Criseyde, he is also using
her to enjoy and honor that merciful love which binds in its
holy bonds the whole universe, including these two lovers,
whose hearts, at this point, are participating in "thilke love
that governeth hevene."[39]

With Troilus thus inspired and transported by love, Criseyde seems almost forgotten. Indeed, she finds it necessary to call Troilus back down from his lyrical and spiritual flights in praise of love, to remind him that she and her body are there waiting.

> But lat us falle awey fro this matere,
> For it suffiseth, this that seyd is heere,
> And at o word, withouten repentaunce,
> Welcome, my knyght, my pees, my suffisaunce.
>
> (III.1306–9)

If she had not intervened one suspects Troilus would still be praising love. If this is simply cupidity, it is the strangest cupidity ever imagined! For all the comedy and irony here—the comedy of the sexual lover who forgets sex, the irony of finding peace and sufficiency in worldly love—there is in this scene a genuine contact with the holy.

It is particularly in this scene that Criseyde and Troilus become one in the fullest sense. At long last Criseyde seems like Troilus. Gone are her doubts; she no longer wavers between hot and cold, now this, now that, but gives herself as completely as she can to love. Stylistically, Criseyde now joins Troilus in singing a lyrical *aube*, her one undeniable lyric in the poem. At last, she ceases to debate and speak in "ambages," finding in her peace the harmony which enables her to sing. In their union we see two movements, the movement of Criseyde up toward the high style, her translation for the moment into Troilus's poetic world, and the movement of Troilus downward toward the reality of Criseyde's world. That Troilus's movement downward to join Criseyde is in some ways a fall, a betrayal of his former high ideals, is evident in numerous ways, some of which we have already looked at. We find him, for instance, associated for the first time with "game," his term for the Horaste fiction which he tries, to no avail, to blame completely upon Pandarus. We also see him, seemingly the least sudden of lovers, associated with suddenness, as his "sodeyn comynge" renders Criseyde speechless. Though apparently unable to play the "mannes game" Pandarus and Criseyde call on him to play, once he is alone with Criseyde he announces with a realism hitherto little associated with him,

O swete, as evere mot I gon,
Now be ye kaught, now is ther but we tweyne!
Now yeldeth yow, for other bote is non!

                                              (III.1206-8)

Nonetheless, though both Troilus and Criseyde are in some
ways altered by their union, they both ultimately retain their
own individuality; union is not identity. There is, as Alfred
David points out, a substantial difference between Criseyde's
"contentment" and the "metaphysical quality of Troilus's
happiness."[40]

While their first meeting is climaxed with a kiss, this scene
is bathed in kisses. The kiss itself is an ambiguous symbol,
having, traditionally, both negative and affirmative implications. Negatively, it can represent not only the touching which
cupiditas leads to but betrayal as well, since Judas betrayed
Christ with a kiss. There is an element of betrayal in the
lovers' kisses, in their first kiss, which ratified a covenant in
which the proper spiritual order was distorted, and in their
kisses here, which reveal their commitment to and delight in a
love of the flesh. The kiss of Judas is nowhere nearer than
when Pandarus kisses Criseyde the morning after the consummation, just after Criseyde has accused him of deception and
just prior to the narrator's comparison of Criseyde's forgiveness of Pandarus to Christ's forgiveness of the Crucifixion. We
recall, however, that their first kiss produced harmony, albeit
the ambiguous melody of Venus. So too here, their kisses are
intermixed with song and indeed produce song in praise of
"Benigne Love." In the *Complaint of Nature*, we are told that
God in creating the world "united with mutual and fraternal
kisses things antagonistic from the opposition of their properties."[41] Similarly, in the *Anticlaudian*, Nature is pictured as ending the "civil wars" of the elements "by the bond of faith" and
as imposing "the kisses of peace upon the elements."[42] The
kisses of Troilus and Criseyde also indicate their oneness, the
union, the end both of the hot and cold within Criseyde and of
the distance and opposition between the lovers. Their kisses
signify both their physical and their spiritual union, a peace
which, at least for Troilus and the narrator, passes understanding. The mystery of their union, like the mysteries of the mystic union with God, seems inexpressible.

Agon was every sorwe and every feere;
And bothe, ywys, they hadde, and so they wende,
As muche joie as herte may comprende.

This is no litel thyng of for to seye;
This passeth every wit for to devyse;
For ech of hem gan otheres lust obeye.

(III.1685–90)

The harmony of their wills achieved by love would seem to be
complete and perfect. In his famous discussion of the kisses of
the Bride and the Bridegroom in the Song of Songs, St. Bernard
sees in the kiss not only the mystic union of the soul (and the
Church) with God in the mystic experience and in Paradise, the
marriage of the soul and God in one spirit, but also the Holy
Spirit as well, the love and goodness of the kiss of the Father
and the Son, the same love which creates by bestowing the kiss
of "peace upon the elements."[43] For all the *cupiditas* in their
kisses, Troilus and Criseyde discover in their love and union
something of "Benigne Love," of the Love which is the Holy
Spirit. In the midst of his ecstacy in this scene, Troilus calls
on Imeneus, as well as on Venus and Cupid. Imeneus is, of
course, Hymen, the classical god of marriage. Though the marriage we see here is not the sacramental one of the Church, but
one conducted by nature through the influence of Venus and
the agency of Pandarus, it has some of the same significance
as a Christian marriage, for "Benigne Love" unites with a
holy bond. In *Troilus and Criseyde*, nature itself is sacramental, manifesting in itself the love of God which binds all
together with a kiss. That what is taking place here is in substantial ways similar to what happens in the sacrament of marriage receives support from Alain de Lille's treatment of marriage in the *Complaint of Nature*, where marriage is seen as a
joining of opposites in concord analogous to the union of contraries forming the harmony of God's universe.[44] Though
Hymen is Alain's allegorical representation of this conception, it seems clear that Alain is not thinking of such a natural
union as is described in *Troilus and Criseyde* but of a Christian
sacramental marriage. Chaucer's similar treatment of the
natural bond which unites Troilus and Criseyde as a union of
contraries in imitation of God's *concordia discors* suggests
that he considers it a holy bond, one in ways like the bond

formed in the sacrament of marriage. Perhaps ultimately the narrator is right when he tells us that wise "clerkes" praise such felicity, for all its imperfections.

The basic medieval conception of marriage goes back to St. Paul, who describes the relationship of husband and wife as analogous to the relationship of two other contraries, Christ and the Church, though he does not call them contraries.[45] As Christ is the head of the Church and the Church the body of Christ, so the man is head of the wife, the wife the flesh of the man. The two are one flesh. He goes on to say that no man hates "his own flesh but nourisheth and cherisheth it, even as the Lord the Church." We can perhaps understand better what this meant to the Middle Ages by examining a section of the *Roman de la rose*. When Nature goes to her priest Genius to confess, Genius responds with a diatribe against woman for being unable to keep secrets. To illustrate his point, Genius pictures a husband and wife in bed together, with the wife trying every means from physical enticement to verbal chiding to get a secret out of her husband. Once she gets it, of course, she tells it, thus seemingly proving Genius's point—that it is all right to hold women dear but that one should not trust them, should not commit oneself to them. In the midst of her persuasions, however, the wife utters some wisdom far superior to Genius's cynical notion that women are to be used.

> Quant par mariage assemblasmes,
> Jesus Criz, que pas ne trouvasmes
> De sa grace aver ne eschar,
> Nous fist deus estre en une char;
> E quant nous n'avons char fors une
> Par le dreit de la lei comune,
> N'il ne peut en une char estre
> Fors uns seus cueurs a la senestre;
> Tuit un sont donques li cueur nostre;
> Le mien avez e je le vostre;
> Riens ne peut donc ou vostre aveir
> Que li miens ne deie saveir.

> (IV.16435–46)

However foolish it may be to tell one's wife one's secrets, to give oneself totally to her, even one's heart, such is the mystery of marriage accomplished through the grace of God; such also is the holy folly, the "Seynt Idyot," of love as Book III characterizes it, a love also the product of God's grace. To cherish one's "flesh" is to commit oneself to it in Christ. Though Troilus knows nothing literally about Christ, being a pagan, he has committed himself to Criseyde and to the "Benigne Love" which he perceives in and through her. Those very passages which express his discovery that "mercy passeth right" also reiterate his commitment to her, even to death if she judges he deserves it. Though one may be inclined to feel Troilus is committing too much to Criseyde, the pattern of Christ's love of the Church is a commitment even to death, for, as the narrator says in the proem to Book III, "God loveth, and to love wol nought werne," and he does so even though the world repeatedly crucifies him. Unlike Jean de Meun's Nature, Christ does not repent of making mankind nor will Troilus repent of loving Criseyde when she betrays him.

The value of their gift of themselves to each other is implied in the narrator's reaction to their exchange of rings, and Criseyde's gift of a "broche" in which a ruby was set like a heart, as he proceeds to condemn "nygards" who "blameth love and halt it in despit." He concludes his association of those who despise love with covetous people by wishing that they might be taught that "they ben in the vice," not lovers, "although they holde hem nyce." This characterization of the enemies of love as the covetous recalls Alain de Lille's association of *Largitas*, generosity, with Nature, a virtue in man corresponding to the generosity of nature which accounts for the plenitude of the world.[46] Nature herself is ultimately, at least as Bernardus Silvestris represents her, a manifestation of the generous fecundity of God. If it is God's grace that has made Troilus and Criseyde one, it is their experience of that generosity which inspires theirs. Though neither is ultimately worthy of the other, since both are in some measure false, they nonetheless enter into the mutual and total commitment of a natural marriage. The covetous, those who serve only the self and use the world only for their own aggrandisement, do not know the joy of such holy bonds. Transformed by love, they discover in one another something of the love which made and redeemed them and which restores, through grace, human corruption, even though they are at the same time engaged in something like ravishing.

Such is the house which Pandarus builds. It partakes of all

the ambiguity of Venus, whose priest Pandarus is, as it proves both a place for ravishing and a place for the discovery of the mystery of God's grace. Though it is to last only for a time, it reveals to Troilus and Criseyde a dim perception of the joys of paradise, the joy of perfect love and union. Though Criseyde is its saint and she is all too frail a mortal, in and with her, Troilus discovers something of the holy bond which creates and sustains the universe. In Book V, Troilus takes a final ride by Criseyde's empty house, a place in significance identical to this house, and laments its emptiness—calling it a palace formerly "Enlumyned with sonne of alle blisse." It is a microcosm of which Criseyde is the sun. Though her light is so dim that Pandarus must pick a dark night for Troilus to see it, it is a light mirroring the Light, as we have seen. The poet's approval, however qualified, of this microcosmic house is clear from the fact that it is a microcosm, that love and Pandarus unite the contraries Troilus and Criseyde in a union analogous to God's union of contraries in the universe. They themselves in their love create a little world of harmony and concord, bringing themselves into harmony with the harmony of the universe bound by love. Such is the creative and restorative power of love, when men sufficiently commit themselves to it, even such a natural love as this book celebrates. This natural marriage by Pandarus enables the lovers to participate in the holy bond of love which weds together, through the agency of such forces as Venus and Nature, all things for a time.

The fullest expression of Troilus's love for Criseyde occurs when he sings to Pandarus in the garden a song in praise of Criseyde and love. When Pandarus visits Troilus the day after the consummation, Troilus tells Pandarus that the sun never saw in all its life anyone "so inly fair and goodly as is she." Similarly in this scene, when he makes "a fest" and "a process" of Criseyde, "of hire womanhede,/ And of hire beaute," we find him singing a Boethian song in praise of the binding power of love, thus revealing what he sees in her beauty and what he loves, or at least that portion of what he loves that he can talk about to Pandarus. It is a noble and beautiful song full of what Chaucer undoubtedly considered the highest wisdom and Troilus's realization of its truth affirms the value of his love of Criseyde.[47] In it, he calls on love, which governs the earth and the sea and has its "hestes" in heaven, that is, on divine love, to bind his "accord" with Criseyde. He praises it as the source of order in the universe, as the cause why the discordant elements abide in harmony and the reason the ocean does not drown the land. It is "God, that auctor is of kynde," who encircles hearts and binds them firmly with "his bond of Love." Without love, "al that now loveth asondre sholde lepe," and that all is the house of the universe. Especially significant is the second stanza:

> That that the world with feith, which that is stable,
> Diverseth so his stowndes concordynge,
> That elementz that ben so discordable
> Holden a bond perpetuely durynge,
> That Phebus mote his rosy day forth brynge,
> And that the mone hath lordshipe over the nyghtes,—
> Al this doth Love, ay heried be his myghtes!

(III.1751–57)

The allusions to the progress of the seasons and of day and night remind us both that nature is a world of change and an emblem of stable "feith," and that even its changes, changes which Criseyde will ultimately go through, are the product of love and evidence of the stability of its source.[48] If Nature is the mother of false felicity, she is also a guide to that love which will "falsen no wight." The rest of the poem gives additional evidence of the value of what he sees in her, for he will in his love imitate the truth he sees in her, not the change which is also there, perhaps precisely because he does not see it.

The restoration of Troilus's human nature to something like a prefallen condition through his love is the subject of the remainder of Book III, except for the author's leave-taking. The narrator insists that love has "altered his spirit so withinne" that "Pride, Envye, and Ire, and Avarice,/ He gan to fle; and everich other vice" (III.1805–6). In fact, this "Cupides sone" becomes "benigne." "Benigne," of course, is the very word Troilus used to describe the characteristic of the holy love he experienced in the consummation scene, when he discovered proof in his own experience that "mercy passeth right." Moved by love, guided by Venus, Nature, and Criseyde, he too has become "benigne," Christ's son, as well as Cupid's. Thus it is that love binds together contraries in fallen man—"O Love, O Charite."

Troilus's song echoes the invocation at the beginning of

Book III, both of which praise the love which created and sustains the universe.[49] Book III itself is encircled and bound together by hymns in praise of the binding power of love. It is
itself a little round world, a microcosmic image of God's world,
created in a form analogous to God's creation, through the union of contraries. In it Chaucer unites diverse characters, discordant themes, and contrary styles to create a harmony, a
song inspired by Venus and exemplifying the ambiguous
music of this world. It is the poet's own "place," his palace,
made only for "a time," but revealing that which is forever,
just as God's time and place mirror eternity.

Its basic form is the union of contraries, as it harmonizes all
that is Book I with all that is Book II. Only in Book III do we
find the three characters together in one place at one time. Here
for the only time in the poem they achieve a unity of purpose
and intent—the world that is created satisfies the demands of
each of the individual elements that comprise it, so that all
three, presumably, are in "concord and quiete." It answers to
the nature of each, harmonizing them. We now find Criseyde
in Troilus's world, the bedroom, his place of contemplation,
and Troilus in one of Criseyde's settings, the garden. In Book
III we find united into a rich and harmonious musical whole
the high style and conventions of the romance world of Book
I and the low style and conventions of the realistic world of
Book II, as they blend to form Chaucer's "mixed style." Even
the supreme fabliau moment in the poem—when Pandarus lifts
Troilus into Criseyde's bed and strips him of most of his
clothes—is seen now from a realistic perspective, now from
the courtly one. Beside his "O thef, is this a mannes herte" we
hear "O nece, pes, or we be lost." The whole stanza following
the tossing into bed is a complex mixture of the realistic and
the romantic:

> And seyde, "Nece, but ye helpe us now,
> Allas, youre owen Troilus is lorn!"
> "Iwis, so wolde I, and I wiste how,
> Ful fayn," quod she; "Allas, that I was born!"
> "Yee, nece, wol ye pullen out the thorn
> That stiketh in his herte," quod Pandare,
> "Sey 'al foryeve' and stynt is al this fare!"
>
> (III.1100–1106)

The rapidity of the dialogue suggests realism, as does such a clause as "stynt is al this fare," but "Alas, that I was born" is straight from the world of the romance, as is Pandarus's plea that she save Troilus, pull the thorn from his heart, and forgive him. The profane and the sacred are inextricably mixed in a style perfectly in tune with the two faces and the ambiguous music of this world.

If it is ultimately God who unites "with mutual and fraternal kisses things antagonistic from the opposition of their properties,"[50] it is a task delegated, once originally accomplished, to nature according to the naturalistic tradition in which Chaucer is writing. In the *Complaint of Nature*, we see the goddess Nature join "all things in firmness with the knot of concord and . . . with peace marry heaven to earth."[51] She "cloaks matter with Form," just as in the *Roman de la rose* she is pictured joining the "common form" with matter.[52] Here Venus, and on the human level Pandarus, perform the same function. In the "marriage" of Troilus and Criseyde, we see the union of head and body, of soul and flesh, as Troilus unites with and gives form to the formless flesh of Criseyde. As we have seen, Alain de Lille makes Hymen analogous to Nature; both create similar unions of contraries, though all that is male remains male, all that is female, female. Marriage is union, not identity. In the *Complaint*, Nature describes her creation of the "material" of the body out of "primordial matter." She tells us that she endowed the body with the senses and made it beautiful that it might "be united the more agreeably when it came to marriage with its spouse the spirit," that the spirit would not "in disgust at the baseness of its mate, oppose the marriage."[53] Similarly, Concord in the *Anticlaudian* says that she unites spirit and body, preventing the clash of contraries: "Unless my ties bind souls to bodies, the spirit, disdaining to dwell in these houses, deserting the penitentiaries of the flesh would return to its proper places of origin."[54] Such is Criseyde's beauty and the concord of Troilus and Criseyde. In their union we see the union of the spirit, the divine, eternal, and stable, with the flesh, the earthly, transitory, and changing. Though Troilus seizes Criseyde like a hawk, his repeated tendency to ascend in song recalls Boethius's image of a bird in a cage, an image of the soul, bound to the flesh but forever seeking its true home.[55]

Troilus, as soul, desires both to join with Criseyde and to return to his Maker, just as any level in the Neoplatonic hierarchical universe, a universe in which body is emanated by
soul, tends in two directions, participating in that level which
is above it and seeking to unite with it, and engendering that
level below it, through the outpouring of that which descends
to it.

In the union of Troilus and Criseyde we see not just the
union of the individual soul with an individual body to create
a man, but an image, given the microcosmic character of man,
of the union of the Word with matter to create the universe.
In Book I, Troilus's love of Criseyde is in one sense a response
to her beauty; most of the time, however, we watch him create
an image of her in his mind. Rather like Pygmalion in the
Roman de la rose, first he creates an image of what he loves and
then his love, with the help of Venus, brings that image to
life.[56] In a sense, Criseyde does not even exist in Book I but is
only an idea in the mind of Troilus, just as the world was only
an idea in the mind of God before He, moved by love, created
a time and a place, before he created the universe by uniting
the idea in His mind through such intermediary agencies as
Nature and Venus with the receptacle matter. So Troilus creates Criseyde in his mind and sends out Pandarus to mediate
between his idea and matter. So in Book II, Criseyde is like
uncreated matter, primordial chaos, now hot, now cold, desiring yet fearing union with form. Bound to Criseyde by invisible bonds of love, Troilus, Criseyde's "suffisaunce," stills
the discord in her, just as God in creation united the warring
elements so that "all things, then agreeing through invisible
bonds of union, plurality returned to unity, diversity to identity, dissonance to harmony, discord to concord in peaceful
agreement."[57] That unity which is Troilus's and is expressed
throughout the poem in his lyric monologues becomes Criseyde's, and enables her to sing her *aube*. She is no longer "at
dulcarnoun," now hot, now cold, no longer debating. In
Troilus's union with Criseyde we have an image of the union
of the oneness of God with the multiplicity of chaos to create
the universe. In the activities of Pandarus we can recognize
the intermediary function of such agents for God as Venus,
Nature, and Fate. His activity in encircling Troilus and Criseyde

recalls Boethius's description of God sending forth the World-Soul as his surrogate to create that image of those ideas in His mind which is the universe.[58]

That Criseyde is transformed into an image of Troilus, her peace and her "suffisaunce," is clear from their matching *aubes;* that she is only an image is clear from the significant differences of their songs. Both, as we have seen, lament that their union is only for a time, that it is subject to change, but Criseyde's is addressed to night, the night which she ultimately represents and to which she ultimately must return, the night of nonexistence, since the Light is all and all. Troilus's, though he does not now want the light, enjoying as he does his union with matter, is addressed to that light from which he comes and to which he must return, and to which he instinctively turns even when bound to the flesh of Criseyde. We perhaps ought to recall Bernardus Silvestris's *Cosmographia,* the most important poem behind the *Complaint of Nature* and the *Roman de la rose,* which opens with Nature expressing to Noys primordial matter's desire to be given form. More traditionally, Chaucer locates the impulse of creation in the mind of the creator, Troilus, though finally in Book III Criseyde must call Troilus down from the sufficiency of himself, from his enjoyment of that love which is in his own mind, that the union of spirit and matter may be accomplished—"Welcome, my knyght, my pees, my suffisaunce."

Thus we see that Chaucer has himself created in Book III a round little world in imitation of God. As a poetic world, like God's world, it depends upon false seeming. Just as God's world is only an image of Himself, of the Truth, and not the Truth itself, so the poet's image of that Truth is inevitably a false one, one seeming, at least to the lover of art, that paradise which it is not, but does mirror. If the poet seeks to manifest what is in the mind of God, he, like God, must do so by incarnating the Word, the Truth he seeks to reveal, in the flesh of fable. He, too, must accommodate his revelation, his sentence, to carnal man by uniting it with the flesh of fiction, with solace, that dull and bestial man can be moved, first by the solace, by that which he knows, to that which he does not know, the Truth. That the poet's art is a dangerous art, a perilous mirror, is evident from the behavior of the narrator, who seems little to understand the world he has created and finds so beautiful. To create it the poet has had to invoke the Muses, Muses who Chaucer knew could all too easily be what Lady Philosophy told Boethius they were. If loving the world is a hazardous way to God, so creating poetry is, for it, too, as a human and spiritual activity depends upon nature. It is a gift which even the pagans had. Chaucer ends *Troilus and Criseyde* by rejecting the world as a vanity and his poem as mere pagan poetry, directing his readers to God. But if the little round world of Book III is a Zero, a vanity, a nothing, mere "feynede" love, it is also an image of God's totality, a perilous mirror of it, just as God's world is both a vanity and a manifestation of Himself and His stable Love. Though Book III describes the ruby which will shortly fall out of the circular ring of the poem's progress from woe to "wele" to woe, in its light we can see the Light. It is a vanity made of false seeming, but made, to the best of the poet's powers, in the image of God. It is an imitation of this world, of its union of the false and the stable, of time and eternity, of day and night, of spirit and matter, of *caritas* and *cupiditas*, of heaven and hell. When the poet turns to pray at the end of the poem, he not only prays to Jesus and His "benigne" mother, "benigne" being the last word of the poem as well as the key word in Book III, in a sense the Word, he also prays to the Trinity, which though uncircumscribed, "al maist circumscrive." That which God's love circumscribes is the world, that vanity which God in His love creates and sustains, just as the world of Book III is circumscribed by hymns in praise of that circumscribing love. So Troilus creates and sustains Criseyde, his vanity, and Chaucer, his poem.

4

Tragedy and Comedy

Book IV begins with a proem lamenting the fact that Fortune's wheel now turns, casting Troilus down and raising Diomede up.[1] Though the progress of the poem's action in time suggests a linear movement, the poet's original characterization of this action as "Fro wo to wele, and after out of joie," the image of Fortune's wheel, and the use of allusions to the cycles of the seasons and of day and night to depict the passage of time all suggest a circular movement, an end which is a return to the beginning. Though the reader is told that the love of Troilus and Criseyde lasted three years, for instance, the poem's imagery associates it with the passage of a single summer.[2] Troilus first saw Criseyde in April, "of lusty Veer the pryme," Pandarus began wooing her in May, "that winter dede made," and now it is late July or early August, as we approach the inevitable harvest of sorrow which is the fruit of "feynede" love.[3] Imagery associated with Troilus suggests a similar circular movement. When he first falls in love, Troilus says that Criseyde is cold toward him "as frost in wynter moone." Pandarus's early successes cause him to revive as a flower in morning and to rejoice as "thise holtes and thise hayes" do when May "revesten hem in grene." Now, however, he is like a tree bereft of leaves, "so that ther nys but bark and branche ylaft." The poem's ultimate expression of the cyclical movement of all things subject to fortune and nature is structural. One such cyclical structure is evident in Book IV, for structurally it reiterates the formal structure of the first three books. Its three parts—the first treating Troilus; the second, Criseyde; the third, the two of them together—correspond in their sequence and in much of their action and detail to the first three books, though there are always important and telling differences as well. The sequence of events which brings us to the

bottom of Fortune's wheel mirrors that which brought us to the
top and joins "the endynge to the bygynnynge."

The invocation opening Book IV recalls significantly the invocation to the first book. Once again the subject is sorrow and
the narrator is suffering. If before his verses wept as he wrote,
now the pen with which he writes "Quaketh for drede." Before,
he invoked Tisiphone, a "goddesse of torment," who was
described as herself "sorwynge evere yn peyne." Now he
invokes all three Furies, who are described as endlessly complaining "evere in pyne." Once again we are told that his subject is how Criseyde forsook Troilus, though this time, the narrator, having found Criseyde a joy himself, wishes to mitigate
her offense.

Book I began with a single stanza describing the war "The
ravysshyng to wreken of Eleyne," reported the treason of
Calkas, who knew "by calkulynge,/ And ek by answer of this
Appollo" that Troy was a doomed city, and described the "gret
penaunce" of Criseyde and her visit to Hector in search of pro-
tection, an inspired idea, though we were told that she "nyste
what was best to rede." The beginning of Book IV is significantly similar. We return to the war and the Greek host, with
an "As I have seyd er this" to remind us that we are repeating,
and watch the Trojans suffer defeat. We then revisit Calkas,
who now regrets having betrayed his daughter, and watch him
weep and beg for help. He assures the Greeks that it will cost
them nothing to give him a prisoner with which to "redeem"
Criseyde, since he is certain that Troy shall fall.

> Appollo hath me told it feithfully;
> I have ek founde it be astronomye,
> By sort, and by augurye ek.
>
> (IV.114–16)

The temple scene in Book I is replaced in Book IV by a
Trojan council at which it is decided to exchange Criseyde for
Antenor. In the Trojan council Fortune begins to take away
what she began to give Troilus in the temple. In the council, as
in the temple, Troilus finds it necessary to dissemble, though
now the motive is not fear of mockery but a desire to protect
Criseyde's honor.[4] In the temple scene, as the mocking Troilus
is falling in love, the narrator interrupts the action to mock

Troilus with a lengthy aside beginning "O blynde world." Now
the narrator again interrupts the action, this time to mock the
foolish populace for exchanging Criseyde for the traitor Antenor: "O nyce world."

Once again we follow Troilus home to his bedroom where,
alone, he weeps and wails and calls repeatedly upon death.
While he is thus lying in bed, Pandarus enters, though this
time Pandarus is himself overcome with sorrow, so overcome
that for a moment "he nyste what to say." In Book I he had
immediately accused Troilus in mocking tones of fearing the
Greeks and called on God to save them for thus bringing
"oure lusty folk to holynesse." Then the narrator told us that

> Thise wordes seyde he for the nones alle,
> That with swich thing he myght hym angry maken,
> And with an angre don his wo to falle.

> (I.561–63)

Now, after recovering from his speechlessness and sententi-
ously observing that their misfortune proves the untrustworthi-
ness of Fortune, he again tries to light a fire under Troilus by
suggesting that he get another girl. Once again the narrator
assures us that

> Thise wordes seyde he for the nones alle,
> To help his frend, lest he for sorwe deyde;
> For douteles, to don his wo to falle,
> He roughte nought what unthrift that he seyde.

> (IV.428–31)

Now, as before, Pandarus tries to help his friend, though
Troilus is again convinced nothing will help. Once again Pandarus gradually brings Troilus around to his way of thinking,
though there are significant differences in the two scenes.[5] Both,
for instance, feel more deeply grieved and now even Pandarus
feels nearly helpless. The sudden collapse of their joy causes
them both to speak rather abruptly and harshly. Troilus rejects
Pandarus's advice that he take another as fiendish and responds to his suggestion that he ravish her with the observation that he himself has already thought of that, and Pandarus
rather curtly tells him, "Frend, thow maist, for me,/ Don as
the list" (IV. 582–83).

Finally, as the scene draws to a close, Troilus assents to

Pandarus's advice that he ravish Criseyde, though he qualifies
this assent.

> But certeynly thow maist nat so me priken,
> Ne peyne non ne may me so tormente,
> That, for no cas, it is nat myn entente,
> At shorte wordes, though I deyen sholde,
> To ravysshe hire, but if hireself it wolde.
>
> (IV.633–37)

At the end of Book I Troilus similarly agreed to do as Pandarus recommended, adding, however, a similar proviso.

> But herke, Pandare, o word, for I nolde
> That thow in me wendest so great folie,
> That to my lady I desiren sholde
> That toucheth harm or any vilenye;
> For dredeles me were levere dye
> Than she of me aught elles understode
> But that that myghte sownen into goode.
>
> (I.1030–36)

Pandarus's response in both cases is substantially identical, revealing the distance between the two characters, for all their
apparent oneness of purpose. In Book I the narrator observes
"Tho lough this Pandare" and Pandarus blithely answers: "And
I thi borugh? fy! no wight doth but so." He is just as cavalier
about significant moral distinctions now: " 'Why so mene I,'
quod Pandarus, 'all this day.' " This conveniently forgets his
earlier observation that though it might grieve Criseyde to be
ravished, they could afterward make a peace. With the two
thus in apparent agreement, the first part of Book IV ends just
as Book I then ended, with Pandarus going out to find a time
and a place.

The second part of Book IV, the sequence depicting Criseyde and Pandarus's visit to her, repeats Book II, though at
first appearance it seems radically different from the earlier
book, its contrary, not its image. Seemingly transformed by
love, Criseyde now looks like Troilus. Though once again we
see her in a social scene, surrounded by her friends, she no
longer seems one of them and must dissemble, like Troilus in
the Trojan council scene, when they congratulate her on her
expected reunion with her father. Like Troilus, she retires to

her bedroom to be alone, and there weeps and wails, tears her
hair and wrings her fingers, curses her fate, and calls on death.
A careful reading of the scene reveals, however, that she is
ultimately still the same Criseyde. Upon first hearing the
rumors that she is to be exchanged for Antenor, we are told
that "she nyste what was best to reede," precisely what we
were told when her father first abandoned her. Presented with
the same problem, she will arrive at the same solution, and reveal in the process that change is still her essence.

When Pandarus suggested to Troilus that he take another
lady, Troilus insisted that Criseyde could not be compared to
"any creature formed by kynde." He sees their union as the
work of the gods and Criseyde as divine. Criseyde, true to herself, draws her comparisons from nature when she laments
their impending separation, feeling that she can no more live
without Troilus than a fish without water or a plant that has
been uprooted. For Criseyde, Troilus is her "kynde noriture."
She sees their love as rooted in nature, and nature is pre-emi-
nently a world of change. Though she concludes from these
analogies that death awaits her, her subsequent complaining
reveals that she is not ready to die but, like nature, to change.
The course of action she resolves upon is "slydying," to say
the least.

> I shal doon thus, syn neither swerd ne darte
> Dar I noon handle, for the crueltee,
> That ilke day that I from yow departe,
> If sorwe of that nyl nat my bane be,
> Thanne shal no mete or drynke come in me
> Til I my soule out of my breste unshethe;
> And thus myselven wol I don to dethe.
>
> And, Troilus, my clothes everychon
> Shul blake ben in tokenyng, herte swete,
> That I am as out of the world agon,
> That wont was yow to setten in quiete;
> And of myn ordre, ay til deth me mete,
> The observance evere, in youre absence,
> Shal sorwe ben, compleynt, and abstinence.
>
> (IV.771–89)

One need not recall her later contradictory assertion that had
Troilus slain himself with a sword, she would have done the

same to see the irony and falling-off here. In two verses she
moves from starving herself to death, since she fears swords, to
the life of a widow, a life of mourning and abstinence. Her very
resolution to be true reveals she is still the debating, now-this,
now-that Criseyde of Book II. She is describing herself as she
was when we first met her dressed in widow's black. Then she
responded to Pandarus's suggestion that she do observance to
May by asserting that "It sate me wel bet ay in a cave/ To
bidde and rede on holy seyntes lyves" (II. 117–18). So it is to
live "as out of the world agon." Though it might suit her, we
know Criseyde will never choose to lead even such a life of
abstinence for long, at least not if past is prologue to future.

In the next stanza she manages to echo Troilus almost perfectly, while at the same time revealing both their different
natures and their different experience of love.

> Myn herte and eke the woful goost therinne
> Byquethe I, with youre spirit to compleyne
> Eternaly, for they shal nevere twynne.
> For though in erthe ytwynned be we tweyne,
> Yet in the feld of pite, out of peyne,
> That highte Elisos, shal we ben yfeere,
> As Orpheus with Erudice, his fere.
>
> (IV.785–91)

Earlier Troilus told Pandarus that

> The deth may wel out of my brest departe
> The lif, so longe may this sorwe myne;
> But fro my soule shal Criseydes darte
> Out nevere mo; but down with Proserpyne,
> When I am ded, I wol go wone in pyne;
> And ther I wol eternaly compleyne
> My wo, and how that twynned be we tweyne.
>
> (IV.470–76)

Whereas Troilus pictures himself as eternally complaining,
ever in pain in Hades with Proserpina, Criseyde pictures herself
as eternally complaining in the Elysian fields, "the feld of pite,
out of peyne." Criseyde's easy translation of herself and Troilus to the pagan equivalent of heaven sharply contrasts with
Troilus's imagined eternity alone in hell. Criseyde, for all her
intended constancy, can only imagine a change, an end to

sorrow and suffering. As their *aubes* simultaneously revealed their oneness and their difference, here in their common sorrow, their union in grief, we also see that essential difference.[6] Troilus is ever one; Criseyde, ever double.

After Pandarus arrives we also recognize significant reiterations of the substance of Book II. Trolius's first words to Pandarus when Pandarus joins him in Book IV are "Lo, Pandare, I am ded, withouten more." Criseyde's first words to Pandarus when he makes a similar entrance here recall not Troilus, but the old Criseyde, as she asks him,

> Wher shal I seye to yow welcom or no,
> That alderfirst me broughte unto servyse
> Of love, allas! that endeth in swich wise?
>
> (IV.831–33)

Unlike Troilus, she is able to regret what has passed, to wonder if it has all been worth it, just as before, between hot and cold, she could debate whether it would be worth it to accept Troilus as a lover. Once again Pandarus stills her doubts and persuades her to save Troilus from his death. This time, however, he does deliver his message briefly and trusts to her wits, before disparaged, to save the day. Significantly he does not specifically mention the only plan he has any confidence in, glossing it over with a "destourbe youre goynge." Perhaps he is ashamed to admit to his niece how much he prefers Troilus's pleasure to her honor, or perhaps, in spite of his assertion to Troilus that if she loves him she will not leave him, he knows that such a plan would be unacceptable to her, for all her certainty that she would exchange all the world for love. Having advised her to advise herself and having lectured her on the proper use of time, both things we saw him do as he led Criseyde "by the lappe" toward Troilus in the final moments of Book II, he goes forth to find Troilus, with the final meeting of the love arranged.

The structural reiteration in Book IV of the patter first three books is completed in its third and final meeting of the two lovers, a scene which echoes in ways the climactic scene in Book III. One recalls earlier book Troilus covered his absence from ho ing that he has gone to the temple to make a sa an answer from Apollo concerning the war. He then, of course, went and waited in Pandarus's "stuwe." Once Pandarus had put everyone to bed, he came to Troilus to tell him to make ready to enter the bliss of heaven. In response, Troilus began to pray at length to the gods for help, until Pandarus mocks him—"Thow wrecched mouses herte,/Artow agast so that she wol the bite?" (III.736–37). This time Troilus actually does go to a temple to pray, being unable to wait. Both recourses to prayer are true to his character and to his experience of love as overwhelming.[7] Now, especially, it would seem that only the gods can help him. Once again, having everything arranged, Pandarus goes to him, mocks him for praying, imitating his "Almyghty Jove in trone," and implies that he is not acting the man: " 'O myghty God,' quod Pandarus, 'in trone,/I! who say evere a wis man faren so?' " (IV.1086–87). This time, however, he does not go with him, being both no longer needed as he once was and no longer able to help. This time Troilus goes alone, not to the bliss of heaven but to its contrary, the pains of hell, the agony of separation, not the joy of union. Just as Pandarus's absence indicates at the dramatic level of the poem the helplessness of the lovers, so on the symbolic level it indicates the impending desolation of their union, since an intermediary is necessary to join contraries.

However different the sufferings of hell may be from the joys of heaven, they have much the same transporting effect upon the lovers. If before when Criseyde kissed Troilus he was so moved "That where his spirit was, for joie he nyste," now when they meet and kiss, "The lasse woful of hem bothe nyste/ Wher that he was." Just as Troilus swooned before so that he could scarcely be revived, so now Criseyde does, and Troilus kisses her time and again in hopes of reviving her. If before Criseyde found it necessary to recall Troilus to herself when he was in the ecstacy of love, "But lat us falle away fro this matere/For it suffiseth, this that seyd is heere" (III.1306–7), now when they are talking of death, just after Troilus has ly killed himself and she has asserted she would do the e brings them back to the present.

> But hoo, for we han right ynough of this,
> And let us rise, and streght to bedde go,
> And there lat us speken of oure wo.
>
> (IV.1242–44)

Whether it is the joys of love or its sorrows, Criseyde remains herself, in touch with the reality of this world. Neither joy nor sorrow can transport her to another world.

Once again they achieve one will. After Criseyde explains her plan, Troilus, though his heart "mysforyaf," manages "To trusten hire," and they begin once more "for joie th'amorouse daunce." For one brief stanza the winter of sorrow returns to its former summer of joy, "And as the briddes, whanne the sonne is shene,/ Deliten in hire song in leves grene" (II.1432–33), so they delight in their words together. They cannot forget their impending separation, however, and lament it, as they earlier lamented the coming of day. Now, of course, they are only acting out the inevitable fate there prefigured and predicted. However inevitable it may be, Troilus, in spite of his fatalism, repeatedly resists Criseyde's plan. Now he is "at dulcarnoun," so that Criseyde, who will serve herself, though she insists she will do whatever Troilus commands "for that is no demaunde," must use as much pressure to bend Troilus to her will as Pandarus and Troilus used in getting her to yield in the consummation scenes. Now, in a sense, it is Criseyde that ravishes Troilus.

Book IV ends in much the same way as Book III ended, as now Criseyde, rather than Troilus, speaks of what she loves. She assures Troilus that he need not fear that "lengthe of yeres" or "remuable Fortune" will destroy her love because it is not based on anything subject to nature or fortune. She insists that it was not such things as "pompe, array, nobleye" nor his "estat roial" that moved her to love him, but his "moral vertu, grounded upon trouthe" (IV.1672). We need not remember what it was that first appealed to her when Troilus rode by looking like Mars to the cheers of the crowd to see Criseyde's self-deception.[8] Though she asserts her love of his "moral vertu" and his "despit" for all that "souned into badde," when she particularizes the bad, it is "rudenesse and peoplissh appetit." We slide from moral virtue to social virtue and see that Criseyde is concerned for appearances. Criseyde's ability to love Diomede, a fine figure of a man, but one possessing absolutely no "moral vertu" or "trouthe" reveals this concern all too clearly. While Troilus is something less than "trouthe,"[9] Criseyde's argument that a love of "moral vertu, grounded upon trouthe" is not subject to change only proves that hers

was not such a love, for the constancy of Troilus's love of
Criseyde proves that the love of "trouthe," even as it is reflected in such a distored mirror as Criseyde, can make a
man true.

As so often before, the morning comes and forces the lovers
to part. When Troilus saw that she might not remain, "Which
that his soule out of his herte rente,/Withouten more, out of
the chaumbre he wente" (IV.1700–1701). Their separation, his
departure from the bedroom which has ever been the place of
their union, tears the soul from his heart, since his heart is with
Criseyde. We remember that the proem to Book IV announced
that it would recount "the losse of lyf and love yfere/ Of
Troilus" and that Troilus has just been described "as he that
felte dethes cares colde," and we realize that we ought, perhaps,
on one level to take such statements seriously, for if in the
union in Book III of Troilus and Criseyde we can see the union
of soul and body, here we see the destruction of that union, the
inevitable separation after a time of the soul from the house of
the body. At one level at least, Troilus has already lost his life
and his love, and lost them together, since he found them both
in and through the body from which he is now separated.

Though the above examination of the parallels between Book
IV and the first three books has been necessarily selective, it
should be sufficient to demonstrate that the repetition goes
beyond the merely incidental to become a fundamental aspect
of the poem's structure.[10] It leaves us, however, not where the
third book ended, in the paradise of union, but where we began, in the hell of separation. The same sequence of events
which united the lovers separates them. Now the world's dark
face, very real though only dimly visible in Book III, emerges
to be predominant. In what is perhaps the most interesting
analysis of the poem's structure to date, "Narrative Structure
in Chaucer's *Troilus and Criseyde*," Gerry Brenner sees "the
poem's dialectic of dualities" in its "two types of narrative
structure": "One type of narrative structure, the surface harmony that narrative repetition creates, lends itself easily to a
metaphor of harmony. The other type, the underlying chaos
that inverted parallels, ironic foreshadowings, and multiple
points of view wreak upon the surface structure, lends tself to
a metaphor of cacaphony and disorder."[11] Many of the paral-

lels we have been looking at are what Brenner calls "inverted parallels." It is essential to see that though such parallels characterize the discord and mutability of the world, they are part of the poem's larger order. Just as God's universe orders the discordant, the two faces of this world, so Chaucer's poem orders them.

The fact that the same pattern of events which built Pandarus's house now destroys it suggests that its construction and its destruction are the consequence of the same fundamental laws. "Natural justice," the order of the created, is just. Just as Troilus ravished Criseyde, though she yielded, to unite them, so Criseyde now ravises Troilus, though he yields, to separate them. Chaucer's references to the "Proserpine" story when Troilus imagines himself complaining his separation from Criseyde for an eternity and when Troilus dreams of "Escaphilo" illuminate this justice. As Ovid tells it, Pluto, moved by Venus, ravishes Proserpina and carries her off to hell, where Jove decrees she must reside for six months of each year since she eats of the fruit of the underworld.[12] In her absence, her mother, Ceres, the goddess of fertility, laments and the earth is barren. The Pluto and Proserpina story, a pagan myth in many ways the equivalent of the Christian myth of the Fall, informs Chaucer's treatment of ravishing. Though Troilus imagines that Criseyde is Alceste, constancy in love, she is another Proserpina, having the same two faces Ovid gives to Proserpina, a melancholy one and a joyful one, "as when the sun breaks through and drives away the watery clouds that formerly covered him."[13] Just as Proserpina's fate is just, the result of her own violation of the prohibition not to eat the fruit of the underworld, so Criseyde's is. She too will fail in her vow of total abstinence, her declared intention to live "as out of the world agon." More important than the implied parallel between Criseyde and Proserpina is the implied parallel between Troilus and Pluto. Just as Troy's fall is an inevitable and just consequence of Paris's ravishing of Helen, so Troilus's loss of Criseyde is an inevitable and just consequence of his ravishment of her. When the Trojan council exchanges Criseyde for Antenor, in contradiction of Hector's insistence that Trojans are not accustomed to selling their women, they insure the fall of Troy, for Antenor will betray them by giving the

Palladium to the Greeks. Though Troilus is silent at the council
in order to protect Criseyde's honor, his devotion to that good
causes him to betray a larger good and to participate in the
selling of Criseyde, whom he first saw at a service honoring
the Palladium. One cannot love a "feynede" good and not
betray the Good. Though man lives in a fallen, two-faced
world because of Adam's and Eve's original ravishment of
God's forbidden fruit in the Christian myth, each man insures
the justice of that fate by duplicating that sin. Chaucer's treatment of the themes of ravishing and consequent vengeance
implies Troilus's freedom—if he had not ravished her he would
not have lost her—at the same time that it demonstrates the
inevitability in this fallen world of such ravishment and loss.
By structuring Troilus's loss of Criseyde in imitation of his
winning of her, Chaucer orders his poem in imitation of natural
justice, those laws which order both the creation and dissolution of all things in this world, and reveals that the two-faced
order of this world is a just and harmonious one.

Though the order of Book IV is the order of the union of
Troilus and Criseyde, it leaves us with the two forever separated. The wheels of Fortune and Nature turn in that stable
circle which returns all things at their end to their beginning.
As Lady Philosophy can help us understand, this order mirrors
divine providence. She teaches Boethius that "the engendrynge
of alle thinges, . . . and alle the progressiouns of muable nature,
and al that moeveth in any manere, taketh his causes, his ordre,
and his formes, of the stablenesse of the devyne thought"
(IV.pr.vi.42–47) and that that order is one which unites beginning and end to keep a stable course. She attributes the harmonious order of this world to the harmonious order of the
heavens, for the "accordance" of the heavens "atempryth" the
elements, making peace among them, and orders the passing
seasons. The same "accordance" ultimately dissolves this
world's union of contraries: "This atempraunce norysscheth
and bryngeth forth alle thinges that brethith lif in this world;
and thilke same attempraunce, ravysschynge, hideth and byny-
meth, and drencheth undir the laste deth, alle things iborn"
(IV.m.vi.34–39). This circular order, the stable ordinance of all
things, is the stable and harmonious order of Chaucer's tragedy. The same "benigne love" which created the heaven of

Book III creates the hell of Book IV. As we shall see, this painful process is merciful as well as just, insuring that life's tragic cycle is only part of a larger divine comedy.

Book V is composed of juxtaposed scenes in the Trojan and Greek camps, scenes which further define for us Criseyde and Troilus and reveal that the one is ultimately rooted in *cupiditas;* the other, in *caritas.* It begins by introducing us to a new character, "sodeyn" Diomede, but an old and familiar sequence of events in the wooing of Criseyde. Chaucer alters the *Filostrato* to increase Diomede's suddenness by having him begin to court Criseyde immediately and to make his courtship of her systematically reiterate the progress of Pandarus's efforts on Troilus's behalf. In the short time that it takes Diomede to lead her "by the bridel" from the plain between the two camps to her father's tent, he burlesques the whole progress of the narrative from Troilus's first sight of Criseyde to his first meeting with her at Deiphebus's house. He promises, for instance, in one stanza to be her friend and in the very next asks her to treat him as her brother. Ida Gordon has noted this parodic duplication and suggests that its function is to force the reader to reassess Troilus's courtship of Criseyde, asking whether or not, for all Troilus's superior gentility, there is any real moral difference between Diomede and Troilus.[14] While this duplication does force us to reassess Troilus's love and Pandarus's labors and reveals real similarities, it also forces us to recognize real differences, not differences so much in behavior as in intention. Chaucer's consistent concern for the intentions of his characters becomes, if anything, even more pronounced in Book V and it is here that we understand once and for all who intends what.

Diomede is the only significant character in the poem whose intentions are completely unambiguous and totally clear—he intends to serve himself. For all the similarities of his and Troilus's rhetoric of love, we recognize a fundamental difference. Diomede intends deception; his rhetoric is only words. Even Pandarus will not reduce to Diomede. Though Diomede's "he that naught n'asaieth, naught n'acheveth" reminds us of Pandarus's "Unknowe, unkist, and lost, that is unsought," Pandarus follows this assertion with his appeal to Troilus to "thynk it is a guerdon, hire to serve," not Diomede's "I shal

namore lesen but my speche." It is ultimately Criseyde who is
revealed to be essentially similar to Diomede.[15] Just as Criseyde could think that it is no wonder that Troilus loves her
since she is, as everyone admits, one of the fairest and "good-
lieste" women in all of Troy, so Diomede can follow the assertion that Criseyde can find among the Greeks a "moore parfit
love, er it be nyght" than with "any Troian" by recommending
himself—"I am, al be it yow no joie,/ As gentil man as any
wight in Troie" (V.930–31). Unlike Troilus, whose love of
Criseyde prevents him from being sudden and whose love
ultimately causes him to forget himself, "sodeyn" Diomede
judges that "He is a fool that wole foryete hymselve." For all
Criseyde's fine words of love at the end of Book IV, we recognize in her decision to leave Troy a similar unwillingness to
forget herself.

Though we are told that Criseyde "naught his tales herde/
But her and ther, now here a word or two," she thanks him for
his offers of friendship and accepts it, adding that "trusten
hym she wolde, and wel she myghte" (V.188). Once again we
recognize her too easy acceptance of the appearance of things
and realize that if Fortune's nature insures Diomede's chance,
Criseyde's nature will insure his success. When Diomede, "in
his nedes prest," comes on the ninth day and declares quite
openly his love, Criseyde answers him with "ambages," with
"double wordes slye,/ Swiche as men clepen a word with two
visages" (V.898–99). Though she intends to deceive him with
her assertions that she loves no one in Troy and that she will
love him, if she ever loves a Greek, she only deceives herself,
for we see in her, as no doubt Diomede does, the same po-
tential for change we have seen before. Though she insists that
she is disposed "to pleyne and maken wo" until she dies, just
as she responded to Pandarus's invitation to love with the assertion that it would better suit her "ay in a cave/ To bidde,
and rede on holy seyntes lyves," she goes on to add, "What I
shal after don, I kan nat seye;/ But trewelich, as yet me list nat
pleye" (V.986–87). Given her nature, we know she will play,
and that in the last analysis it will only be "pleye." Her now
hot, now cold temperment is perfectly reflected at the conclusion of this ambiguous response to Diomede, just before she
once again "caste hire eyen down,"

> I say nat therfore that I wol yow love,
> N'y say nat nay; but in conclusioun,
> I mene wel, by God that sit above!

> (V.1002–4)

Diomede leaves that night, the ninth, with a promise that he may visit again the next day, though she had earlier vowed, "bityde what bityde,/ I shal tomorwe at nyght" go to Troy. Night comes, the moon rises, and Criseyde goes to bed to repeat herself once more:

> Retornyng in hire soule ay up and down
> The wordes of this sodeyn Diomede,
> His grete estat, the perel of the town,
> And that she was allone and hadde nede
> Of frendes help, and thus bygan to brede
> The cause whi, the sothe for to telle,
> That she took fully purpos for to dwelle.

> (V.1023–29)

We recognize here a repetition of Criseyde's initial reaction to Troilus when he rode by on wounded horse, except now there is no mention of "distresse" or "trouthe."

We also recognize here an implicit defense of Criseyde on the narrator's part—"and thus began to brede/ The cause"—which parallels his defense of her then against the charge of "a sodeyn love." Then he told us that she only began to incline to love Troilus. The narrator continues his efforts to defend Criseyde and to avoid the truth—"men seyn—I not—that she yaf hym hire herte." Though he will not confirm her new love, he insists that "trewely, the storie telleth us" that no woman ever made such woe as she did when she betrayed Troilus. The lament she is given as an instance of her sorrow at betraying Troilus is as much or more concerned with her loss of honor, her damage to her good name, as it is with him. Chaucer also condenses time here, describing now what will only happen later, making her, as it were, look worse than she is that we may see what the narrator refuses to see. This is a sudden love, as was Criseyde's love of Troilus, for her love never contains any of that wonder and awe which characterizes true love. She and Diomede do justly deserve each other.

The fact that Criseyde finds a new love when she is once more placed in a situation where she "nyste what was best to rede" (I.96; V.18) indicates that she is of fortune and nature in a way that Troilus is not. The human tragedy of this world is figured primarily in Criseyde, not Troilus. When we first see Troilus, he is aloft in the temple; it is Criseyde who is standing "ful lowe" by the door, dressed in "blake wede," as one in winter or in death. When we come to know her in Book II, we see in her the now hot, now cold character of the things of this world, a reflection of the fact that the things of this world are born of the chaotic elements. Though she ascends to the fullness of life in Book III, so that for a brief time she is no longer "at dulcarnoun," but contraries harmonized, the life she manifests there is consonant with the nature of earthly things—she has this world's two faces. When she leaves Troy, she returns to her life of mourning and, shortly, to her now hot, now cold nature, as she begins a new life with a new lover. Just as Fortune turns "hire brighte face" from Troilus and "on hire whiel she sette up Diomede," so Criseyde turns her bright face from Troilus and sets Diomede up on her wheel. Like the chaotic dust from which she arose to love Troilus and to which she has returned, she rises again to clothe another soul in flesh for a time—"To Diomede algate I wol be trewe." We know, however, that she will be true to Diomede, as she was true to Troilus, only for a brief while, for ultimately she is true to her own nature, inevitable change. The narrator's resigned, philosophical statements in Book V when he is forced to admit Criseyde's falseness—"thus goth the world"; "swich is this world"—are, in a sense, precisely correct, for Criseyde is a mirror of this world, "whoso it kan byholde." The truth we see in Criseyde is the truth we see in nature and fortune, the endless, cyclical coming-to-be and passing-away of the things of this world. Caught in her own *cupiditas*, Criseyde can only vow to be true "algate" tomorrow, while ever remaining true to her love of self and the inconstancy that produces. Paradoxically even this tragedy is good; its cycle mirrors providence. Though the Criseydes of this world pass as "soone as flowres faire," there is goodness both in their flowering and in their fading, for both their ascent into life and their descent into death reveal the beauty, order, and harmony of God.

If Criseyde's essence is change, Troilus's is constancy. From the first moment he sees Criseyde until he is killed by Achilles, he remains remarkably true to his love of her and what he understands that love to require of him. Though he is clearly not the love that "nyl falsen no wight," not Christ, his truth in loving makes him a mirror, though a distorted one, of *caritas.* Ironically, he is himself a flawed incarnation of that love he believes is perfectly incarnated in Criseyde. Troilus, of course, fell in love with extreme suddenness. He saw Criseyde once and then went home to create an image of her and to worship that image. In the process, he creates her an image of the love that is in him. Though she is not the "benigne love" he thinks she is, he is of that love, or is at least transformed into something like it, if we can trust the narrator's assertion at the end of Book III that Troilus had become "benigne." Just what he thinks he sees in Criseyde is evident when he accuses Cassandra of lying after she explains that his dream indicates that Criseyde now loves Diomede. He tells Cassandra she might as well lie about Alceste, that best of creatures,

> For whan hire husbonde was in jupertye
> To dye hymself, but if she wolde dye,
> She ches for hym to dye and gon to helle,
> And starf anon.
>
> (V.1530–33)

Though Troilus is mistaken in this conviction that Criseyde is another Alceste, another almost perfect manifestation of that love which died and went to hell that man might live, this mistake is a consequence both of Criseyde's own dissimilar similitude to that love and of Troilus's own much greater similitude to the love which created and redeemed man.

Troilus's dissimilar similitude to the love that is Christ is especially evident in his refusal to ravish Criseyde, his refusal in the face of all Pandarus's urgings to commit the sin which transformed Troy into a besieged city. A brief examination of the implications of the Christian ideal of marriage as St. Paul presents it in the fifth chapter of his Epistle to the Ephesians will help us to understand the significance of Troilus's refusal, though he is neither married nor a Christian. Paul explains that as Christ is the head of the Church and the Church the body of Christ, so the husband is the head of the wife, the wife the body of the husband. He advises husbands to love their "wives even as Christ also loved the church, and gave himself for it," and "to love their wives as their own bodies," and wives to be obedient to their husbands "as the church is subject unto Christ." To love and cherish one's wife as Christ loves and cherishes the Church is above all else to leave one's wife free as Christ leaves the Church free.[16] A husband should refuse to ravish his wife presumably for the same reason Christ refuses to ravish the Church. Where there is mastery, there can be no love. To love one's wife as Christ loves the Church is also to be willing to suffer for her, for where there is freedom, there will also be pain, since man invariably does or says amiss. Indeed, the history of Christ's love of the Church suggests that the price of freedom is crucifixion. This high ideal of love also requires that one maintain one's commitment to one's wife, as Christ continued to love the world though it crucified him. One recalls Jean de Meun's Nature announcing, in response to man's infidelity to her: "Si m'aïst Deus li crucefis,/ Mout me repent don ome fis" (IV.259.19209–10). Though it may be natural to repent of loving that which betrays one, man is called to imitate Christ, who bore the cross Nature swears by as evidence that he did not repent of making man, who bore the cross to redeem that world which he knew would crucify him when he created it.

Though Pandarus urges Troilus to ravish Criseyde and though Criseyde insists that she will do whatever he commands "for that is no demaunde," Troilus neither can nor will ravish Criseyde against her will. He will not serve himself by imposing his will upon her. He leaves her free even though he is virtually certain, given his fatalism, that she will never be able to return. One recalls that when Pandarus recommended ravishing Criseyde, he advised Troilus to have mercy on himself, that he "manly sette the world on six and seven;/ And if thow deye a martyr, go to hevene" (IV.622–23). It is, of course, precisely by not ravishing Criseyde, by having mercy on her rather than on himself, that he dies a martyr to love. In that, presumably, rests a large part of his chance to go to heaven. In the scene where Criseyde is exchanged for Antenor, we watch Troilus repeatedly ask himself why he does not prevent Criseyde's going. "Why nyl I helpen to myn owen cure?" Though Troilus himself does not fully know why, he cannot serve himself. The narrator tells us that Troilus refrains for fear Criseyde will be killed. Rather like Alceste, Troilus dies the death of separation from Criseyde, his life, and chooses the hell of that separation that she may live.

If Chaucer's picture of Troilus in Book V makes him appear at times pathetic, at times comic in his blindness, it also makes him appear saintly in his fidelity. The whole presentation of Troilus in the fifth book recalls in general medieval characterizations of Christ as lover-knight either ignored or betrayed by those he loves yet faithful in his love of them.[17] Though Pandarus repeatedly urges Troilus to get another girl, realistically observing that if one can sing, another can dance, Troilus continues to love Criseyde even after he at long last recognizes the truth. When Pandarus learns of Criseyde's infidelity, he can only say, "What sholde I seyen? I hate, ywys, Criseyde;/ And God woot, I wol hate hire evermore!" (V.1732–33) In a sense, like Jean's Nature, Pandarus repents that he ever made the house he made and that he ever loved it himself. In striking contrast, Troilus can only reiterate his love of her:

> Thorugh which I se that clene out of youre mynde
> Ye han me cast; and I ne kan nor may,
> For al this world, withinne myn herte fynde
> To unloven yow a quarter of a day!
> In corsed tyme I born was, weilaway,
> That yow, that doon me al this wo endure,
> Yet love I best of any creature!
>
> (V.1695–1701)

Though much of this lament, Troilus's final statement in this world, is self-righteous—I didn't deserve it—and self-deceiving—all my pity is that your "name of trouthe is now fordon"—it reveals once again the constancy of his love of Criseyde even though she has crucified him. The limitations of such a love as Troilus had for Criseyde, limitations evident in this final lament which simultaneously proves its worth, are also evident in Troilus's subsequent behavior. No longer do we get glowing descriptions of Troilus's "gentillesse," as he is transformed into something like one of the avenging Furies the poet invoked, as he is consumed with a desire for revenge and becomes like the Greeks we meet at the beginning of the poem, who wage war "in diverse wise and oon entente," to avenge ravishing. Troilus's charity extends to no one accept Criseyde. He curses virtually everybody else. His love is still a mixture of *cupiditas*, of the first Adam, and *caritas*, the second Adam, Christ. However ahistorical it may be, we should perhaps quote some lines from John Donne's "Hymn to God, my God, in my sicknesse," lines which serve as an excellent commentary on Troilus and his sickness and upon the hymn of his songs as he journeys through this world.

> We thinke that *Paradise* and *Calvarie,*
>   *Christs* cross and *Adams* tree, stood in one place;
> Look Lord, and finde both Adams met in me.[18]

In his song in Book V, a song echoing the one he sang in Book I, Troilus laments that he no longer has Criseyde as a light to steer by. Though we are inclined to believe that one can only guide a boat on the North Star, the one constant star, by Christ, who alone will "falsen no wight," we have seen Troilus steer by a star that does change, yet steer ultimately, for all his ups and downs and all the buffeting from the contrary winds within and without him, a straight path. There is in Troilus a "trouthe," a fidelity in love, like Christ's, for all his similarity to Diomede, that sudden ravisher.

Just as Criseyde's story reveals the tragic cycle of fortune and nature, that stable circle of all things unstable, of all things that are born only to die, so Troilus reveals the comic cycle of all things divine, of all things which come from God and return to him, thus joining their ending to their beginning in a stable circle. Though the narrator begins *Troilus and Criseyde* by characterizing its structure as tragic—"Fro wo to wele, and after out of joie"—and declares his work a tragedy in his fond farewell to it, the whole poem, which is by no means over when the narrator says goodbye to it, encloses the world's tragic cycle in God's divine cycle. When we first see Troilus, he is high in the temple of Pallas Athena laughing. He has not yet fallen into his first sorrow. When we last see him, after the narrator has said goodbye to his tragedy and prayed for the power "to make in som comedye," he is again laughing, this time from the height of the eighth sphere to which he ascended upon his death.[19] The poem's total account of Troilus's history returns him at his end to his beginning, to a laughter after his final ascent which echoes his laughter prior to his initial fall.

As Kemp Malone has pointed out, a diagram of the poem's total progress would be a W.[20] Troilus begins on high, falls into his first sorrow to experience the world's tragedy with Criseyde, and then ascends on high again. The poem's tragic pattern of ascending to descend is contained within its comic cycle, a descending to ascend. Its union of the human tragedy with God's comedy is reflected in a form simultaneously tragic and comic. This is its ultimate union of contraries.

Diagrammed, the poem's structure would seem to be a gradual ascent from the hell of Book I through the purgatory of Book II to the heaven of Book III to return by similar gradations to the hell of Book V. Its form would seem to be a mirror of the tragedy which results from the "feynede" love of a "worldly vanyte." If we look at the poem from the heavenly perspective of the retraction and take its implications seriously, however, we will come to the opposite conclusion, for if Troilus's love of Criseyde is a vanity, a false love, than Book III, when Troilus is most one with Criseyde, is the poem's low point, its nadir, not its zenith. From this point of view, Books I and II are a gradual descent into the fleshly net of Book III; Books IV and V are a gradual ascent up from that total involvement with this world. To take these implications seriously is to ask whether or not the poem's ambiguities are such that they reveal that the ascending action of the first two books is also a descending one and that the descending action of the last two books is also an ascending one. From a Christian point of view, the ultimate false seeming of this world is that life is a tragedy, for God makes evil work for good and transforms the tragedy of man's sin into the comedy of God's grace. Similarly, it is the poem's ultimate false seeming to appear only the tragedy of man's sin. When the narrator prays to God in the last stanza of the poem, he characterizes the Trinity as "uncircumscript" yet circumscribing all. Part of what God's love circumscribes is this world's tragedy and the vanity of its "feynede loves." Just as we can see in Criseyde this world's tragedy, so we can see in Troilus a distorted mirror of that circumscribing love, that love which descends into this world to create, sustain and redeem it and to return it to its true source. The poem's tragic structure, as we shall see, is paradoxically a comic structure, a movement from alpha to omega.

Chaucer's picture of Troilus before he falls in love emphasizes his apparent freedom. Not yet devoted to any lady nor subject to love and its law, Troilus looks "now here, now there," praising and disparaging "whom hym leste." That his sudden love enslaves him is evident, for instance, both from the servant role he shortly adopts and from Chaucer's use of images of nets and snares to characterize Troilus's new condition. We can understand something of the significance of this fall by remembering Boethius's characterization of the psychology of sin, the process by which the mind loses the freedom natural to it by becoming enslaved by ignorance and "felonous talentz": "But the soules of men moten nedes be more fre whan thei loken hem in the speculacioun or lokynge of the devyne thought; and lasse fre whan thei slyden into the bodyes; and yit lasse fre whan thei ben gadrid togidre and comprehended in erthli membres. But the last servage is whan that thei ben yeven to vices and han ifalle fro the possessioun of hir propre resoun. For aftir that thei han cast awey hir eyghen fro the lyght of the sovereyn sothfastnesse to lowe thingis and derke, anon thei derken by the cloude of ignoraunce and ben troubled by felonous talentz; to the whiche talentz whan thei approchen and assenten, thei hepen and encrecen the servage which thei han joyned to hemself; and in this manere thei ben caytifs fro hir propre liberte" (V.*pr*.ii.26–43). Boethius's characterization of the process by which the soul becomes enslaved is modeled after the Platonic theory of the soul's descent, its original freedom on its proper star, its gradual descent into the body, and its all too frequent corruption through its union with matter. Though it is not altogether clear just what psychological distinction Boethius is making when he distinguishes between sliding into the body and being comprehended in earthly members, it is clear that that distinction is based upon the stages of the soul's descent into the flesh. Macrobius, for instance, tells us that the soul "does not suddenly assume a defiled body out of a state of complete incorporeality, but, gradually sustaining imperceptible losses and departing further from its simple and absolutely pure state, swells out with certain increase of a planetary body: in each of the spheres that lie below the sky it puts on another ethereal envelopment."[21] The soul's acquisition of a "planetary body" gradually prepares it "for assuming this earthly dress." The process by which man loses his spiritual freedom duplicates the process by which free souls become imprisoned in the flesh. Each mirrors the other. The progress of Troilus in the first three books is modeled in part upon this Boethian psychology of sin and the corresponding theory of the descent of the soul. From the heavenly perspective of the retraction, we are forced to recognize that though Troilus discovers something of "the lyght of sovereyn sothfastnesse" in his union with Criseyde, his union with her on that darkest of nights is also "blynde lust," a "servage" full of ignorance and "felonous talentz" which makes them "caytifs fro hir propre liberte." Though Troilus is free when he first sees Criseyde, his freedom is not that of "the speculacioun or lokynge of the devyne thought." Only after he falls in love is he concerned with such speculation, as he goes to his room to ponder the paradoxical mysteries of love and to create that image of Criseyde which enables him to wonder if she is woman or goddess. His original experience of love is psychologically liberating, for it frees him of his love of self and proves this fall a fortunate one. If freedom is contemplating divine thought, then, paradoxically, the helpless lover of Book I is free. Troilus's union with Criseyde is essentially a two-stage process which mirrors significantly the two stages by which Boethius and Macrobius depict the soul's loss of its original freedom, its gradual envelopment in a planetary body and its comprehension in earthly members. The first stage culminates in the first meeting of Troilus and Criseyde and the covenant between the two which is ratified by Criseyde's first kiss. That it constitutes a loss of freedom and a fall away from divine thought is evident from the fact that he subordinates himself to Criseyde, becoming her servant. That Troilus retains a considerable measure of his original freedom is clear from the nature of the covenant that is established. It is founded upon the reason of divine justice; he is to be rewarded as he deserves. The first stage of Troilus's union with Criseyde brings them for a time into "concord" and "quiete." The second stage in Troilus's loss of spiritual freedom is completed in the next meeting of the two Chaucer dramatizes, the consummation scene. Pandarus finally leaves and Troilus suddenly grows sudden, announcing, "Now be ye kaught, now is ther but we tweyne,/ Now yeldeth yow." Ironically, it is Troilus who is caught, who yields his soul completely to his love of Criseyde and consequently grows sudden. That there is also in Troilus some of the "servage" of a soul given over to vice is clear from the Horaste fiction, though it is equally clear from Troilus's praise of "Benigne Love" that the light of divine truth has not been totally extinguished in his soul.

Other elements in Troilus's progress toward union with Criseyde also reflect the theory of the descent of the soul and suggest that Chaucer also sought to mirror in that progress the creative process by which the soul descends to this world's life, not just to parallel the Boethian psychology of sin.[22] This is, indeed, what we would expect from our examination of the *concordia discors* tradition and its use of the myth of the descent of the soul to dramatize the creation of man the microcosm. Troilus's weeping and wailing in Book I recall the terrified weeping of the "numberless throng of souls clustered about the abode of Cancer" which Nature sees in her ascent to get the soul of man in Bernardus's *Cosmographia* (II.iii.95–96). They were weeping because they were "destined to descend, pure as they were, and simple, from splendor into shadow, from heaven to the kingdom of Pluto, from eternal life to that of the body." Though Troilus does not weep in terror but in desire, reflecting Macrobius's picture of the soul falling because a "secret yearning" for the life of the body creeps "into its thoughts,"[23] Bernardus's description of the fate awaiting these souls describes Troilus's. He is in Book I relatively pure and simple, he has the oneness of a soul undefiled by the flesh, and he is to descend "from splendor into [the] shadow" of his dark night with Criseyde, his own Prosperina in the Kingdom of Pluto.[24] Similarly, when Troilus repeatedly calls on death in Book I, he does so because he is dying to one life to be born to another, just as the soul dies, according to Marobius, in its descent to reach "the stage which on earth is called life."[25] Certain of the poem's astronomical references support such a reading of Troilus's progress toward Criseyde. Jove and Saturn are in Cancer, the portal of souls descending to this world, on the night when Troilus unites with the flesh of Criseyde.[26] Similarly, part of the reason Chaucer has Troilus pray to all seven of the planets (except Saturn) before entering the heaven

of the consummation scene and thank them all immediately
after demanding that Criseyde yield is their intermediary
function in the soul's descent from its pure and simple contemplation of the light of truth to its mysterious and harmonious union with the body.

We have already seen in examining Book III that the union
of Troilus and Criseyde mirrors the soul's union with the body.
What we see there is an image of the dual nature of man as
Bernardus, for instance, describes it in the *Cosmographia*:[27]
"He will derive his understanding from the heavens, his body
from the elements, so that while his body sojourns on earth his
mind may dwell far above. His mind and body, though of
diverse natures, will be joined into one, such that a mysterious
union will render the work harmonious. He shall be both
divine and earthly, comprehend the universe about him
through knowledge, and commune in worship with the gods.
Thus he will be able to conform to his two natures, and remain
in harmony with the dual principles of his existence" (II.x.113).
If the union of Troilus and Criseyde mirrors the creation and
nature of man, it ought also to mirror the creation and nature
of the macrocosm, since man is a microcosm. We have already
seen that Book III is such a mirror; a brief reconsideration of
Troilus's progress toward union with Criseyde and of the
intermediary role of Pandarus will demonstrate that part of
what Chaucer dramatizes in the first three books is the descent
of God's love to create the universe.

Troilus is in Book I virtually an incarnation of the love that
overwhelms him, a love which in its union of contraries is a
distorted reflection of the love that is God. For all the feelings
of unworthiness and insufficiency which love creates in Troilus,
his behavior parodies that of one self-sufficient. Though he
desires Criseyde, he does nothing to win her, but contents himself with his own thoughts. He contemplates that image of
perfection that is the Criseyde of his mind, that is an image
more of himself than of Criseyde, but does nothing to actualize
it. Even Pandarus cannot bring him out of himself until, in one
of the poem's supremely ambiguous moments, he tells Troilus
that nothing ventured is nothing gained and that he should
"thynk it is a guerdon, hire to serve" (I.819). Though it may
well be largely the self-serving advice that moves Troilus, the

radical idealism of "thynk it is a guerdon, hire to serve" reminds us that it is for some such reason that God emerged from the perfect self-sufficiency of his own thought and love to create the universe an image of himself, since he could not possibly gain anything from it.

St. Bernard's explanation of the incarnation of Christ will help us to understand Chaucer's reflection in Troilus of God's gift of himself which is the creation. St. Bernard argues that God became man because fallen man can only love carnally and implies that Christ's separation of himself from the Godhead to put on man's defiled flesh is as much God's redemptive sacrifice as the Crucifixion.[28] By having Troilus echo Christ on the cross immediately after he commits himself to love—"O Lord, now youres is/ My spirit, which that oughte youres be" —Chaucer dramatizes not only Troilus's death to one life and birth into another but something of God's sacrifice of himself in the creation as well, for, given God's omniscient eternal present, even his original creation is a sacrifice of the self, a passion.

After Troilus consents to let Pandarus seek Criseyde for him, Chaucer pictures Pandarus as going forth from the world of Troilus's bedroom to find a time and a place, to actualize what is in his own mind, or as an agent of Troilus, what is in Troilus's mind, to the degree that he understands that. Chaucer dignifies Pandarus's undertaking by picturing it as a creative activity in a magnificent stanza which implicitly compares Pandarus to God, or more accurately, to God's subordinate creative agents.

> For everi wight that hath an hous to founde
> Ne renneth naught the werk for to bygynne
> With rakel hond, but he wol bide a stounde,
> And sende his hertes line out fro withinne
> Aldirfirst his purpos for to wynne.
> Al this Pandare in his herte thoughte,
> And caste his werk ful wisely or he wroughte.
>
> (I.1065-71)

One remembers, as no doubt Chaucer wished his readers to, Boethius's celebrated description of God's creation of the universe in *Metrum* ix of the third book of the *Consolation* in which Boethius tells us that God, freely moved by his own goodness, created "this world to the lyknesse semblable of that faire world" in his thought. After describing the harmonizing of the elements and the ordering of the physical universe, Boethius describes God's creation of the World-Soul which moves all things. First, he divides it into two harmonious parts, "and whan it es thus divyded [and] it hath assembled a moevynge into two rowndes, it gooth to torne ayen to hymself, and envyrouneth a ful deep thought and turneth the hevene by semblable ymage" (III.*m*.ix.27–32). Though Pandarus's characterization is informed by numerous subordinate, creative agencies of the *concordia discors* tradition, his divided nature and his movement mirror in particular this picture of the World-Soul. Just as it moves all, Pandarus moves both Troilus and Criseyde. Just as the World-Soul gives life to the created by revolving in two contrary circles, the circles of the Same and the Different, so Pandarus's many comings and goings form ultimately two contrary circles.[29] We see him go forth at the end of Book I to get Criseyde and return at the end of Book II leading her "by the lappe" to Troilus. After he has assigned Criseyde to the inner chamber of his house on the consummation night, we see him go forth to get Troilus from his hiding place and return leading him "by the lappe" to complete his creation of this house of love. Only then does he "torne ayen to hymself."

The structure and action of the first three books reveal that the little universe of love created in Book III is the product of two contrary movements. Troilus's sudden fall into love is a fall into a hell of suffering. Chaucer invokes Tisiphone, one of the Furies and hence a daughter of Night and, at least in Dante, of hell, to help him describe it.[30] Troilus ascends from the depths of Book I to the heaven of Book III through the purgatory of Book II, a purgatory which Chaucer introduces by echoing the opening lines of Dante's *Purgatorio*. Paradoxically, the ascending action is also a descending one, as it mirrors in reverse, as mirrors do, the descent of God's self-sufficient love to create. The destruction of this little world produces two similar contrary movements, as in its descent we can see mirrored the ascending return of God's love to himself.

As we saw at the beginning of this chapter, Book IV duplicates the sequence of the three books, not to unite the lovers, however, but to separate them. If the creation of that little world mirrored the passion, so does its destruction, as Troilus once more echoes Christ on the cross, "And thow, Criseyde, o sweete herte deere,/ Receyve now my spirit" (IV.1209–10). This is the passion of death. Though Troilus does not kill himself after uttering these words, since Criseyde, who has swooned and whom Troilus thinks dead, revives, their separation is a death. In the proem to Book IV the narrator tells us that it will recount together "the losse of lyf and love yfeere/ Of Troilus" (IV.27–28). That it does so on one level is clear from the final lines of the book,

> For whan he saugh that she ne myghte dwelle,
> Which that his soule out of his herte rente,
> Withouten more, out of the chaumbre he wente.
> (IV.1699–1701)

When we leave Book IV we are not only leaving the chamber of love which Pandarus built but also, in a sense, the world itself, since that chamber is a microcosm. In Book IV Chaucer has both Troilus and Criseyde imagine life without the other in terms of a life in the other world. Troilus imagines an eternity of complaining with Pluto and Proserpina in Hades; Criseyde imagines a life of joy in Elysium together with her Orpheus. Criseyde's imagined new life follows immediately her conception of herself living without Troilus "as out of this world agon" (IV.780). In Book V we are "as out of this world agon."

Book V begins with Criseyde leaving besieged Troy, another of the poem's images of this world, to join the Greeks, who in their efforts to avenge the ravishing of Helen are like the avenging Furies, those spirits of hell, the poet invokes. Though Criseyde begins a new life with Diomede here, it is not really a life of joy but one of regret. Criseyde is not Eurydice, but Proserpina, and Diomede is not a new Orpheus, but an old Pluto, a ravisher of women. Criseyde has journeyed, in a sense, to Hades. Just as Dante has Paolo and Francesca relive their love in hell in complete awareness of its true barrenness, Chaucer pictures Criseyde reliving her love of Troilus with Diomede.[31] His picture of that new life reveals all the barrenness of Criseyde's love, making it an image of the hell of a love with no truth in it. Diomede's and Criseyde's mutual love is revealed to be only mutual ravishing. Criseyde's ascending movement into new life with Diomede is, paradoxically, actually a continuing descent into hell, into a love that is death.

Troilus's movement after Book III, though it is a descent into the hell of separation which leads ultimately to his death in the epilogue, is also, paradoxically, an ascent. As we have seen, Book IV is a sudden return for Troilus to a hell of suffering like the one his sudden love plunged him into, and begins for us another Dantean progression from hell through purgatory to heaven. Though Book V pictures Troilus suffering even more intensively, it is for Troilus a second purgatory. Gradually and painfully he learns the falseness of what he has loved and is prepared for his flight into the heavens which occurs in the epilogue after his death. Though Chaucer does not picture heaven for us, he does direct us to it, both through Troilus's advice that we "all oure herte on heven caste" and through his narrator's advice that we love Christ, who "nyl falsen no wight." The image of purgatorial suffering in Troilus's suffering in Book V is, of course, a distorted image, just as Book III is only a distorted mirror of heaven. He is only "as out of the world agon." If Troilus learns in Book V that Criseyde is false, the self-righteousness and the self-deception we see in his final lament reveal that he has not fully understood the degree to which his love was "feynede," the degree to which it was betrayal and ravishing. In his return to his first laughter, he joins his ending to his beginning to make a stable circle, but there is some question as to whether he has learned much of anything from his experience of this world and its two faces, its union of the sacred and the profane. He ends condemning love as he began mocking it, seemingly unaware that it was his experience of some of God's *caritas* in the joy and the double sorrow of "his lovynge of Criseyde" which has brought him to the height from which he originally fell. He now recognizes, in a sense, that it was a fall, but not that it was a fortunate fall. When he began he loved only himself; now his heart is directed toward heaven. Though his love of Criseyde was in many ways a "feynede" love of a "worldly vanyte," the vanity which is the world is a reflection of the "Benigne Love" and "trouthe" of its Creator.

Troilus's ascent to the eighth shpere, the sphere of the fixed stars, which is in the myth of the cosmic cycle of the soul the origin and end of souls, mirrors the return of the soul to God, or perhaps we should say to its judgment before God, since Chaucer does not tell where Mercury "sorted hym to dwelle."[32] Given the microcosmic nature of man and his creation by God in a manner similar to the creation of all things, we can also see in Troilus the return of all things to God, an image of that time when this world will be no more, having been separated out into heaven and hell. Indeed, in Troilus's and Criseyde's history we can also see an image in little of all history; of the creation according to the laws of justice, a justice mirrored in the original covenant between Troilus and Criseyde; of the fall, evident in the Horaste fiction and the change in the nature of the union of Troilus and Criseyde, a union which is rightly characterized as merciful since the law of justice requires not a fallen union but an end to their little world altogether; of the passion of the redemption, mirrored in Troilus's crucifixion by Criseyde as a result of his refusal to ravish her; and of the final end of all things, mirrored in Criseyde's return to chaos and fall into a love that is only hell and in Troilus's return to his source. On this level, to turn to God in the final stanza of the poem is precisely right, for at the end of time God will be all in all.

In the last stanza of the poem the narrator directs us to the Trinity, characterizing it, though perhaps unwittingly, as a circle: "Thow oon, and two, and thre, eterne on lyve,/ That regnest ay in thre, and two, and oon." He also characterizes it as "uncircumscript" yet circumscribing all. That which God's love circumscribes is this world, as the structure of Chaucer's poem demonstrates. If it pictures for us the tragedy of this world's "blynde lust," of all things that come to be only to pass away, it also pictures for us the divine comedy of the love which descends from God to return to Him. If we see mirrored in Criseyde the nature and fate of all things ruled by nature and fortune, we can see mirrored in Troilus, however dimly, the nature and fate of all things divine. Both of these circles, the circle of *cupiditas* which is ultimately of hell and the circle of *caritas* which is of God, unite to create this world and are proof of the stable source of all things. Though Troilus's history mirrors the divine comedy, he unites both circles, as he falls into this world to experience its tragedy before returning to the heights from which he fell, the sphere of the fixed stars, the true home of the soul. His course is ultimately a spiral, as he is turned one way by God's circumscribing love, just as the planets are turned by the divine motion of the fixed stars, at the same time that his own cupidity turns him in the opposite direction, just as each of the planets has its own contrary circular motion.[33] Thus it is that God harmonizes contraries in man and in the cosmos: "O Love, O Charite!"

5

Chaucer and His Narrator

That Chaucer begins *Troilus and Criseyde* not only with a declaration of his subject and an invocation of a muse but also with an assertion of his reasons for writing it, that he includes in his epilogue a farewell to his poem, and that he repeatedly interrupts his narrative to comment not only on the action of the poem but also on the story as story—all, taken together, indicate that *Troilus and Criseyde*, in some sense, is a poem about poetry. Though the poet's high calling is to mediate between his audience and truth, poets are not parsons; they do not reject either "rym" or "rum, ram, ruf" that they may preach the naked Word. They tell fables, clothing truth in the false seeming of fiction.[1] As we have seen, *Troilus and Criseyde* reveals God's truth in a way analogous to the way in which the world reveals that truth. It is a similar mirror through which we can see darkly the truth. Chaucer sought to incarnate the Word in his poem as the Word is incarnated in the time and place of this world, since carnal man can only know the truth if it is accommodated to his limited "wit" and can only be moved to love it if it is first revealed to him in the flesh. Such a celebration of the Trinity as that ending the poem can only come at the end, after we have passed through its world and have been prepared intellectually and emotionally to see truth face to face.

This is not only a high calling but a presumptuous and quite possibly a futile one as well. Can any man to whom the truth must be accommodated understand the truth sufficiently to accommodate it to his fellow man? Does any man possess the skill to incarnate that truth in the flesh of his art so that one will ultimately be moved to love it and not the flesh of poetry? That Chaucer had his doubts at least about his own capabilities is evident in the successive evaluation of his poem in the epilogue, his tender and loving address to it to "kis the steppes, where as thow seest pace/ Virgile, Ovide, Omer, Lucan, and Stace" (V.1791–92) and his contemptuous "Lo here, the forme of olde clerkis speche/ In poetrie, if ye hire bokes seche" (V.1854–55). At the same time that Chaucer presumes to create in imitation of God by ornamenting with form the chaotic matter of the Troilus story, he dramatizes and confesses his own inevitable failure to achieve perfectly the sacred ends of art through his characterization of the narrator's own limited understanding and often misguided love of that matter. It is to the narrator that we must turn, then, if we are to understand the poem's ambiguous evaluation of the nature, function, and worth of poetry.[2]

One of the ways in which Chaucer defines the artist's task and its hazards is by establishing parallels between the narrator and Pandarus. Both are presented as unsuccessful in love—the narrator implies that he has never even dared to try—and see themselves as servants of love's servants. Both affirm that love is a good and take upon themselves substantial labors in love's behalf, insisting that they do so only for the benefit of others. If the poem questions Pandarus's motives and function, forcing us to ask why Pandarus labors so diligently and whether or not the Herculean task of boosting Troilus into bed is a worthy one, it also questions the narrator's function and motives. Can the translation of a pagan poem help young lovers, especially given the narrator's intellectual and moral confusion and his own inevitably less than perfectly pure motives, since he too is a fallen man? One recalls that when Dante meets the lovers Paolo and Francesca in hell and asks Francesca what first moved them to the love which led to their sorry end, she tells him that they fell in love and yielded while reading of Lancelot and Guinevere and that "*Galeotto fu il libro e chi lo scrisse.*"[3] Galeotto was, of course, the intermediary going between Lancelot and Guinevere, the Pandarus of that romance. Chaucer no doubt remembered this characterization of book and author as pander and recognized in it the very real hazards in writing pagan poetry, hazards he dramatizes by paralleling the narrator as author with Pandarus the go-between. Though Chaucer no doubt hoped to lead young lovers, to whom he addresses his poem, to Christ, this is a perilous undertaking, given the delights of Book III, delights which, as we shall see, ensnare to no little degree the narrator. The danger is that Chaucer's Herculean task of creating the poem, a task dramatized in the narrator's Herculean task of translating it, may only serve to boost young lovers into bed.

In the opening proem the narrator takes his stance at some distance from his poem. His perspective is that of a fourteenth-century Christian looking back at the pagan past, and he asserts a Christian purpose for writing the poem,

> For so hope I my sowle best avaunce
> To prey for hem that Loves servauntz be,
> And write hire wo, and lyve in charite,
>
> And for to have of hem compassioun,
> As though I were hire owne brother dere.

(I.47–51)

He begins the proem by announcing the full scope of his story, the double sorrow of Troilus, and ends it with the fact that Criseyde will forsake Troilus. Both his foreknowledge of the end of his tale and his Christian perspective place him in a position superior to his matter. It is beneath him, so to speak. There is also perhaps a trace of superiority in his declared intention of having compassion on the servants of Love "as though I were hire owene brother dere."

Other elements in the proem, however, suggest that this superiority is more illusory than real. Though his insistence that he is not a lover and that he does not dare to pray to Love because of his "unliklynesse" may suggest that he has passed through his youth, the time of love, to sufficient age to recognize that love is folly, it also reminds us of Troilus in Book I, who is persuaded that he is such a wretch he will never have success in love and that he will "therefore sterve." Both the ease with which he puts on a "sory chere" to become a "sorwful instrument" and his picture of himself far from Love's "help in darknesse" indicate that he is experiencing his own psychological and spiritual crisis. The narrator's situation at the beginning of the *Troilus* is similar to Boethius's at the beginning of the *Consolation* and Dante's at the beginning of the *Divine Comedy*. The *Consolation* opens, we recall, with Boethius both literally in prison and metaphorically imprisoned, lost in the darkness of ignorance so far from his true home that he does not even recognize Lady Philosophy, his mentor and guide. He is complaining, writing "the drery vers of wretchidnesse" which wet his "face with verray teres," just as the narrator is writing "woful vers, that wepen" as he writes them.[4] No doubt, if Lady Philosophy were to enter the narrator's dark prison as she did Boethius's, she would recognize in him the same illness she discovered in Boethius, that ignorance of self which is ignorance of God, and would begin the cure by banishing the Muse who helps him weep, Tisiphone, that daughter of night and spirit of hell, just as she banished Boethius's Muses on the grounds that such "comune strompettis" nourish him "with sweete venym" instead of curing him.[5] The *Divine Comedy* opens with Dante awaking one morning in the middle of his life to discover that he is lost in a dark wood and that he is incapable of ascending directly to the sun.[6] Dante will have to descend through hell that he may ascend to the sun, just as Lady Philosophy will have to lead Boethius through Fortune's false goods that she may turn him in the opposite direction in the middle of Book III toward the true good. The narrator's sorrow would seem to be Boethius's and Dante's sorrow, that of a man who finds himself lost in the dark prison of this world far from his true home in heaven and, seemingly, so full of despair that though he can pray for others, he does not dare to pray to Love for himself.[7] If love is what vivifies the soul, the narrator would appear to be spiritually dead. Like Dante and Boethius, he will have to descend that he may ascend; he will have to journey through the joy and sorrow of this world's heaven and hell that he may come to the Love that "nyl falsen no wight" at the end of the poem, when he will at last be able to pray for himself.

The undercurrent of superiority evident in the first proem surfaces in the narrator's reaction to Troilus's self-satisfied mockery of lovers, as he mocks him for mocking—"O blynde world, O bynde entencioun!" In his mockery he sounds almost precisely like Troilus and reveals that he, in spite of his intention to be compassionate, is guilty of a similar pride. Apparently, he has not yet learned that Troilus really is his "brother dere." Caught up in his enthusiasm for Cupid's revenge, he leaps into the poem, as it were, to affirm unequivo-

cally that love of "kynde" is a good.[8] At the end of the poem
he will just as unequivocally reject it and affirm, by implication,
what he now mocks Troilus for asserting, that lovers are fools.
Were we to accept his final judgment as the whole truth about
love of "kynde," we might be inclined to mock him now ourselves with a similar "O blynde world" and a similar "But
alday faileth thing that fooles wenden" (I.217). Like Pandarus,
the narrator seems somewhat too prone to reactions "for the
nones." He seems to have forgotten what he began by knowing, that Troilus's love would fail in significant ways. Though
the superiority of his reaction to Troilus's "surguidrie" demonstrates that the narrator has maintained some distance from
him, the blindness of his own reaction and the total enthusiasm
with which he reacts reveal that he is getting caught up in
his poem.

The unqualified enthusiasm with which he praises Troilus at
the end of the first book and his seemingly total obliviousness
to the ambiguity of so much that takes place in it suggest that
he in his own sorrow identifies with Troilus in his. Now Troilus
does apparently seem like a brother. Thus, at the beginning of
Book II the narrator employs the same metaphor for his poetic
progress through the poem as Troilus uses to characterize his
agony in Book I. Just as Troilus sees himself as a ship sailing
toward his port, one tossed about by contrary winds, so the
narrator tells us that the boat of his "cunnyng" is at last sailing
out of the tempestuous waters of Troilus's despair. In his own
despair, he has found a kindred soul in Troilus. The narrator's
metaphor for the progress of his poetic efforts is taken from the
opening of the *Purgatorio*, where Dante describes the boat of
his wit as sailing through better waters now that he has left
behind the cruel sea of hell.[9] Chaucer's use of this image to
characterize the narrator's progress in conjunction with his use
of similar images to characterize Troilus identifies the suffering
each experienced in Book I as hellish.

Freed from the "tempestous matere" of Troilus's despair and
from some of his own sorrow, the narrator now reasserts his
distance and appears, for the first time dispassionate. He invokes a new Muse, Clio, the Muse of history, telling us that
he needs to use no other art here. He goes on to apologize that
he writes without "sentement," dissociating himself from

lovers in words which associate him with Pandarus, "A blynd man kan nat juggen wel in hewis" (II.21). He is, he explains, only translating. He also explains that if the behavior of his characters seems strange, his audience should remember that "In sondry londes, sondry ben usages" (II.28) and that his story is of another time and another place. He ends the proem by asserting that since he began, he will follow his author as best he can. The narrator has returned, as it were, to the four-teenth century, but in the process he has so dissociated himself both from love and from his story that we are forced to ques-tion whether there is any reason to continue other than "syn I have bigonne."

In the proem to Book II Chaucer is not only characterizing his narrator's present psychology but also using his narrator to characterize some of the dilemmas of his art. In the very words with which Chaucer has his narrator emphasize the otherness of the past, Chaucer makes us recognize the basic similarity of past and present, their oneness: "For every wight which that to Rome went/ Halt nat o path, or alwey o manere" (II.36–37). "Ecch contree hath his lawes," but there is also a "law of kynde." The ways may be different, but the goal is the same, Rome. Just how a story about Troy can lead us to Rome is not clear, however, especially since the narrator has himself, in a sense, never been there. How can one who is not a lover lead us to true love? If the Rome to which Chaucer hopes his pagan poem will lead us is that love which "nyl falsen no wight," if he hopes to lead us to the Trinity, how can he, while he himself is still in this world? Part of the answer to this question lies in such a Muse as Clio and such an activity as translating. If Chaucer wishes to make his poem a mirror of the love which is the other world, a world he has never seen, he must do so, paradoxically, by making it an accurate mirror of this world, for this world is a mirror of God. In a sense, the only way he can mirror God is by mirroring that which is not God, this "worldly vanyte." The only way he can lead us to the timeless and placeless One that is Rome is through such a time and a place as Troy. Chaucer's characterization of his narrator's dis-passionate stance suggests that we can only see God reflected in this world if we view it dispassionately, as a historian should. This very necessity causes another problem for the poet, how-

ever; for if he makes his poem dispassionate so that we may
understand, he may well leave us unmoved. In a sense, Chaucer
must keep us simultaneously at a distance that we may know
and in the poem that we may feel. His narrator seems at this
point, at least, only capable of being now this, now that. He
cannot yet unite both contrary ways of knowing.

In the course of the second book, the narrator has difficulty
keeping his distance and perspective. Just after Criseyde first
sees Troilus, for instance, he leaps in to react to what is taking
place, just as he did when Troilus first saw Criseyde. His
response this time is very much the contrary of his earlier
response. If then he rejoiced in Troilus's sudden fall into love,
mocking him for mocking lovers, he now defends Criseyde,
telling us that though "som envious" man might "jangle" that
"This was a sodeyn love" (II.667), a light love born at first
sight, the truth is "that she gan enclyne/ To like hym"
(II.674–75) and only later, after much service and suffering on
his part, came to love him. One such "envious" man was, of
course, the narrator's author, Boccaccio.[10] It is not, apparently,
an easy thing to translate accurately, at least not when the
honor of a lady is being impuned. From the rational perspective
of a historian no doubt love at first sight does seem sudden
and light. The subsequent history of Troilus and Criseyde, a
history the narrator knows, suggests that such sudden falls as
Troilus's produce truer lovers than such a gradual, reasoned
submission to love as Criseyde's. Once again we are forced to
see that the narrator's reaction is both "for the nones" and not
a little blind. But then this is the same narrator who will tell us
at the end of his tale that he told it to warn women against
false men. Clearly, he cannot keep himself from becoming
emotionally involved with his own story and intruding into it
with, at times, alarming suddenness. His reaction here is less
sudden than his reaction to Troilus's fall. That event drew
from him the exclamation of an apostrophe. Here he specu-
lates—"Now myghte som." Though this fact suggests that he
now has better control of his emotions, he will shortly be
totally involved in the action and once again urging love on.
The next time Criseyde sees Troilus ride by, for instance, he
will observe,

> To God hope I, she hath now kaught a thorn,
> She shall nat pulle it out this nexte wyke.
> God sende mo swich thornes on to pike!
>
> (II.1272–74)

Having defended Criseyde against the charge of haste, he would now, it seems, have her hurry up. The exclamation here indicates that our translator is learning to write with "sentement," but losing perspective.

We remember that the second book ends in midscene, with Criseyde and Pandarus whispering together just outside the door to the bedroom in which Troilus lies "recordyng his lesson" (III.51). The last line of the second book reveals the narrator's almost total empathy with Troilus—"O myghty God, what shal he seye?" If Pandarus could hear him, he would probably mock him as he mocks Troilus—" 'O myghty God,' quod Pandarus, 'in trone,/ I! who say evere a wis man faren so?' " (IV.1086–87). The narrator is no longer a translator who has already read the whole book, it would seem, but an observer, almost a participant. Like the reader, he awaits what is to come with anticipation, with his authorial foreknowledge totally eradicated. He is no longer, as he was at the beginning, above the poem viewing its total history as an eternal present, like God, but in the poem. Looked at in terms of the narrator, the proem to Book III is another sudden interruption of the drama he is recounting, another exclamation full of apostrophes. Like his other reactions to his poem, this one is also "for the nones" and blind, for if the proem is a masterful depiction of the ambiguity of Venus looked at as a timeless whole, as a single image, as it were, read as a continuous narrative, a series of observations in time, where the narrator is now located, it is a hodgepodge of contradictions. It indicates the narrator's confusion and lack of control, a seeming inability to distinguish the Holy Spirit from Jove the ravisher. The more he becomes involved in the poem the less he is able to see its totality as a timeless whole. Reacting to parts, he loses the whole.

In Book III his vision is almost totally "for the nones" and consequently more partial than ever. If he began the poem hoping to advance his soul by telling the double sorrow of

Troilus, now that he is narrating Troilus's joy he participates
so wholeheartedly in it that he even asks why he has not sold
his own soul for one such "blisful nyght." Though he began
as a mentor and guide to young lovers, now he calls on them,
those who have feeling "in loves art," to correct him. How
totally he is one with the emotions of his characters is clear
from the fact that just as they end their nights together with
aubes lamenting the coming of day, so he ends his summary
account of their nights together and their indescribable bliss
with his own pained lament that day comes—"But cruel day,
so wailaway the stounde!/ Gan for t'aproche" (III.1695–96).
Though he goes on to describe their grief that day comes, this
"cruel" and "wailaway" express his own grief.

With this enthusiasm goes a corresponding and consequen-
tial blindness. It is just before he characterizes day as cruel that
he declares that "Felicite, which that thise clerkes wise/
Comenden so" (III.1691–92), cannot describe their joy. His
phraseology recalls Criseyde's proof that "worldly selynesse,/
Which clerkes callen fals felicitee" (III.813–14), is a false happiness shortly before she welcomes Troilus as her "suffisaunce." Though a truly wise clerk might indeed commend
this happiness as ultimately a good, both because its goodness
mirrors God and thus proves God good and because it will
fail and thus prove it is not the Good it mirrors, this would not
seem the narrator's point, given his "cruel day" lament that it
passes. He seems merely to have forgotten that such joy does
not last and cannot. Just as he blindly overvalues the goodness
he sees here, so he brushes aside with impatience the dark side
of this paradise. This is evident from his treatment of what is
unquestionably Trolius's moment of greatest moral failure in
the poem. When Criseyde asks him about his jealousy, a jealousy Pandarus has used to get her to admit Troilus fully into
her favors, he lies and thus proves himself at least to some
degree a ravisher, not the perfection the narrator tells us he
is at the end of the book. The narrator tells us that Troilus had
to lie "for the lasse harm," as though this vice were a virtue,
and explains that

> He seyde hire, whan she was at swich a feste,
> She myght on hym han loked at the leste,—

Noot I nought what, al deere ynough a rysshe,
As he that nedes most a cause fisshe.

(III.1159–62)

In short, he dismisses it out of hand, almost without seeing it.
One suspects, however, that at this moment his blindness is
willful. Emotionally committed to the paradise of love he is
celebrating, he will not see its dark side, even if he has to
ravish the truth of history and alter his source to make both
what he wants them to be. We might, for instance, recall the
reason his author does not say whether or not Criseyde believed Pandarus when he said that Troilus was out of town.
Boccaccio does not say because his version of this history has
Criseyde initiate the consummation scene by having Pandarus
go get Troilus when he is out of town.[11] Ever sensitive to the
honor of ladies and himself not a little in love with Criseyde,
the narrator changed the story in an effort to make Criseyde
an innocent victim of Pandarus and the stars that brought the
rain. All his efforts to make her more innocent than she really
is fail, however, just as his efforts to make Book III seem a perfect paradise fail.[12]

To accuse the narrator of a blind ravishing of history in Book
III similar to Troilus's blind ravishing of Criseyde is to see only
half of the effects of the poem on the narrator to this point, for
it has had benign effects upon him as well. Though he began in
sorrow and darkness unable to pray to Love, in a spiritual state
of paralysis, he is now able to pray to Love. Indeed, his proem
to Venus is precisely that, a prayer to Love. However ambiguous that prayer, it is a necessary prologue to his prayer to true
love at the end of the poem. Carnal man, including the narrator,
must first be moved by such flawed and distorted incarnations
of the Word before he can love the Word. He now can feel and
can love. If his picture of Troilus's and Criseyde's paradise is
a blind one, this is partly a consequence of the narrator's
charity, of his desire to love and think well of his characters.
There is in him no envy of the happiness of the world he creates
and he, like Troilus, no longer japes at lovers.

We must see that the narrator has come to his present psychological condition by a path similar to Troilus's, one the
poem requires us to see as simultaneously ascending and descending. He has risen from the hell of his own spiritual dead-

ness in Book I through the purgatory of Book II to his present joy; he has fallen from his position above the poem, a position from which he knew the whole as a single present, like God in his knowledge, into the poem and its time. He has been ensnared by it and only gives up his celebration of love in Book III because he must, because, as he says, Venus, Cupid, and the nine Muses, all of whom have been his guides, "wol wende" so that he "kan namore" (III.1812). To create Book III he had to descend in suffering and in love to vivify it, to make it live that it may move us, just as God creates with descending love the world that it may move us. The remainder of the poem will similarly move the narrator simultaneously in two contrary directions, down into a second empathetic sorrow with Troilus, back up above the poem to a position from which he will again be able to see it as a whole.

The proem to Book IV opens with a lament.

> But al to litel, weylaway the whyle,
> Lasteth swich joie, ythonked be Fortune,
> That semeth trewest whan she wol bygyle,
> And kan to fooles so hire song entune,
> That she hem hent and blent, traitour comune!
>
> (IV.1–5)

That the narrator himself has to some degree been seduced by the song he has been singing—he ends Book III by characterizing it as a song—is evident from his own distress. This is his lament. He is apparently to be counted among those fools Fortune, like that other two-faced goddess, Venus, seizes and blinds with her music, for the joys of love and the delights of the Muses, themselves tempting sirens and common traitors, as Boethius tells us,[13] caused him to forget what he insisted was his subject—the double sorrow of Troilus, not his joy. He is not merely victim, however. Armed with foreknowledge of his story and with at least the theoretical knowledge that Fortune is a siren, his all too willing suspension of disbelief and his all too delighted and delightful description of the pleasures of worldly happiness make him as much seducer as seduced. Many a young lover, not to mention many a critic, has no doubt been ravished by his "speche," however well forewarned.[14] Transported by the narrator's picture of the heaven

of love, some no doubt have stopped reading in order to seek
out a Criseyde and a bed.

If the narrator's present sudden sorrow is a fall, it gradually
frees him from his love of the worldly paradise he has been
picturing and thus proves that bad fortune is good fortune for
him, as well as for Troilus. Like Troilus, the narrator must
suffer in order to learn the unalterable fact that the heavenly
places of poetry, like the world's heavenly places, are only for
a time. The difficulty the narrator has in accepting God's unalterable laws are evident in his handling of Books IV and V.
We can recognize his unwillingness to see the truth in his
apostrophe—"O nyce world" (IV.206)—castigating the Trojans for exchanging Criseyde for the traitor Antenor. Instead
of mocking them for not knowing what they cannot know, he
ought, perhaps, to mock himself for having loved what he
should have known could not last. Though his history tells
him otherwise and will not be denied, he tries to deny Criseyde's untruth. Indeed, even here in the proem to Book IV we
hear him try to deny and mitigate it.

> For how Criseyde Troilus forsook,
> Or at the leeste, how that she was unkynde,
> Moot hennesforth ben matere of my book,
> As writen folk thorugh which it is in mynde.
> Allas! that they sholde evere cause fynde
> To speke hire harm, and if they on hire lye,
> Iwis, hemself sholde han the vilanye.
>
> (IV.15–21)

He seems nearly as reluctant as Troilus to see the truth, the
light of day, and nearly as hurt by his discovery of the world's
frailty. His efforts to resist the truth climax in Book V when he
must tell us that Criseyde "took fully purpos" to stay among
the Greeks. He begins three straight stanzas with a reference to
his story, resisting it in the first two to conclude "Men seyn—
I not—that she yaf hym hire herte" (V.1050), but affirming in
the third that it "trewely" tells us that no woman ever had
greater sorrow than Criseyde did for her untruth. The narrator's own picture refutes his refusal to admit the truth, however, as he narrates now what is only to happen later so that
instead of looking victimized by circumstances, Criseyde looks

sudden. In his descent into suffering, however, we see him gain
again some distance on his subject, as he adopts a stance of
philosophical resignation.

> Swich is this world, whoso it kan byholde:
> In ech estat is litel hertes reste.
> God leve us for to take it for the beste!
>
> (V.1748–50)

This is clearly true of the "estat" of poet as well as that of lover.
His efforts to achieve a fourteenth-century Christian per-
spective are also evident in his efforts to transform his love of
Criseyde into compassion.

> Hire name, allas! is punysshed so wide,
> That for hire gilt it oughte ynough suffise.
> And if I myghte excuse hire any wise,
> For she so sory was for hire untrouthe,
> Iwis, I wolde excuse hire yet for routhe.
>
> (V.1095–99)

Like Troilus, he is learning that true love is not ravishing but
relinquishing. One can be neither a true historian nor a true
poet if one bends the world to one's own will, making it serve
the self. Though the world and even poetry may offer only
false happiness, the proper response is not to hate them for
their falsity as Pandarus hates Criseyde nor to continue to love
them blindly as Troilus does Criseyde. One must see the truth
of their inadequacy and yet continue to love them, for they
mirror the truth which is not inadequate. In a sense, for a time
in Book V the narrator manages both to be dispassionate, to
see the whole truth, and to be involved in his poem, to love it
and its truth. This is, of course, what the reader must do if the
poem is to come to life for him, as it has come to life for the
narrator, and in that life lead him to truth.

The narrator's efforts to deal with the poem he has created
continue in the epilogue and remain inadequate, ambiguous,
and often comic.[15] After telling us that he has written what
he set out to write, the story of Troilus's love, and telling those
who wish to know more about the war to read "Dares," he
turns to the ladies in the audience and apologizes for having
written of an untrue woman, asking them not to blame him and
asserting that he would rather write of "Penelopeë's trouthe

and good Alceste." This is a decidedly comic and "for the nones" reaction. He knew the whole story when he chose to write it rather than Penelope's or Alceste's story. He continues his blind and "for the nones" response in the next stanza as he tells the ladies that he did not tell the story only for the advantage of men but mostly for women, who are betrayed by the "grete wit and subtilte" of man. Though this indeed must be part of any total moral of the tale, Pandarus and Troilus having betrayed with wit and subtlety Criseyde, it will not do to thus slight her equivalent betrayal of them. He seems no more able to face her betrayal now than he could face theirs then, though we might offer the mitigating excuse that he was himself transported by the ecstacy of love when they betrayed her and hence, like Criseyde, largely oblivious to it. No doubt the powerful ladies in his audience, ladies who he clearly fears may take offense, provide a mitigating excuse for his present unwillingness to face the facts equitably. Part of the reason for his unwillingness to face the truth, however, is that he, like Troilus, is still in love with Criseyde, or rather, with the image of her he created. Similarly, he is still identifying with Troilus, still seeing in a sense through the eyes of his hero. The result of this continued involvement is continued narrative confusion.

After two stanzas to bid fond farewell to his "litel bok," stanzas in which he addresses it as though it were a living, breathing thing, he suddenly returns to his narrative, and affirms that Troilus was "withouten any peere, save Hector," a motif we have heard before, and invariably with cause to doubt the objectivity of the speaker. He describes the death of Troilus, his ascension to the "holughnesse of the eighthe spere," and his subsequent rejection of the world as a vanity. He tells us that Troilus "dampned al oure werk that foloweth so/The blynde lust." Taking his cue from Troilus, he then himself adopts a *contemptus mundi* attitude and speaks condemningly in sharp tonal contrast to his "weilaway" four stanzas earlier when he was describing Troilus's death.

> Swich fyn hath, lo, this Troilus for love!
> Swich fyn hath al his grete worthynesse!
> Swich fyn hath his estat real above,
> Swich fyn his lust, swich fyn hath his noblesse!
> Swich fyn hath false worldes brotelnesse!

> And thus bigan his lovyng of Criseyde,
> As I have told, and in this wise he deyde.
>
> (V.1828–34)

Thus, like Troilus, he condemns this world, though without any of his laughter. While we are not surprised that in his pain and sorrow he should reject all as a vanity, the tone and the position of this outburst are suspect. It would make much better logical and emotional sense to react in this way after Troilus's death, but before he is translated to the heavens and himself learns once again to laugh. That is the location of the stanza in Boccaccio.[16] Though we do not know what "fyn" Troilus has—he ultimately goes where "Mercurye sorted hym to dwelle"—the fact that he is granted even such a reward as this final encompassing vision suggests that his "lovyng of Criseyde" has been something more than a vanity, though Troilus himself does not seem aware of it.

The narrator continues to imitate Troilus, though his Christian perspective allows him to be a little more precise in his recommended action. If Troilus condemns the world as a vanity "To respect of the pleyn felicite/ That is in hevene above" and recognizes that we "sholden al oure herte on heven caste," the narrator tells us to return "hom fro worldly vanyte" and directs us to Christ, who "nyl falsen no wight." At long last, he is securely back in the fourteenth century. Just as Troilus in the eighth sphere "gan despise/ This wrecched world," so the narrator rejects it and his poem depicting it:

> Lo here, of payens corsed olde rites,
> Lo here, what alle hire goddes may availle;
> Lo here, thise wrecched worldes appetites;
> Lo here, the fyn and guerdoun for travaille
> Of Jove, Appollo, of Mars, of swich rascaille!
> Lo here, the forme of olde clerkis speche
> In poetrie, if ye hire bokes seche!
>
> (V.1849–55)

Perhaps he ought not so totally to condemn all that, since it is his presentation of all that and his imitation of Troilus that have brought him home to Christ. It is his poem about Troilus that has been his guide, not Christ, through this false world to this truth, just as Criseyde has been Troilus's guide. The false leads finally to the true; the world's tragedy, to its comedy.

Though the end of the poem explicitly condemns such a love as Troilus experienced and such an activity as secular poetry, it implicitly affirms the very real value of the world and of poetry, though neither Troilus nor the narrator seems to be aware of its real value and can only see in it a negative lesson. The narrator ends his advice to "yonge, fresshe folkes" to reject the world and turn to Christ by asking a question only seemingly rhetorical: "What nedeth feynede loves for to seke?" Men need to seek "feynede loves" such as the poem has described and such as poetry is because, as the narrator himself earlier insisted, love is a "lawe of kynde." Pandarus is no doubt right when he asserts that there is an impulse to love in all people and that it can take one of two forms, love "celestial, or elles love of kynde," and the narrator is no doubt right that it is better to embrace love celestial. Pandarus is also right, however, in his faith that Criseyde will choose to love and cherish "a worthi knyght," however wrong he may be in asserting that it would not suit her "to ben celestial as yet." Young people will choose "love of knyde." One is reminded of Reason's efforts in the *Roman de la rose* to persuade the Lover to abandon his love of the rose by depicting old age, though full of suffering and remorse, as preferable to youth, a time of foolish delights.[17] Though no doubt Reason is right that it would be better for the Lover to skip his youth altogether and to embrace old age straightway, such expectations are contrary to the "law of kynde," if not to reason itself. As the authority on vanities, the Preacher says, "All things have their season, and in their times all things pass under the sun," including "a time to mourn and a time to dance."[18] Though it is nice to think that a tragedy depicting the folly inherent in worldly love will persuade young people to reject it, Chaucer no doubt was tolerant enough to live with the fact that it probably would not. Young men will seek "feynede loves," and, as Chaucer's poem demonstrates, will be led by that law of nature which turns man from God back to God. Indeed, for those like Troilus and the narrator at the beginning of the poem, those lost in the dark, the only way home to God is through such vanities as Criseyde and poetry. One must fall that one may rise.

When the narrator tells us to reject the world and love God "that after his ymage/Yow made," he unwittingly affirms the value of such worldly vanities as Criseyde and poetry—for all their falsity, they are images of God. When the narrator, at long last able to pray to the God of Love, prays to Him in the poem's final stanza, his prayer, paradoxically, returns us to the world.

> Thow oon, and two, and thre, eterne on lyve,
> That regnest ay in thre, and two, and oon,
> Uncircumscript, and al maist circumscrive,
> Us from visible and invisible foon
> Defende, and to thy mercy, everichon,
> So make us, Jesus, for thi mercy digne,
> For love of mayde and moder thyn benigne.
>
> (V.1863–69)

It ends not with God, but with Mary, that human in whom all human goodness is united. In appealing to Christ for mercy through that benign "mayde and moder" it reminds us that Christ did not scorn to take on human flesh, to love man even though man would and does betray him. In characterizing the circle of love which is God as circumscribing, it reminds us that part of what God's love creates and sustains with his binding, circumscribing love is this world, insuring that its vanity and its tragedy are a divine comedy not in vain. Thus, ironically and paradoxically, Chaucer makes the narrator's "for the nones" rejection of this world demonstrate that we cannot and ought not to reject it. The end of the poem simultaneously rejects the world to affirm God and sends us back into the world. Having led us to the truth and moved us by its tragedy to love that truth, the poem insists that we return from this joyous contemplation of truth to the world. Though Chaucer's epilogue rejects poetry, it also affirms his intention to write another poem, to make a comedy. After the poem forces us to learn the painful truth that God alone "nyl falsen no wight," it returns us to the world and our fellowman, in all their beauty and falsity, that we may love them with compassion as brothers, as Christ loves man. Through his poem, Chaucer seeks to teach us this true art of loving.

Chaucer does not, however, merely seek to teach us this true art of loving truly as an abstraction. Though he of necessity leaves his readers free, in a sense he seeks to ravish us out of our involvement with ourselves with his poem's beauty, with his "speche," that we may become involved in the poem's progress to this end and, thus, be able at the end to love more wisely. The narrator is our guide through the poem, one who, for better or worse, constantly orders our reactions to the poem, just as Troilus is the narrator's guide. Since the two follow much the same course, the narrator's efforts to inform our reactions reinforce our involvement with Troilus and his story. Our experience of reading the poem is thus parallel to the narrator's experience in writing it. We have seen that the narrator's experience in creating the poem, as Troilus's experience of loving Criseyde, must be viewed as forming two circles, a comic circle, which returns him at the end to a position above the poem from which he began, and a tragic circle, a movement from his own sorrow, in which he identifies with Troilus, upward to "wele, and after out of joie." For Chaucer, these two movements in particular characterize the motions of the soul as it journeys to God. The tragic circle within the mind is the motion of cupidity and irrationality, thought when it goes "from things corruptible to the Creator and back again to things corruptible."[19] This is the pattern of the poem's tragic progress, its movement from sorrow to the "wele" of "Benigne Love" darkly glimpsed in Book III back to things corruptible. The poem's central moment, the high point of its tragic movement, forms precisely this pattern for Troilus, the narrator, and the reader. It begins with the narrator describing Criseyde naked:

> Hire armes smale, hire streghte bak and softe,
> Hire sydes longe, flesshly, smothe, and white
> He gan to stroke, and good thrift bad ful ofte
> Hire snowisshe throte, hire brestes rounde and lite:
> Thus in this hevene he gan hym to delite,
> And therwithal a thousand tyme hire kiste,
> That what to don, for joie unnethe he wiste.
>
> (III.1247–53)

The narrator is clearly as pleased as Troilus with this heaven, as the reader must be, given the beauty of the poetry. We and the narrator then follow Troilus in his ascent in song to praise

"Benigne Love," an ascent which ends with Criseyde calling
Troilus and us back down by reminding him that she is lying
there naked.

> But lat us falle awey fro this matere,
> For it suffiseth, this that seyd is heere,
> And at o word, withouten repentaunce,
> Welcome, my knyght, my pees, my suffisaunce!
>
> (III.1306–9)

As if to insure our descent, the narrator then protests his inability to describe their joy and invites those of us "that han
ben at the feste/ Of swich gladnesse" (III.1312–13) to judge
whether "hem liste pleye!" The word "pleye" indicates what
joy he has in mind; the appeal to those who have been there
insures that we in our minds return our thoughts to that
"pleye." If the poem repeatedly moves us in this way, as it
returns us to things corruptible, it ultimately forces us to realize
with pain that things are corruptible, and thus forces our
thoughts ultimately toward that which is not corruptible, to
that which we glimpsed even in irrationality.

Ultimately, the poem moves our minds, as we follow its hero
and narrator, in rational motion, when "thought goes from the
Creator through the creatures to the Creator and there rests."[20]
This is the dominant pattern, for instance, of the third book,
with its opening proem to Venus and its praise of that love
which creates and sustains the universe near its end. It is also
the pattern of the whole poem. Though the narrator begins
unable to pray for himself, he does begin with his mind on the
Creator, asserting that he undertakes the work to advance his
soul and asking others to pray. He appeals to us on the basis
of our experience in love and asks us to pray to God for those
in some way less fortunate. Though his experience of writing
the poem and ours in reading it ensnare us for a time in the
poem's picture of this world, causing us to love it with not a
little of what Chaucer would have finally judged irrationality,
it does not rest there, but returns at its end to that love which
"nyl falsen no wight." Just as Chaucer dramatizes in the
Troilus both irrationality and rationality in his narrator, so he
seeks to move our minds. He seeks to "ravish" us into loving
the world he creates in the first three books, even though such

a love will inevitably involve us in patterns of irrational thought, for carnal man can only first be moved by manifestations of truth which appeal to his fallen nature, his irrationality. Once Chaucer has moved us to love such a false paradise, he reveals its falsity, trusting that that purgative process will cleanse us of our love of what was false in that paradise and turn us to the truth we saw mirrored there, however dimly. Thus, he seeks to restore in us that rational love which is for a medieval Christian not only man's source and end but his true nature as well.

Though Chaucer returns us at the end of the poem to the Creator and though his narrator seems content to rest there, the end, as we have seen, returns us to the world of the poem, hopefully wiser and prepared to see the order which led us to that end. The end of the poem does not merely send us back to the poem, however. It sends us back into the world properly ordered at least for a time. Chaucer, after all, presumably did not write his poem for future monks, but for such men of the world as made up his audience in London, Troynovant. In a sense, he created his poem as a retreat from the real world for them, a religious retreat on a mountain of contemplation from which they would have to return to the real world. Though such a return to the world inevitably involves one again in irrationality and cupidity, Chaucer no doubt hoped that the poem would strengthen that love which is rational in its readers.

If we are to understand Chaucer's poem we must see it as a progress in time and as a stable whole, a single image. Chaucer created it to be, like history, a moving image of eternity, of that love which created, redeemed, and returns all things to it. If we see in it the tragic circle of this world and of our own cupidity, we must also see that God's love encircles even that tragedy and cupidity and turns it to good. At the same time that Chaucer orders *Troilus and Criseyde* to make it a mirror of divine truth, he dramatizes through his narrator's inability to understand and love truly his own inevitable failure to understand and love perfectly the truth and his own inevitable failure perfectly to mirror that truth in his poem. If we look at the poem's structure as a consequence of the narrator, we see it as an almost accidental consequence of the narrator's failures, of his inability to control himself and his art. In making its order appear the consequence of the narrator's blunders, a result of chance, Chaucer is dramatically suggesting that any true value his poem may have must be attributed to God, "of whom," as Chaucer says in the retraction to the *Canterbury Tales*, "procedeth al wit and goodness." Though Chaucer created *Troilus and Criseyde* to be a sacramental revelation of God, through his dramatization of his narrator's limitations, he confesses his own limitations and his own conviction that if his poem does reveal God and move men to love Him, the credit for that must be given to God. In the end, the last of last analyses, for Chaucer, God is all in all. Men can only write poems which, if vivified by God, will move the lover of poetry to reject the music of poetry for heavenly harmony. Until that end, the poet returns to writing poetry.

Notes   Index

Notes

CHAPTER 1: THE DYNAMIC PRINCIPLE OF THE TROILUS

1. *Troilus and Criseyde*, in *The Works of Geoffrey Chaucer*, ed. F. N. Robinson, 2d ed. (Boston: Houghton Mifflin Co., 1957), I, 400–420. All quotations from Chaucer are from this edition.

2. D. W. Robertson, Jr., "Chaucerian Tragedy," *ELH*, 19 (1952), 1–37. See also his *Preface to Chaucer* (Princeton, N.J.: Princeton Univ. Press, 1962).

3. Ida L. Gordon, *The Double Sorrow of Troilus: A Study of Ambiguities in Troilus and Criseyde* (Oxford: Clarendon Press, 1970).

4. *Ibid.*, pp. 12–15.

5. Several critics have noted that the poem intentionally brings together the antithetical. See, especially, Sanford B. Meech, *Design in Chaucer's Troilus* (Syracuse Univ. Press, 1959); Charles Muscatine, *Chaucer and the French Tradition* (Berkeley and Los Angeles: Univ. of California Press, 1957), pp. 124–65; and Robert O. Payne, *The Key to Remembrance* (New Haven: Yale Univ. Press, 1963), pp. 171–216. This study is a product both of their pioneering work and of my conviction that they failed to grasp the real significance of Chaucer's use of contraries.

6. Robertson, *Preface to Chaucer*, especially the introductory chapter, pp. 1–35.

7. *Ibid.*, p. 26.

8. *De operibus sex dierum*, prol., *PL* CLXXXIX, 1515–16; quoted in M. D. Chenu, O.P., *Nature, Man, and Society in the Twelfth Century*, selected, ed., and trans., Jerome Taylor and Lester K. Little (Chicago and London: Univ. of Chicago Press, 1968), p. 9.

9. *The Consolation of Philosophy* III.pr.xii.30–39. Quotations from the *Consolation* are from Robinson's edition of Chaucer's translation. The obvious logic of using Chaucer's translation of the *Consolation* in a study of the *Troilus* is strengthened by the fact that the glosses incorporated into it from Nicholas Trivet derive in part from Guillaume de Conches and thus constitute one more link between Chaucer and the school of Chartres, the focal point of much of the background examined in this study. On the glosses of Conches and Trivet, see Charles Jourdain, "Des Commentaires inédits de Guillaume de Conches et de Nicholas Triveth sur la Consolation de la philosophie de Boèce," *Notices et extraits des manuscrits de la Bibliothèque Impériale*, 20, No. 2 (1862), 40–82. Influenced no doubt by Boethius, the Chartrians similarly use *concordia*

discors as evidence of God's existence. See J. M. Parent, O.P., *La Doctrine de la création dans l'école de Chartres* (Paris: Libr. Philosophique J. Vrin, 1938), pp. 31–34.

10. Arthur O. Lovejoy, *The Great Chain of Being* (Cambridge, Mass.: Harvard Univ. Press, 1936), pp. 45–66.

11. Most notably, Rosamund Tuve, "A Medieval Commonplace in Spenser's Cosmology," *SP*, 30 (1933), 33–47; and Earl R. Wasserman, *The Subtler Language* (Baltimore: Johns Hopkins Press, 1958), esp. pp. 35–168.

12. *Expans'd Hieroglyphicks: A Critical Edition of Sir John Denham's Cooper's Hill* (Berkeley and Los Angeles: Univ. of California Press, 1969), p. 171, n.10. Spitzer's monumental work was originally published in *Traditio: Studies in Ancient and Medieval History, Thought, and Religion*, 25 vols. (New York: Fordham Univ. Press, 1944–69), II, 409–64; III, 306–65.

13. The Platonic rationalism which was the dominant philosophy of the first half of the twelfth century has been traditionally associated with the school of Chartres, though it was much more broadly based. Indeed, there is considerable reason to doubt that the school at Chartres was the intellectual center of this school of thought. See R. W. Southern, "Humanism and the School of Chartres," *Medieval Humanism and Other Studies* (Oxford: Basil Blackwell, 1970), pp. 61–85. On the varieties of Platonism in the later Middle Ages, with particular reference to the twelfth century, see Chenu, *Man, Nature, and Society in the Twelfth Century*. For a discussion of the influence of medieval Platonism and particularly Platonic rationalism on the literature of the twelfth century, see Winthrop Wetherbee, *Platonism and Poetry in the Twelfth Century* (Princeton: Princeton Univ. Press, 1972). Anyone familiar with the work of Chenu and Wetherbee will recognize my substantial debt to these two studies.

14. There is no question but that Chaucer knew thoroughly the *Consolation*, the *Complaint*, and the *Roman*. The only concrete evidence that Chaucer knew the *Anticlaudian* is his reference to it in the *House of Fame* (lines 985–90), a reference indicating nothing more than an awareness that it describes the heavens, though Chaucer certainly implies familiarity with the work. On the question of whether or not Chaucer knew the whole of Macrobius's *Commentary* or just the *Dream of Scipio* itself, see Stahl's introduction to Macrobius, *Commentary on the Dream of Scipio*, trans. William H. Stahl (New York: Columbia Univ. Press, 1952), pp. 52–55; and J. A. W. Bennett, *The Parliament of Fowls* (Oxford: Clarendon Press, 1957), esp. pp. 30–61. Bennett demonstrates that Chaucer's account of the *Dream of Scipio* depends at times upon Macrobius's *Commentary*. Chaucer's parody of verses from the *Megacosmos*, the first half of the *Cosmographia*, in the *Man of Law's Tale* (lines 197–203) indicates some knowledge of this crucial work, though not necessarily at the time he wrote the *Troilus*. See Robinson's "Explanatory Notes," p. 693, note to lines 197 ff; and Chaucey Wood, *Chaucer and the Country of the Stars* (Princeton: Princeton Univ. Press, 1970), pp. 208–19.

15. Calcidius's translation with running commentary of Plato's

Timaeus extends only as far as 53C. See *Timaeus a Calcidio translatus commentarioque instructus*, ed. J. H. Waszink (London: Warburg Institute, 1962). My discussion of the *Timaeus* is sufficiently general to enable me to rely primarily upon F. M. Cornford's translation and commentary, *Plato's Cosmology* (New York: Harcourt, Brace and Co., 1937).

16. *Platonism and Poetry*, p. 29.

17. *De institutione arithmetica*, in *De institutione arithmetica; De institutione musica*, ed. Godofredus Friedlein (1867; rpt. Frankfurt: Minerva, 1966), II. xxvii. 129. See also Concord's description of herself in Alain de Lille's *Anticlaudian*, trans. William H. Cornog (Philadelphia, 1935), II.v.70–71.

18. The import for medieval allegories of love of the conception of the creation of macrocosm and microcosm as a sacred marriage has yet to be explored. Something of this import is suggested by Alain de Lille's characterization of Hymen as a harmony analogous to the harmony of Nature herself. See *The Complaint of Nature*, trans. Douglas M. Moffat (New York: Henry Holt and Co., 1908), *pr.* viii. 76–78; and Winthrop Wetherbee's discussion of the significance of Alain's characterization of Hymen, "The Function of Poetry in the *De planctu naturae* of Alain de Lille," *Traditio*, XXV, 110–11.

19. On the revival of interest in nature and human nature in the twelfth century, see Chenu, *Nature, Man, and Society in the Twelfth Century*; and Southern, "Medieval Humanism," *Medieval Humanism and Other Studies*, pp. 29–60.

20. See Wetherbee, *Platonism and Poetry*, pp. 34–35.

21. The idea that the universe is composed of contrary elements drawn together by love and torn asunder by hate would seem to derive ultimately from Empedocles. See Frederick Copleston, S.J., *A History of Philosophy* (Westminster, Md.: Newman Press, 1948), I, 62–64.

22. *Hexameron*, trans. John J. Savage, *Fathers of the Church*, XLII (New York: Cima Pub. Co., 1961), III.ix.xvii.81.

23. See, for instance, Isidore of Seville, *De natura rerum*, ed. Gustavus Becker (1857; rpt. Amsterdam: Adolf M. Hakhert, 1967), VII.iv.19.

24. *Commentary* I.vi.59–60.111–12.

25. Jean Seznec, *The Survival of the Pagan Gods*, trans. Barbara F. Sessions (New York: Pantheon Books, 1953), pp. 45–47.

26. Spitzer, *Traditio*, II, 431.

27. *Elucidarium*, I, ii, *PL* CLXXII, 1116; quoted in Chenu, *Nature, Man, and Society in the Twelfth Century*, p. 33, n.74.

28. See Rudolf Allers, "Microcosmus," *Traditio*, II, 345.

29. *De natura rerum* XI (*De partibus mundi*).ii–iii.24–25. The diagram is reproduced from a manuscript of *De natura rerum* now in the possession of the Bodleian Library, MS. Auct. F 3 14, fol. 7ᵛ.

30. *The Cosmographia of Bernardus Silvestris*, trans. Winthrop Wetherbee (New York and London: Columbia Univ. Press, 1973). The work was titled *De mundi universitate* by its modern editors, Barach and Wrobel, but *Cosmographia* is the title usually assigned to it in the manuscripts (*Cosmographia*, p. 130, n.9).

31. On the use of the idea of chaos at the school of Chartres, see
Parent, *La Doctrine de la création*, pp. 41–43. Guillaume de Conches, for
instance, affirms the existence of chaos *"ante mundi exornationem, non
ante creationem (Glosae super Platonem*, ed. Edouard Jeauneau [Paris:
Libr. Philosophique J. Vrin, 1965], clxxv–clxxvi, pp. 289–90). See also the
Anticlaudian I. v.56–57, where Nature is pictured as redeeming "ancient
chaos" and the "primeval tumult" by binding together contraries; and
Guillaume de Lorris and Jean de Meun, *Le Roman de la rose*, ed. Ernest
Langlois (Paris: Firmin-Didot and Co., 1922), IV.159.16729 ff. How
thoroughly commonplace the picture of creation as a two-stage process
in which God first created chaos and then ornamented or ordered it is, is
evident from its appearance in such a handbook of commonplaces as *De
proprietatibus rerum* of Bartholomaeus Anglicus. See the Renaissance
recension quoted by Tuve ("A Medieval Commonplace on Spenser's
Cosmology," pp. 135–36), *Batman upon Bartholome* (London, 1582), VIII,
and X.iii.
32. On the popularity of the heterodox concept of the World-Soul in
the twelfth century, see Wetherbee, *Platonism and Poetry*, pp. 28–35. On
the importance of speculation about the World-Soul on the formation of
twelfth-century concepts of Nature, that prima donna of allegorical abstraction in the literature we are examining, see Tullio Gregory, *Pla-
tonismo medievale: studi e ricerche* (Rome, 1958), pp. 135–50.
33. The contemporary understanding of the poem as some variety of
allegorical fable was initiated by Etienne Gilson, who denied its literal
paganism by interpreting it allegorically, equating Noys with the Word
and the World-Soul with the Holy Spirit. See "La Cosmogonie de
Bernardus Silvestris," *Archives d'histoire doctrinale et littéraire du moyen
âge*, III (1928), 5–24. Silverstein and Wetherbee, who follow Silverstein
generally in this regard, both stress the fable more than the allegory,
reading the poem neither literally nor as a consistent allegory but as a
tertium quid, a fabulous representation of creation intended to metaphorically suggest rather than assert truth. See Theodore Silverstein, "The
Fabulous Cosmogony of Bernardus Silvestris," *MP*, 46 (1948–49), 92–116;
and Wetherbee, *Platonism and Poetry*, esp. pp. 158–186, as well as the
introduction to Wetherbee's translation.
34. See, for instance, John Gower, *Confessio Amantis, The Complete
Works of John Gower*, ed. G. C. Macaulay, II (Oxford: Clarendon Press,
1901), 31–32, *Prologus*, 971 ff.; and the *Roman de la rose* IV.169.16975 ff.
35. On the pervasive ambiguity in Bernardus's representation of the
nature and destiny of man, see the *Cosmographia*, pp. 45–55.
36. The description of the goddess Nature here summarized occurs in
pr.i of *The Complaint*, pp. 5–17.
37. See Spitzer, "Classical and Christian Concepts of World Harmony,"
Traditio, III, 307 ff.
38. For Nature's long and digressive complaint in the *Roman*, see *Le
Roman de la rose* IV.140.16285 ff. She does not actually get around to explicitly indicting man until lines 19021 ff.
39. On the virtues and vices of trees rooted in *caritas* and *cupiditas*

respectively, see Chenu, *Nature, Man, and Society in the Twelfth Century*, p. 113.

40. *The Allegory of Love* (Oxford: Clarendon Press, 1936), p. 73.

41. *Psychomachia, Prudentius*, trans. H. J. Thomson (Cambridge, Mass. and London: Loeb Classical Library, 1949), I, 343.

42. *Commentary* I.xi.10.132. There is also account of the cycle of the soul in the *Timaeus* 41D–42D.

43. *Commentary* I.xi.11–12.132–33.

44. *Ibid.*, xii.14.136–37.

45. Man's return to the Creator through the created is both the theme of their own works and the theme the Chartrians, with the help of varying degrees of allegorical exegesis, discovered in Virgil's *Aeneid*, Martianus Capella's *Marriage of Philology and Mercury*, and Boethius's *Consolation*. See Wetherbee, *Platonism and Poetry*, pp. 104–25.

46. On Bernardus's conception of these *Genii*, see the *Cosmographia*, pp. 44–55; p. 140, n.155; and p. 157, n.9.

47. On the restoration of man as a regaining of Eden and the natural justice which characterized prelapsarian man in the *Divine Comedy*, see Charles S. Singleton, *Dante Studies* (Cambridge, Mass.: Harvard Univ. Press, 1958), Vol. II, *Journey to Beatrice*, esp. pp. 57–69.

48. *The City of God*, trans. Marcus Dods (New York: The Modern Library, 1950), XI.ii.346–47.

49. See the *Complaint of Nature*, pr. ix.91–92; and, for explication, Wetherbee, *Traditio*, XXV, 114 ff.

50. On the personification of Nature in the literature we are examining, see George D. Economou, *The Goddess Natura in Medieval Literature* (Cambridge, Mass.: Harvard Univ. Press, 1972).

51. On the relationship of Nature to the World-Soul in Chartrian thought and literature, see n. 31 above. Hugh of St. Victor identifies the "archetypal Exemplar of all things which exist in the divine Mind" as one definition "men of former times" attributed to the term "nature." See Hugh of St. Victor, *Didascalicon*, trans. Jerome Taylor (New York: Columbia Univ. Press, 1961), I.x.57. For numerous references to these "men of former times," see Taylor's notes to Book I, esp. pp. 192–93, n. 69.

52. On the association of Nature with the superlunary world, especially by the astronomers, and its intermediary function as a link between ideas and matter in macrocosm and microcosm, see Economou, *The Goddess Natura*, esp. pp. 64–66. On the historically important characterization of Nature as such an intermediary link in Calcidius, see *The Goddess Natura*, pp. 20–21.

53. On his inability to describe her, see the *Roman* IV.135.16165 ff. On Nature as chambermaid, a term she applies to herself, at the same time that Jean implies Nature's affinity to the World-Soul, see the *Roman* IV.162.16785 ff.

54. Chaucer would seem to be dealing with the issue of Nature's limitations as former and reformer of man in Fragment VI of the *Canterbury Tales*, where he juxtaposes Virginia as Nature's paragon and the malformed Pardoner.

55. Alain's doubts about the power of love to reform men are evident in his treatment of Venus. Drawing upon the tradition that there are two Venuses—a Venus *caelestis* who signifies harmony and natural justice and a Venus *scelestis* who is the mother of lechery and fornication—he unites the two figures in a single Venus and pictures her as formerly a source of harmony but now one of discord, since she has fallen and deserted Hymen for Antigamus. See Economou, *The Goddess Natura*, pp. 85–87.

56. The history of the association of rationality and irrationality in man with the contrary movements of the heavenly spheres has been extensively documented by A. B. Chambers, "Goodfriday, 1613. Riding Westward: The Poem and the Tradition," *JEGP*, 28 (1961), 31–53; and John Freccero, "Dante's Pilgrim in a Gyre," *PMLA*, 76 (1961), 168–81. See also Wood, *Chaucer and the Country of the Stars*, pp. 231–34. To their citations should be added *Anulfi Aurelianensis glosule super Lucanum*, ed. Berthe M. Marti (Rome: American Academy, 1958), IX.iv.40–55.432.

57. *Timaeus* 36B–36D.

58. *Ibid.*, 44D.

59. One finds the two interrelated ideas—the myth of the cosmic cycle of the soul and the motions of rationality and irrationality in macrocosm and microcosm—presented as a single whole in *Anulfi Aurelianensis glosule super Lucanum*, IX.iv.431–33.

60. Lynn Thorndike, *The Sphere of Sacrobosco and its Commentators* (Chicago: Univ. of Chicago Press, 1949), p. 1.

61. *Ibid.*, p. 123.

62. *De caelo* II.iii.286a.

63. *Ibid.*, 286a–b; *De generatione at corruptione* II.iii.4.

64. This passage is quoted in the commentary on *The Sphere of Sacrobosco* attributed to Michael Scot as a description of the circle of the firmament of reason (*The Sphere of Sacrobosco*, p. 303). Though Boethius never makes the parallel between the two motions of the World-Soul and those of the human soul explicit, his picture of the contrary motions of the World-Soul in the ninth meter of the third book was understood as descriptive of the human soul (Freccero, "Dante's Pilgrim in a Gyre," pp. 174–75). Boethius's description (V.*pr.* ii.26–43) of how the human soul gradually loses its freedom by becoming ensnared in thoughts of earthy things draws upon the myth of the cycle of the soul and upon the theory of the two heavenly motions.

65. On the ascent of pride and the descent of humility, see D. C. Allen, "Milton and the Descent to Light," *JEGP*, 55 (1961), 614–30.

66. On Christ's three advents, see Singleton, *Dante Studies, II*, 72–84.

67. *The Confessions of St. Augustine*, trans. E. B. Pusey (London: Thomas Nelson and Sons, n.d.), p. 72.

68. *The City of God* XII.ii.382.

69. *Ibid.* iii.382. One finds essentially the same argument in Dionysius the Areopagite, *The Divine Names*, trans. the Editors of the Shrine of Wisdom (Surry, 1957), p. 43. See also Augustine's *Faith, Hope, and Charity*, trans., Bernard M. Peebles, *Fathers of the Church*, IV (New York: Cima Pub. Co., 1947), IV.xiv.379.

70. *The City of God* XI.xxxiii.378.

71. *Ibid.*, XIV.xiii.461.

72. That the theatre with its temples is intended to characterize the microcosm, as well as the macrocosm, is most evident in Chaucer's presentation of Theseus, who begins the poem serving Mars and Venus but has become by the second book a servant of Diana.

73. For an interpretation of Saturn as beneficent, one for which there is ample precedent but little evidence in poem in my judgment, see P. M. Kean, *The Art of Narrative, Chaucer and the History of English Poetry*, (London and Boston: Routledge and Kegan Paul, 1972), II, 28–34.

74. On the blindness of Theseus's speech on necessity, and his failure to recognize his own freedom and responsibility, both of which the poem recognizes, see Dale Underwood, "The First of the *Canterbury Tales*," *ELH*, 26 (1959), 455–69.

75. On the marriage as a union of opposites and a comic ascent to the "thyng that parfit is and stable," see P. M. Kean, *The Art of Narrative*, pp. 49–52.

76. Copleston, *A History of Philosophy*, I, 34.

77. *Commentary* I.v.3.95.

78. *Timaeus* 32B–C. For Plato, the number four is not necessary to create the world, but four numbers in geometrical progression (see Cornford, *Plato's Cosmology*, pp. 43–52). The harmony of the world is in the geometrical progression of its four numbers. Macrobius also transmits some of this to the medieval world. See the *Commentary* I.vi.24–28.104–5.

79. *The Mind's Road to God*, trans. George Boas (New York: Liberal Arts Press, 1953), II.x.20. I have slightly altered Boas's translation, translating *numerosa* as "full of numbers" rather than as "rhythmical." See also Boethius, *De institutione arithmetica* I.ii: *Omnia quaecumque a primaeva rerum natura constructa sunt, numerorum videntur ratione formata. Hoc enim fuit principale in animo conditoris exemplar;* and Alain de Lille, *Anticlaudian* III.iv.84–86, where much that I am endeavoring to explain here lies compacted.

80. *Commentary* I.vi.7–9.100–101.

81. See Spitzer, *Traditio*, II, 432 ff.

82. On the numbers of music and poetry as Augustine treats them, see *On Music*, trans. Robert Catesby Taliaferro, *Fathers of the Church*, II (New York: Cima Pub. Co., 1947). On the whole tradition, see Spitzer, "Classical and Christian Ideas of World Harmony."

83. *De Institutione Musica* I.ii.187–88: "*Et primum ea, quae est mundana, in his maxime, perspicienda est, quae in ipso caelo vel compage elementorum vel temporum varietate visuntur. Qui enim fieri potest, ut tam velox caeli machina tacito silentique cursu moveatur? . . . Iam vero quattuor elementorum diversitates contrariasque potentias nisi quaedam armonia coniungeret, qui fieri posset, ut in unum corpus ac machinam convenirent? Sed haec omnis diversitas ita et temporum varietatem parit et fructuum, ut tamen unum anni corpur efficiat.*" See also Alain de Lille, *Anticlaudian* III.v.87–88.

84. *De Institutione Musica* I.ii.188–89: "*Humanam vero musicam quisquis in sese ipsum descendit intellegit. Quid est enim quod illam*

incorpoream rationis vivacitatem corpori misceat, nisi quaedam coaptatio et veluti gravium leviumque vocum quasi unam consonantiam efficiens temperatio?"

85. *Didascalicon* II.xii.69.

86. *Ibid.*

87. *Ibid.*

88. *Ibid.*

89. See Spitzer, *Traditio*, II, 440 ff.

90. *Liber xii quaest.*, ii, *PL* CLXXII, 1179; quoted in Chenu, *Nature, Man, and Society in the Twelfth Century*, p. 8.

91. See especially the sixth book of *De Musica*.

92. *Commentary* II.i.2.185.

93. *The City of God*. XI.xviii.361–62.

94. See the *Troilus* I.400–420, I.624–51, I.946–52, III. 1744–71.

95. Meech, *Design in Chaucer's Troilus*, pp. 15–19.

96. Muscatine, *Chaucer and the French Tradition*, pp. 133–61; Meech, *Design in Chaucer's Troilus*, esp. chap. 3; Payne, *The Key of Remembrance*, pp. 197 ff.

97. Muscatine, *Chaucer and the French Tradition*, p. 133.

98. *Ibid.*, pp. 133 ff.

99. Payne, *The Key of Remembrance*, p. 187; Muscatine, *Chaucer and the French Tradition*, p. 135.

100. Payne, *The Key of Remembrance*, p. 197.

101. Though Pandarus uses nearly as many proverbs when talking with Criseyde as he does with Troilus, his "sententious remarks" are directed almost exclusively to Troilus. See B. J. Whiting, *Chaucer's Use of Proverbs* (Cambridge, Mass.: Harvard Univ. Press, 1934), pp. 55–61.

102. Robertson, "Chaucerian Tragedy," p. 18.

103. Muscatine, *Chaucer and the French Tradition*, p. 158.

104. Payne notes that even when Criseyde is alone and begins to use a style like Troilus, Chaucer invariably ends up externalizing her feelings, rather than letting her express them directly (*The Key of Remembrance*, pp. 199–200).

105. Muscatine, *Chaucer and the French Tradition*, pp. 148–53.

CHAPTER 2: PSYCHOLOGICAL AND SACRAMENTAL CHARACTERIZATION

1. A useful "sample" of critical opinions about the three major characters can be found in Meech, *Design in Chaucer's Troilus*: Criseyde, pp. 395–97; Troilus, pp. 402–4; Pandarus, pp. 412–14. I have not sought to document the critical origin of most of the commonplaces reiterated here about Chaucer's characters, trusting that the reader will recognize how virtually impossible that is and that I do not claim them as my own. I stand in this chapter particularly on the shoulders of many of my critical betters, without, I fear, adequately thanking them in the notes.

2. Robertson, for whom Troilus is another Adam and Criseyde another Eve, is a notable exception to the predominant fashion of understanding

them literally, though he sees nothing transcendent in Criseyde. See "Chaucerian Tragedy," and the *Preface to Chaucer*, 475–503.

3. Though the idea is a medieval commonplace, the phraseology here employed to express it is borrowed of course from St. Augustine, *On Christian Doctrine*, trans. D. W. Robertson (Indianapolis and New York: Bobbs-Merrill Co., Inc., 1958).

4. For a judicious appreciation of the importance of both the literal and the symbolic with reference to the "Pardoner's Tale," see Alfred David, "Criticism and the Old Man in Chaucer's *Pardoner's Tale*," CE, 27 (1965), 39–44.

5. On the importance of the literal-historical level as the foundation of the allegorical, see Henri De Lubac, *Exégèse médiéval* (Paris: Aubier, 1959), II, 426–87. For evidence of the increasing awareness in the later Middle Ages of the importance of history and the inseparability of allegory from it, see Beryl Smalley, *The Study of the Bible in the Middle Ages* (Oxford: Basil Blackwell, 1952), especially the chapters on Hugh of St. Victor and his followers (chaps. 3 and 4) and her discussion of how the study of Aristotle altered the conception of the relationship of the literal and allegorical, pp. 292–308. See also the chapters on "Allegory" and "Symbolism" and especially the "Appendix: The Two Kinds of Allegory" in Charles Singleton, *Dante Studies* (Cambridge, Mass: Harvard Univ. Press, 1954), Vol. I, *Commedia: Elements of Structure*.

6. Singleton, *Dante Studies*, I, 89–90.

7. M. D. Chenu, *Nature, Man, and Society in the Twelfth Century*, pp. 123 ff. The following distinction between an Augustinian sign and a Dionysian symbol is indebted to Chenu.

8. Dionysius the Areopagite, *The Divine Names*, p. 21.

9. Chenu, *Nature, Man, and Society in the Twelfth Century*, p. 133.

10. Dionysius the Areopagite, *The Divine Names*, p. 77. See also Chenu, *Nature, Man, and Society in the Twelfth Century*, pp. 131 ff.

11. *In apocalypsim Libri Septem*, i, PL CXCVI, 689; quoted by Chenu, *Nature, Man, and Society in the Twelfth Century*, p. 140, n.77.

12. Chenu, *Nature, Man, and Society in the Twelfth Century*, p. 132. Robertson argues that the distortion common in medieval narrative serves a similar function: "The incoherence of the surface materials is almost essential to the formation of the abstract pattern, for if the surface materials—the concrete elements in the figures—were consistent or spontaneously satisfying in an emotional way, there would be no stimulus to seek something beyond them" (*Preface to Chaucer*, p. 56).

13. *The Ecclesiastical Hierarchy* is basically an explication of the symbolic revelations of God in the sacraments. The sensible symbols are a principal means by which God's grace illuminates the initiate; one contemplates "through" the visible symbol the Invisible of which it is an illumination. Hugh of St. Victor defines a sacrament as "a corporeal or material element set before the senses without, representing by similitude and signifying by institution and containing by sanctification some invisible and spiritual grace." On the necessity of the similitude, he observes that "every sacrament ought to have a kind of similitude to the

thing itself of which it is the sacrament, according to which it is capable of representing the same thing." See *On the Sacraments of the Christian Faith,* trans. Roy J. Defarrari (Cambridge, Mass: The Medieval Academy of America, 1951), I.ix.2.155.

14. See, for instance, *The Divine Names,* chap. 1; and Dom Denys Rutledge, *Cosmic Theology: The Ecclesiastical Hierarchy of Pseudo-Denys: An Introduction* (London: Routledge and Kegan Paul, 1964), pp. 47–59.

15. The comparison begins at line 20279, *Roman de la rose* V. 47–59.

16. Lewis, *The Allegory of Love,* pp. 151–53.

17. *Roman de la rose* IV. 217.18135 ff.

18. *Ibid.,* 174.17101 ff.

19. *Ibid.,* 252.19021 ff.

20. *Ibid.,* 254.19055 ff.

21. Helen F. Dunbar, *Symbolism in Medieval Thought* (1929; rpt. New York: Russell and Russell, 1961), pp. 278–80; Lewis, *The Allegory of Love,* pp. 44 ff.

22. On the differing conceptions of how the world reveals God and the consequent differing evaluations of the worth of poetry among the Chartrians and the Victorines, see Wetherbee, *Traditio,* XXV, 91–99; and *Platonism and Poetry,* pp. 11–73.

23. *Roman de la rose* IV.123.15891 ff.

24. For the term *heterocosmos,* see M. H. Abrams, *The Mirror and the Lamp* (1953; rpt. New York: W. W. Norton & Co., Inc., 1958), pp. 272–85.

25. Robertson, *Preface to Chaucer,* p. 56.

26. St. Gregory, *Super Cantica Canticorum Expositio, PL* LXXIX, 471–73. The enigma suggests (*insinuat*) the love which the frigid soul does not know since it is fallen.

27. Dionysius the Areopagite, *The Divine Names,* p. 10.

28. For a discussion of Bernard's conception of carnal love and its function in the ascent to God, see Pierre Pourrat, *Christian Spirituality in the Middle Ages* (Westminster, Md.: The Newman Press, 1953), II, 30–33.

29. *Life and Works of St. Bernard,* ed. John Mabillon, Vol. IV, *Sermons on the Canticles,* trans. and ed. Samuel J. Eales (London, 1896), Sermon xx on Cant. vi.113: "I consider that a principal cause why God, who is invisible, willed to render Himself visible in the Flesh, and to dwell as a Man among men, was to draw, in the first place, to the salutary love of His sacred Flesh all the affections of carnal man who were unable to love otherwise than in a carnal manner, and so by degrees to draw them to a pure and spiritual affection."

30. See for instance, Macrobius, *Commentary* I.vi.1–3.99 and Alain de Lille, *Anticlaudian* III.iv.85.

31. The most sustained insistence upon Troilus's heroic manhood is found in Thomas A. Kirby, *Chaucer's "Troilus": A Study in Courtly Love* (Baton Rouge: Louisiana State Univ. Press, 1940). For an interpretation of Troilus's behavior as effeminate as a consequence of his submission of reason to passion, see Robertson *Preface to Chaucer,* p. 488.

32. Numerous critics have noted in the characterization of Troilus and

Criseyde a rather unconventional analysis of male and female. See, for instance, Robert E. Kaske, "The Aube in Chaucer's *Troilus*," in *Chaucer Criticism*, ed. Richard J. Schoeck and Jerome Taylor (Notre Dame: Notre Dame Univ. Press, 1961), II, 171 ff.

33. St. Bonaventure, *The Mind's Road to God*, pp. xvi–xix. See also, for instance, Denys Rutledge, *Cosmic Theology*, pp. 68 ff.

34. Ernest H. Wilkins, "Canticus Troili," *ELH*, 12 (1949), 169–70. Wilkins includes *S'amor non è* and discusses the significant variants.

35. *The Complaint of Nature*, m.v.46–48; *Roman de la rose* II.212.4293 ff. The passage in the *Roman* is based upon that in the *Complaint*.

36. See *The Complaint of Nature*, pr.v.54–57.

37. *The City of God* XIV.xxviii.477.

38. Chenu, *Nature, Man, and Society in the Twelfth Century*, p. 136.

39. For the great fire on the seventh circle of Purgatory, see the *Purgatorio*, cantos xxv–xxvii. Canto xxvii ends with Virgil's declaration that Dante's will is now a sufficient guide to right action. Having but little medieval Italian, I have used the edition by John D. Sinclair, with an English translation facing the Italian text: *The Divine Comedy of Dante Alighieri*, 3 vols. (New York: Oxford Univ. Press, 1939).

40. See Alfred David's observation that "Troilus's first sorrow may be viewed as a type of penitential suffering, and perhaps it was with this idea in mind that Chaucer modeled the first line of Book II on the grand opening of the *Purgatorio* ("The Hero of the *Troilus*," p. 572).

41. Though Ida Gordon allows that Troilus is more "gentil" than Diomede according to the code of courtly love, she sees little essential difference (*The Double Sorrow of Troilus*, pp. 123–24).

42. John Spiers states what is now, perhaps, the consensus view when he terms Diomede "an inferior and degraded replica" of Troilus (*Chaucer, The Maker* [London: Faber and Faber, 1951], p. 79).

43. Richard Green, "Alan of Lille's *De planctu naturae*," p. 661, n.24.

44. As a literary form the *débat* or *conflictus* is ideally suited to the presentation of contraries in conflict. There are numerous medieval debates in which personified abstractions representing various of the great opposites in life (Summer and Winter, Youth and Old Age, Body and Soul, Winner and Waster) debate, and where the main point is, as often as not, that both are a part of the total scheme of things. Chaucer's companion poems "The Complaint of Venus" and "The Complaint of Mars" could profitably be analyzed from this perspective.

45. We should perhaps note that in the *Complaint of Nature* the goddess Nature explains that she, unlike theology, attains "faith by reason," knowing that she may believe (*pr.iii.30*). So it is with Criseyde, who, as we shall see, represents nature.

46. That Criseyde is closely associated with fortune and nature has, of course, been suggested before. See, for instance, Muscatine's observation that "Criseyde's ambiguity is as the world's" (*Chaucer and the French Tradition*, p. 165).

47. Though Christianity denied that primordial matter existed prior to creation, it employed frequently a "two stage" creation: First God created

the *hyle*, chaotic matter, potentiality; then he ornamented and ordered it to create the universe in which we live. See Silverstein, "The Fabulous Cosmogony of Bernardus Silvestris," pp. 98–102. It is perhaps worth noting that in their treatment of the two opposed principles from which the world was formed according to the *Timaeus*, the Chartrian Platonists identified "the same" with God, *unitas*, and "the different," *diversitas*, with the *hyle*, and derive the diverse from the same. Silverstein points out that Thierry of Chartres, following Chalcidius, uses *unitas* and *binarius* for the *idem* and *diversum* of the *Timaeus* precisely because such a numerical metaphor indicates the dependence of the *Hyle* on God, two deriving from one (The Fabulous Cosmogony of Bernardus Silvestris," pp. 101–3). Criseyde's duality similarly characterizes *hyle*, it seems to me, whether or not Chaucer knew Chalcidius's *Commentary* or *De operibus sex dierum.*

48. Muscatine, *Chaucer and the French Tradition*, p. 138–39.

49. *Ibid.*, p. 140.

50. The phraseology comes from Winthrop Wetherbee, whose interpretation of Genius I follow ("The Function of Poetry in the *De planctu naturae* of Alain de Lille," p. 112). See also, Wetherbee, *Platonism and Poetry*, esp. pp. 181–85, 202–10, and his discussion of *ingenium*, pp. 94–98; and *Cosmographia*, pp. 56–57. See also Lewis, *The Allegory of Love*, pp. 36–63; and "Genius and Genius," *RES*, 12 (1936), 189–94; and Robertson, *Preface to Chaucer*, p. 199, and n.101.

51. *Roman de la rose* III.23.6928 ff.

52. *Poetria nova*, trans. Margaret F. Nims (Toronto: Pontifical Institute of Medieval Studies, 1967) I.43.16–17. Geoffrey stresses the need to construct the matter in the mind before clothing it in words.

CHAPTER 3: THE MARRIAGE OF HEAVEN AND HELL

1. On the intimations of the Holy Spirit in these lines, see Robert K. Root, *The Book of Troilus and Criseyde* (Princeton, N.J.: Princeton Univ. Press, 1926), p. 464, note to lines 15–17. See, for an example, the second selection from Guillaume de Conches' commentary on the *Consolation*, "De L'âme du monde et de l'âme humaine," in Charles Jourdain, "Des Commentaires inédits de Guillaume de Conches et de Nicholas Triveth sur la Consolation de la philosophie de Boèce." p. 75. Commenting on Boethius's picture of the World-Soul in *m*.ix of Book III, Guillaume similarly characterizes its vivifying power and equates it with the Holy Spirit, *"divina et benigna concordia."*

2. See Robertson, *Preface to Chaucer*, pp 124–27.

3. Bernardus Silvestris, *Commentum super sex libros Eneidos Virgilli*, ed. Guillelmus Riedel (Griefswald: J. Abel, 1924), I, 9.

4. For the genealogy of Aeneas, Cupid, and Jocus according to Bernardus, see *Commentum super sex libros Eneidos Vergilli*, I, 10: *"Ubi ergo invenies Venerem uxorem Vulcani matrem Ioci et Cupidinis, intellige voluptatem carnis, quia naturali calori iuncta est et iocum et cohitum parit. Ubi vero legeris Venerem et Anchisem Eneam filium habere,*

intelligere per Venerem mundana musicam, per Eneam humanum spiritum."

5. Richard Green, "Alan of Lille's *De planctu naturae,*" *Speculum,* 31 (1956), 667–72; Economou, *The Goddess Natura,* pp. 85–87.

6. On Venus in the *Complaint,* see *pr.* v, esp. pp. 54–57. On Hymen as the sacrament of marriage, see Wetherbee, *Traditio,* XXV, 110.

7. For Troilo's song, see *Il Filostrato* III.74–89; Chaucer borrows only from stanzas 74–79. As Root as pointed out, Troilo's song is itself indebted to the *Consolation* II.*m.*8 (*The Book of Troilus and Criseyde,* p. 465, notes to lines 1–38).

8. F. N. Robinson, "Explanatory Notes," *The Works of Geoffrey Chaucer,* p. 822, note to III.1–49.

9. Concerning the effect of Venus upon Mars, Root (*The Book of Troilus and Criseyde,* p. 465, note to line 22) succinctly observes that "philosophically, Love, as the spirit of unity (cf. 3.29), appeases the wrath of War; astrologically Venus, as benefic planet, mitigates the malefic influence of Mars (see *Complaint of Mars* 36–42); mythologically, Mars became the Lover of the goddess Venus (cf. 3.725)."

10. For a survey of the variety of medieval conceptions of *Natura* and her functions among the allegorical poets of interest for this study, see Economou, *The Goddess Natura.*

11. For Bernardus's conception of nature, see Tullio Gregory, *Anima Mundi: La filosofia di Gulielmo di Conches et la Scuola di Chartres* (Florence: G. C. Sansoni, 1955), pp. 187 ff; Economou, pp. 63–72.

12. *Roman de la rose* IV.169.16955–74.

13. For the image of Fortune's "double visage" see Boethius, *Consolation* II.*pr.*i.57–61.

14. See *The City of God* VII.vii–x.214–18. The association of Janus with the beginning and end of things makes him the perfect figure to invoke as we enter the natural world of Book II and meet Criseyde, herself a symbol of nature, for the order of nature according to Boethius is an order which joins "the endynge to the bygynnynge." See the *Consolation* III.*m.*ii.

15. The best study of light imagery and metaphysics is contained in Joseph Mazzeo's *Medieval Cultural Tradition in Dante's Comedy.* (Ithaca, N.Y.: Cornell Univ. Press, 1960), pp. 56–132.

16. *The City of God* X.ii.305–6.

17. *The City of God* VIII.iii.246. Augustine's particular use of the term nature here suggests the possibility that he was one of the "men of former times" Hugh of St. Victor identifies as associating nature with the divine mind.

18. *Medieval Cultural Tradition in Dante's Comedy,* pp. 58–59. See *The Republic* 508B,C; 509B.

19. *Medieval Cultural Tradition in Dante's Comedy,* p. 60. See Augustine, *Soliloquia* I.i.3, *PL* XXXII, 870.

20. On the influence of Pseudo-Dionysius on Dante, see Gardner, *Dante and the Mystics* (1913; rpt. New York: Octagon Books, Inc., 1968), pp. 77–110.

21. *Divine Names,* IV, 30.

22. On the universe of Dionysius as a hierarchy of light, see Rutledge, *Cosmic Theology*, pp. 11 ff.

23. *Divine Names*, I, 14.

24. For Dionysius the universe would seem to be the consequence both of the outpouring of light from the Light and the desire of the things that are to participate in that Light. See Ronald F. Hathaway, *Hierarchy and the Definition of Order in the Letters of Pseudo-Dionysius* (The Hague: Martinus Highoff, 1969), pp. 51–60.

25. *Inferno* xi.46–51.146.

26. See *Il Filostrato* III.21–52.246–62.

27. Griffin translates stanza 21 of Part III (*donde fessi Criseida a chiamar Pandaro, e monstrato Tutto gliet' ha*) as though the initiative were Pandaro's. The context makes it clear that it is Criseida who summons Pandaro. It would make no sense for Pandaro to arrange a meeting at a time when Troilo is absent nor does it make sense for Boccaccio to characterize Pandaro as concerned about Troilo's absence unless Criseida has suggested that now is the time.

28. On the rain as an intervention by God to bring the two together, but one which in no way causes Criseyde's "surrender," see Robert P. apRoberts, "The Central Episodes in Chaucer's *Troilus*," *PMLA*, 77 (1962), 378–80. The same thing can be said of Chaucer's version ("The Legend of Dido") of the Dido and Aeneas cave episode.

29. Unlike Boccaccio's Criseida, who herself insures the consummation of her affair with Troilo, Chaucer's Criseyde yields to the circumstances. Though she may have believed Troilus would be at Pandarus's house, there is no evidence she went there expressly for what transpired, as Robert apRoberts demonstrates ("The Central Episode in Chaucer's *Troilus*," pp. 377–82.)

30. Criseyde's argument comes from the *Consolation* II.pr.iv.118 ff.

31. For an explication of many of the ironies and incongruities in the aubes, see R. E. Kaske, "The Aube in Chaucer's *Troilus*," in *Chaucer Criticism*, ed. Schoeck and Taylor (Notre Dame: Notre Dame Univ. Press, 1961), II, 167–79. Though Kaske sees ironic reference to the future in Criseyde's excessive protestation of her love, he does not comment on the significance of the fact that she addresses the night, Troilus the day.

32. Friend's predilection for deception is evident throughout his advice to the Lover. See, for instance, his insistence that it is a good deed to deceive the deceitful and trick the tricky (*Roman de la rose* III.39.7342–54). For the god of Love's dislike of False Seeming, see *Roman de la rose* III.162–63.10475–92. For his acceptance of him, see III.179.10919 ff.

33. See the *Roman* III.261–62.5535–54.

34. Charles R. Dahlberg, "Love and the *Roman de la rose*," *Speculum*, 44 (1969), 576–77, Dahlberg is commenting upon one of St. Bernard's sermons, *Sermo X de diversis*, 2–4, PL CLXXXIII, 568–69.

35. *Complaint of Nature*, pr.iii.24–25.

36. *Paradiso*, xxxiii.19–21.478.

37. Though this is a commonplace, it is one too often forgotten by many recent critics. If nothing else, Chaucer's familiarity with the *Consolation* would have prevented him from forgetting it, for the *Consolation*

repeatedly insists upon the goodness of creation and of nature, even human nature, which naturally desires the good. See, for instance, III.*pr*.xii.355–57, for the goodness of all nature; and III.*m*.ix.1–11, for creation as a consequence of God's goodness. Like much of the *Consolation*, these parts are heavily Platonic and having nothing to say about man's corrupted will. Most of the time in the *Consolation* the problem is not considered man's fallen will, but his body and the things of the world which blind him and prevent him from loving that which it is natural for his soul to love, the good.

38. Peter Dronke, "The Conclusion of Troilus and Criseyde," *MAE*, 23 (1964), 50–51.

39. *The Consolation* II.*m*.viii.25–26. This *metrum* ends with a prayer that the same love might rule men's hearts as rules the universe, uniting its contraries in harmony. Book III of the *Troilus* is, in a sense, Chaucer's picture of how far the love that harmonizes the universe can harmonize men's hearts and unite them in a harmony where nature is the only guide.

40. David, "The Hero of the *Troilus*," p. 574.

41. *Complaint of Nature, pr.* iv.43.

42. *Alain of Lille, Anticlaudian* I.v.56.

43. For the symbolism of the kiss in St. Bernard, see *Life and Works of St. Bernard*, Vol. IV, esp. Sermon viii, pp. 38–43. For a discussion of the nature of the union of the soul and God signified in the kiss as a harmony of two wills, a marriage, not an identity, see the Introduction to St. Bernard, *The Steps of Humility*, trans. George Bosworth Burch (Cambridge, Mass.: Harvard Univ. Press, 1940), pp. 87–95.

44. For Alain's treatment of Hymen, see the *Complaint, pr.* viii and *m*.ix.76 ff.; for an excellent analysis of Hymen's significance, see Wetherbee, "The Function of Poetry in the *De planctu naturae* of Alain de Lille," pp. 110–11.

45. The passage referred to and quoted from is, of course, Eph. v.21–33.

46. For the significance of *Largitas* in the *Complaint*, see Wetherbee, "The Function of Poetry in the *De planctu naturae* of Alain de Lille," pp. 111–12.

47. It is, of course, based upon the eighth meter of the second book of the *Consolation*.

48. For ordered change as a manifestation of the bond of love, see the *Consolation* IV.*m*.vi, a passage which may also have influenced Troilus's song.

49. In a suggestive article that has been too much ignored, Charles A. Owens point out that the addition of this song to Book III heightens its symmetry, a symmetry which strengthens the poem's images from nature "in which the cycle of growth, maturity, and decay is inevitable," and that its addition, along with the addition of Troilus's ascent to the eighth sphere, strengthens the poem's affirmation of both sexual love and charity, showing Chaucer's "conviction that, however irreconcilable, both were valid." See "The Significance of Chaucer's Revisions of *Troilus and Criseyde*," *MP*, 55 (1957), 1–5.

50. *Complaint of Nature, pr.*iv.43.

51. *Ibid., m.*iv.33.

52. *Roman de la rose* IV.127–29.15973–16018.

53. *Complaint of Nature, pr.*iii.24–5.

54. Alain of Lille, *Anticlaudian* II.v.71.

55. Though Boethius does not literally identify the image of the bird in a cage with the soul trapped in the prison of the flesh, but merely sees it as evidence of how all things wish to return to the place from whence they came, the comparison seems too obvious not to have been intended, especially since Lady Philosophy is trying to get Boethius to remember his true home (*Consolation* III.*m.*ii.21–31).

56. The *Roman de la rose* V.59.20817 ff. Though the allegory of Pygmalion may indeed reveal the self-love inherent in *cupiditas* (John V. Fleming, *The Roman de la rose: A Study in Allegory and Iconography* [Princeton, N.J.: Princeton Univ. Press, 1969], pp. 228–38), it has more important functions in the poem, ones which relate to Jean's conception of how both the artist and lover create. It climaxes the whole last movement of the poem which begins with the entry of Nature and Genius and Jean's discussion of how the artist creates in imitation of nature.

57. *Complaint of Nature, pr.*iv.43.

58. See the *Consolation* III.*m.*ix.

CHAPTER 4: TRAGEDY AND COMEDY

1. On the tradition of Fortune in the Middle Ages, see Howard R. Patch, *The Goddess Fortuna in Medieval Literature* (Cambridge, Mass.: Harvard Univ. Press, 1927). It is no doubt unnecessary to add that for Chaucer, as for Boethius, Fortune is only a manifestation of God's Providence and that all fortune is ultimately good. Numerous critics have stressed the importance of Fortune in *Troilus and Criseyde*. The outstanding spokesman for the viewpoint that the *Troilus* is *de casibus* tragedy, the tragedy resulting from the subordination of self to Fortune, is, of course, D. W. Robertson, "Chaucerian Tragedy." The most deterministic reading is no doubt that of Walter Clyde Curry, "Destiny in *Troilus and Criseyde," Chaucer and the Medieval Science,* 2d ed. (New York: Barnes and Noble, Inc., 1960), pp. 241–98. For differing interpretations of the influence of the *Consolation* on the whole of the form and content of the *Troilus,* see Theodore Stroud, "Boethius' Influence on Chaucer's *Troilus," MP,* 49 (1951–52), 1–9; John P. McCall, "Five-Book Structure in Chaucer's *Troilus," MLQ,* 23 (1962), 297–308.

2. See Henry W. Sams, "The Dual Time-Scheme in Chaucer's *Troilus," MLN,* 56 (1941), 94–100. All the seasonal imagery I allude to with brief quotations in this paragraph is cited by Sams.

3. The evidence that it is late summer is astrological: The sun is in the sign of Leo (IV.31–32).

4. Chaucer allows Troilus more dignity and self-control than Boccaccio allows Troilo, an alteration consistent with his general ennoblement of Boccaccio's hero. See the *Filostrato* IV.14–21.292–95.

5. Alfred David notes some differences to argue the increased sincerity of Troilus in his second sorrow. See "The Hero of the *Troilus*," *Speculum*, 37 (1962), 571–72.

6. Ida Gordon observes that Troilus's vision of unending pain and Criseyde's of an escape from pain are "almost symbolic of the difference of the two characters" (*The Double Sorrow of Troilus*, p. 105).

7. On the dramatic appropriateness of these two prayers, see Alfred David, "The Hero of the *Troilus*," pp. 576–77.

8. Ida Gordon notes the self-deception, asserting that "she may think she loves Troilus for his moral virtue, but what she admires most is his gentlemanly behavior" (*The Double Sorrow of Troilus*, pp. 107–8).

9. For Robertson, Criseyde's "little picture" of Troilus's virtue "could not be more false, more distant from the furtive actions Chaucer has described" (*Preface to Chaucer*, p. 496).

10. The same general pattern of events evident in Book IV of the *Troilus* is present in Boccaccio's *Filostrato*, though there it seems to lack the structural import it possesses in the *Troilus*, both because the structure of Boccaccio's first three parts is different from Chaucer's and because Chaucer has greatly increased the verbal and dramatic echoes to insist upon the structural similarities.

11. Gerry Brenner, "Narrative Structure in Chaucer's *Troilus and Criseyde*," *AnM*, 6 (1965), 13.

12. See the *Metamorphoses*, Vol. I, trans. Frank Justus Miller (New York: G. P. Putman's Sons, 1916), Bk. V, lines 346 ff., pp. 262 ff.

13. *Metamorphoses* V.569–71.262. Though Miller's edition provides a translation, I have supplied my own.

14. *The Double Sorrow of Troilus*, pp. 123–24.

15. Robertson sees the similarity of Diomede and Criseyde and seems to prefer both to Troilus. He has the courage of his convictions: "Neither Criseyde nor Diomede, both of whom seek momentary footholds on the slippery way of the world, is capable of the idolatry of which Troilus is guilty, or of the depths to which he descends" (*Preface to Chaucer*, p. 499).

16. It is of course with man's inevitable distortion of this ideal that Chaucer is primarily concerned in the marriage tales. See especially the Franklin's theorizing, *The Franklin's Tale* V(F).761–98.

17. See Rosemary Woolf's discussion of the betrayed husband and lover-knight characterizations of Christ in the lyric tradition. *The English Religious Lyrics in the Middle Ages* (Oxford: Clarendon Press, 1968), pp. 45–59.

18. *The Divine Poems*, ed. Helen Gardner (Oxford: Clarendon Press, 1952), lines 21–23, p. 50.

19. The questions of whether or not Chaucer wrote "seventh" or "eighth" and whether he was counting outward from the moon or inward from the planets have been recently reexamined in detail with full documentation of the scholarly argument by John M. Steadman, *Disembodied Laughter: Troilus and the Apotheosis Tradition* (Berkeley: Univ. of California Press, 1972), pp. 1–20 and appended notes. On the ques-

tion of whether they are numbered in or out, Dronke's observation that the fact that Venus is referred to as the light of the third heaven in the proem to Book III indicates that Chaucer is numbering the planets outward from the moon seems to me telling as to Chaucer's intention ("The Conclusion of *Troilus and Criseyde*," *MAE*, 33 [1964], p. 47). Steadman's examination of the apotheosis tradition seems to favor, in my judgment, the sphere of the fixed stars as the point from which Troilus looks back.

20. *Chapters on Chaucer* (Baltimore: Johns Hopkins Press, 1961), pp. 105–8.

21. *Commentary* I.xi.11–12.132–33.

22. See chap. I, this book.

23. *Commentary* I.xi.11.132–33.

24. Boethius similarly identifies the Kingdom of Pluto as this world in his explanation of Orpheus's failure to rescue Eurydice from Hades as the soul's looking back from the light of sovereign good to the low and dark things of this world (IV.*m*.xii.60–70). This myth and Boethius's interpretation of it is relevant to the *Troilus*, of course, given Criseyde's ironic imagined picture of Troilus and her together in Elysium like Orpheus and Eurydice. See also *Commentary* I.xii.3.134.

25. *Commentary* I.xi.12.133.

26. On Cancer as the portal of souls descending, see *Commentary* I.xii.1–3.133–34; and *Cosmographia* II.iii.95–96.

27. See also Alain de Lille's picture of Concord uniting soul and body, *Anticlaudian* VII.ii.130, a passage quoted in part in chap. 1.

28. See n.29, chap. 2 above.

29. We should note that some Chartrians, following Calcidius, identified the same, termed *unitas*, with God and the different, termed *binarius*, with chaos, using number terminology to show the dependence of chaos for existence upon God. See Silverstein, "The Fabulous Cosmogony of Bernardus Silvestris," pp. 101–2.

30. See Robinson, "Explanatory Notes," *The Works of Chaucer*, p. 813, note to lines 1 ff.

31. *Inferno* v.25.72–79.

32. On the ascent of the soul in the epilogue see Steadman, *Disembodied Laughter*, esp. pp. 1–20, 42–65. Steadman notes the two motions of the soul in macrocosm and microcosm and characterizes Troilus's return to the eighth sphere as a return to reason, the eighth sphere's motion being rationality (pp. 60–62). Steadman does not, however, associate either this theory or the related theory of the cycle of the soul, both of which he rightly sees help explain the end of the poem, with any of the poem, apparently, except the end.

33. Virtually everything Freccero observes about the significance of linear, circular, and spiral movement in the *Divine Comedy* could be said about the same three movements in the *Troilus*, since Chaucer's poem dramatizes all three. See "Dante's Pilgrim in a Gyre," *PMLA*, 76 (1961), pp. 168–81.

CHAPTER 5: CHAUCER AND HIS NARRATOR

1. See Macrobius's defense of fables, one much cited in medieval times. *Commentary* I.ii.1–20.83–87. The charges against Plato for writing fables there attributed to Colotes the Epicurean might well be leveled against Chaucer: "If you wished to impart to us a conception of the heavenly realms and reveal the condition of souls why . . . did you not do so in a simple, a straightforward manner, instead of defiling the very portals of truth with imaginary character, event, and setting, in a vile imitation of a playwright?" (I.ii.4.84). It is in a sense the question that this chapter seeks to answer. See Wetherbee, *Platonism and Poetry*, pp. 36–48.

2. Almost all critics presently writing on Chaucer's poetry speak of his narrators, though they seem to conceive of his relation to Chaucer and his function differently. Perhaps the best analysis of how Chaucer uses the narrator as a poetic devise to reveal truth is in Gordon, *The Double Sorrow of Troilus*, pp. 61–92.

3. *Inferno* v.137.78.

4. See the *Consolation* I.m.i. See also the related condition of Alain de Lille's dreamer at the beginning of the *Complaint of Nature* and his related progress. On the spiritual condition of dreamers in the dream vision tradition, see Paul Piehler, *The Visionary Landscape: A Study in Medieval Allegory* (London: Edward Arnold, 1971), pp. 27–30, 47–78. Both Robinson (p. 814, note to line 7) and Stroud ("Boethius' Influence on Chaucer's *Troilus*," *MP*, 49 [1951–52], 2) point out that Chaucer's picture of his weepy verses recalls the *Consolation*. For a discussion of certain aspects of the *Consolation*'s influence on the character of the narrator, see McCall, "Five-Book Structure in Chaucer's *Troilus*," *MLQ*, 23 (1962), 297–308.

5. See the *Consolation* I.pr.i.

6. *Inferno* i.1–136.22–29. On the mountain as the equivalent of purgatory and Dante's efforts to reach the sun as the soul's ascent to God, see Dorothy Sayers, *Hell, The Comedy of Dante Alighieri* (Baltimore: Penguin Books, 1949), I, 75. The descent through hell is, of course, an image of a descent both through the world's evil and the evil in the self.

7. Chaucer's use of the terms "love," "god of love," and "god" in the opening proem, in some ways a proem to the whole of the *Troilus*, is, as has been recognized, ambiguous.

8. For a valuable interpretation of the fluctuating distance between the narrator and his tale which the reading offered here hopes to supplement, see Morton W. Bloomfield, "Distance and Predestination in *Troilus and Criseyde*," *PMLA*, 72 (1957), 14–26. Just as the inescapable truth of the story can function as a metaphor for predestination, its resistance to the narrator's efforts to make the story one of paradise on earth functions, like Bernardus's use of the *malignitas* of matter, as a metaphor for the effects of the fall on creation. The truth of human cupidity in Troilus's history prevents the narrator's from creating the world of his poem a paradise, just as the fall "prevents" God's creation

from being an Eden. Ida Gordon points out ambiguities in the narrator's praise of love, but the narrator seems oblivious to them (*The Double Sorrow of Troilus*, pp. 64–67).

9. *Purgatorio* i.1–6.18–19. Robinson notes the parallel (p. 818, note to lines 1–3).

10. Boccaccio tells us that it was a sullen love. *Il Filostrato* II.83.204–5.

11. *Ibid.*, III.21.246 and n.27, chap. 3 above.

12. Chaucer similarly undercuts the narrator's repeated insistence that Criseyde is "al innocent of Pandarus entente (II.1723)" in the scene at Deiphebus's house by telling us that she "avysed wel hire wordes and hire cheere" prior to having Pandarus advise her to advise herself about "what folk ben hire withinne,/ And in what plit oon is" (II.1730–31).

13. Chaucer's translation of the *Consolation* terms them "mermaydenes," the equivalent of Sirens, as Robertson demonstrates (*Preface to Chaucer*, pp. 142–44 and notes appended to those pages). See the *Consolation* I.*pr*.i.68.

14. I allude, of course, to Troilus's fear that Calchas will so praise some Greek "That raysshen he shal yow [Criseyde] with his speche" (IV.1474).

15. The "epilogue" has been the subject of much discussion. For bibliography besides Robinson (p. 837, note to lines 1835–55), see Hans Kasmann, " 'I wolde excuse hire yet for routhe': Chaucer's Einstellung zu Criseyde," *Chaucer und seine Zeit*, ed. Arno Esch (Tübingen: Max Niemayer Verlag, 1968), pp. 98–122. See in particular E. Talbot Donaldson, "The Ending of Chaucer's *Troilus*," *Early English and Norse Studies presented to Hugh Smith*, ed. Arthur Brown and Peter Foote (London: Metheum, 1963), pp. 26–45; and Steadman, *Disembodied Laughter*, particularly chaps. 6 and 7.

16. *Il Filostrato* VIII.27–28.496–97.

17. *Roman de la rose* II.218–26.4421–4628.

18. Ecclus. iii.1,2. I quote from the Douay version, 1609.

19. *The Sphere of Sacrobosco*, p. 123. Let me mention once again Frecerro's study of patterns of motion in Dante's *Comedy*, "Dante's Pilgrim in a Gyre."

20. *The Sphere of Sacrobosco*, p. 123. See also Steadman's observation, drawing on the same tradition, that in returning to the eighth sphere Troilus is returning to rationality (*Disembodied Laughter*, pp. 60–62).

Index